The Scars of Dyslexia

Eight Case Studies in Emotional Reactions

Janice Edwards

CASSELL

Cassell
Villiers House   387 Park Avenue South
41/47 Strand   New York
London WC2N 5JE   NY 10016–8810

First published 1994

British Library Cataloguing-in-Publication Data
A catalogue record for this book is available from the British Library.

Library of Congress Cataloging-in-Publication Data
Edwards, Janice Helena.
  The Scars of Dyslexia : eight case studies in emotional reactions / by
Janice Helena Edwards.
      p.   cm. — (Cassell education)
  ISBN 0-304-32946-0 (hc) : $70.00. — ISBN 0-304-32944-4 (pbk.) : $26.00
  1. Dyslexic children – Education – England – Case studies.
2. Dyslexics – Education – England – Case studies.   I. Title.
II. Series.
LC4709.5.E39   1994
371.91'44—dc20   93–48376
                                                   CIP

ISBN: 0-304-32946-0 (hardback)
       0-304-32944-4 (paperback)

Typeset by Colset Private Limited, Singapore
Printed and bound in Great Britain by Redwood Books, Trowbridge, Wiltshire

Contents

This book is dedicated to my mother, Ruby Edwards.
I wish she had been here to see it published.
I thank her and my father for all their help and support.
Thomas never doubted me!

Acknowledgements

I wish to acknowledge Malcolm Ritchie and Stephen Lushington, past headmasters of Brickwall House Special School, for their contribution to the spirit of this book; and the present headmaster for the opportunity to carry out research. Philip Skelker, head of Carmel College, Oxfordshire, which has an excellent Study Skills and Dyslexia Unit, gave me great support while I was teaching there and finishing my study. Essential experience was gained also from the Dyslexia Institute, Stowe School, Buckinghamshire, and Saxon Mount State Special School, East Sussex. Inspired and caring teachers Molly Gardner, Sue Parkinson and Micky Bull influenced me deeply.

Thanks are necessary to all eight boys participating in the study for allowing me to probe their life experiences and some painful memories, for talking freely to me in their own time and for making helpful suggestions about schools.

I also appreciate the patient help of the parents concerned, many of whom have suffered great anxiety in struggling for their children's welfare.

I am grateful for permission from the relevant councils for allowing me to conduct this study on their grant-aided children.

Note to the Reader

Certain material of a highly confidential nature (psychologists' reports, County Statement forms, reports, etc.) could not be printed in full in this work. I have used such
records for corroboration of memories and details quoted by subjects.

Boys chose to use their own first names, but surnames have been withheld for
privacy and freedom of speech. Parents have been called by the boy's Christian name
initial.

Names of staff and schools have been extracted and replaced by random alphabetical
letters. The boys came from different areas drawn from all over England.

Individual authorities have not been mentioned by name, nor has the particular
specialist boarding school for dyslexics which the students attended. Staff names have
been replaced by random letters.

The foot less prompt to meet the morning dew,
The heart less bounding at emotion new,
And hope, once crushed, less quick to spring again.

Matthew Arnold, *Thyrsis*

The most cruel wounds are those that make no outward show.

Sir Walter Scott, *The Pirate*

We shall never learn to feel and respect our real calling and destiny, unless we have taught ourselves to consider everything as moonshine, compared with the education of the heart.

Scott to Lockhart, quoted in J.G. Lockhart's *Life of Sir Walter Scott*

First of all ... if you can learn a simple trick ... you'll get along a lot better with all kinds of folks. You never really understand a person until you consider things from his point of view ... until you climb into his skin and walk around in it.

Harper Lee, *To Kill a Mockingbird*

Introduction

This book arose from research I carried out for my M.Ed. degree in Learning Difficulties at Bangor, University College of North Wales. My original intention was to
select a sample of eight dyslexic boys who seemed to have survived their difficulties
particularly successfully. I wanted to identify what common factors had enabled them
to achieve stability and good humour despite the frustrations of literacy problems. I
chose my sample group from the age band 16 to 17 at the special school for dyslexics
where I worked. However, in the course of interviewing, it rapidly became evident that
the majority of these boys had suffered extremely bad experiences related to education.
Even these outwardly secure, confident young men had been left with deep emotional
battle 'scars' from their encounters with the educational system.

This book endeavours to communicate their experiences to teachers, and tell the true
story of what it feels like to undergo the dyslexic experience in schools today. Many
of these pupils related events that will shock teachers and parents, and they give some
insight into the repercussions of classroom methods and academic failure.

RESULTS

Four groups of totally unexpected experiences were registered: (1) violence from
teachers, (2) unfair treatment/discrimination, (3) inadequate help/neglect, and (4)
humiliation. These factors appeared to arise from the failure of teachers to acknowledge or understand dyslexia, and their alacrity in labelling a child disruptive or dim.

From interviews with parents and students, participant observation, records, reports
and discussion, much material emerged describing emotional reactions to dyslexic problems at school. This can usefully be classified under the following headings: (1)
truancy/school refusal, (2) psychosomatic pain, (3) isolation/alienation from peers, (4)
lack of communication, (5) lack of confidence, (6) self-doubt/denigration of intellect,
(7) competitiveness disorders, (8) sensitivity to criticism, and (9) behaviour problems.

Six out of my sample of eight experienced incidents of enduring emotional pain connected with their treatment in school. All eight individuals lacked confidence, were

highly sensitive to criticism, and had displayed behaviour problems. Two students only revealed lesser levels of resentment and damaged morale, owing to a milder degree of dyslexia or effective early identification. It was obvious that combinations of differing levels of the emotional reactions identified had had great impact on the personality formation of the students concerned.

The boys themselves emphasized the need for consistent, genuine help, and for teachers who showed they cared for, listened to and respected the individual. They strongly registered the need for specialist help and contact with other dyslexics, but suffered a social alienation through boarding school life. The majority advised that schools should capitalize on their strengths and build up career prospects rather than continuously rubbing the students' noses in their weaknesses. An overwhelming resentment of being treated as 'thick' or 'abnormal' was felt.

CONCLUSION

Teachers need to bear in mind the importance of how individual dyslexics react to failure. The emotional effects of our treatment of the dyslexic pupils in our schools are severely under-estimated.

Part I

An Individual Approach

Chapter 1

What Is Dyslexia?

Dyslexia is recognizable as a measurable discrepancy between cognitive ability and .
literacy level. It can be clearly seen as a substantial difference between tested IQ and
Reading/Spelling Age on traditional scales.

Perhaps the clearest, simplest and most effective definition of dyslexia or specific
learning difficulty is that given by the World Federation of Neurology in 1969, quoted
by Stirling (1978). Dyslexics are categorized as those who 'despite conventional classroom experience fail to attain the language skills of reading, writing and spelling commensurate with their intellectual abilities'.

John   8th January 1980

    my   dad   is   a   sef   in   buide   bidar   he   gos   a
   worc   wen   he   was
  most   & felf   in   bricte·   go   a   werc   wen   you
  wes.   it   iƸ   gotd   mes   sum   its   he   gos   no
  he   is   in   sum   tis   you   can   soe   wot   ea
 it   wos   in   toh   wo   to   he   bos   host

Figure 1.1 An example of dyslexic script

Figure 1.1 is an example of dyslexic script from John, an 11-year-old with an IQ
of 134 Verbal and 97 Performance in the Wechsler Intelligence Scale for Children
(Revised) (WISC(R)) test. He had improved so much that he no longer had b/d, p/q
and u/n reversals. He is part of this study.

A translation of the script might read:

> My dad is a self-employed builder. He goes to work when he wants. Most self-employed
> bricklayers go to work when you want. It is good money. Sometimes he goes no he is in

[doesn't know where he is going]. Sometimes you can see what area it was in town [he] went to. He builds houses.

An analysis shows that the script has many typical dyslexic features:

1.   Approximately 28 per cent error rate even when using very simple words.
2.   Auditory errors where sounds are not heard/recorded: 'sef' for self, 'in buide' for employed, 'bidar' for builder, 'was' for wants, 'ton' for town, 'host' for houses.
3.   Visual errors on common words which need to be remembered by the way they look ('sight' words): 'gos' for goes, 'worc' for work, 'wen' for when, 'wot' for what.
4.   Substitutions: 'a' for to.
5.   Structural confusions: 'you' instead of they, 'sum its he gos no he is in' for sometimes he doesn't know where he is going.
6.   Inconsistencies over spelling the same word: builder as 'bidar'/builds as 'bos', self as 'sef/sfelf', employed as 'in buide/in. . .', work as 'worc/werc'.
7.   Reversals of letters: sometimes as 'sum its/sum tis'.
8.   Omissions of words: self-employed builder becomes 'sfelf in. . .buicte'.
9.   Contractions of words, leaving out letters and sounds: 'bos' for builds, 'ea' for area.
10. Homonym confusions: 'sum' for some.
11. Examples of compound errors abound: e.g. 'host' for houses combines contraction, vowel error and sound error.
12. No punctuation.
13. Printed script and inability to set script directly on the base line indicate problems in handwriting control.
14. He obviously had a very poor memory for words in every aspect, though he had won control by now over sequencing the letters, which he could discriminate phonetically.

It is obvious from looking at John's IQ test profile (Figure 1.2) that he is an exceptionally bright young man, but his pattern of abilities is extremely varied. On three sub-tests his scores place him in the top 1 per cent of the population, revealing spectacular abstract reasoning skill, and a gift for practical judgement and expressive language. This can be summed up as advanced conceptualizing strength. One score is also above average, six are average, and then we see his coding score place him amongst the lowest nine individuals in any hundred tested. This type of erratic, patchy profile might be expected to produce educational confusion within subject disciplines, where different skills may be required at any time on varied tasks. It means that the pupil never really knows what sort of experience is coming next in class and whether he is going to be top or bottom of it, finding work ridiculously easy or impossible. Add to this the confusion and trauma of literacy failure and you have an academically dangerous situation for pupil and teacher to deal with.

The discrepancy between the extremes of the cognitive and perceptual strengths and weaknesses which dyslexics display is greater than that of any of the other learning difficulties which the WISC(R) test scores highlight. Consider the profile examples in Figure 1.3, and compare John's chart to the typical dyslexic pattern as shown in Figure 1.4. Obviously, John's profile follows the dyslexic trend closely in the verbal mode, but at a superior level than an average dyslexic. His performance skills, however, lack the spatial advantage an estimated 1 in 3 dyslexics have (H. Chasty, personal

Verbal scale | Performance scale

Classifications | Scaled scores | Percentiles

Column descriptions:
- Information reflects alertness and interest; measures long-term memory; is influenced by a cultural background; is a measure of orientation to the environment.
- Comprehension measures ability to use practical judgement in everyday social situation.
- Arithmetic measures concentration ability to reason numerically, requires concentration and attention.
- Similarities indicates ability to generalize and reason abstractly. Test of conceptual ability.
- Vocabulary word knowledge acquired from experience and education; expressive language.
- Digit span attention and immediate auditory memory; ability to sequence.
- Picture completion reflects reality perception and observation in identifying missing parts from a whole.
- Picture arrangement ability to comprehend and evaluate a total (social) situation; sequential planning. (Social intelligence.)
- Block design measures ability to analyse and form abstract designs; involves visual motor co-ordination.
- Object assembly is a visual motor task involving perception and organization of concrete forms.
- Coding measures visual memory, speed and accuracy in copying symbols. Associative ability.

Classifications	Scaled scores	Percentiles
Very superior	20	
	19	
	18	
	17	
	16	99
Superior	15	95
	14	91
Above average	13	84
Average	12	75
	11	63
	10	50
	9	37
	8	25
Below average	7	16
	6	9
Borderline	5	5
	4	2
Below normal	3	1
	2	
	1	

Figure 1.2 John: WISC(R) IQ test profile

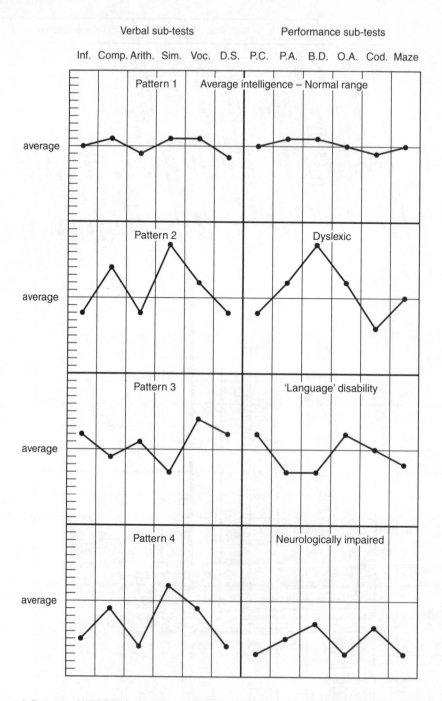

Figure 1.3 Patterns of WISC(R) interest scores. Pattern 1: fairly even level across the scale of scores; Pattern 2: several scores are above average, but patchy abilities; Pattern 3: disability labelled 'language' shows performance deficits also (almost opposite trend to the dyslexic); Pattern 4: generally depressed scores in all but one sub-test.

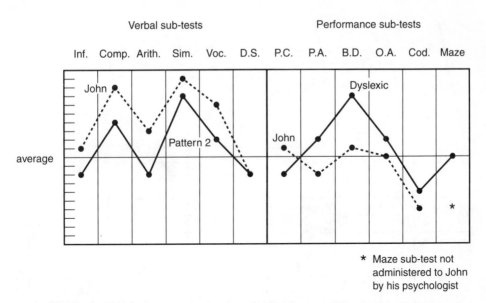

Figure 1.4 Patterns of WISC(R) interest scores (as Figure 1.3) with John's profile superimposed as a dotted line comparable to the typical pattern

communication, 1992; see also p. 16). His three lowest scores, however, clearly show difficulties with auditory and visual memory in the short term, and sequencing. Note that the sub-test scores fluctuate over 13 points in a 20-point marking scheme. Consider also the gap of 37 points between his superior verbal score and his average non-verbal reasoning/performance level. This is charted in Figure 1.5.

DEFINITIONS OF DYSLEXIA

There has been great controversy over the precise definition of dyslexia, with experts focusing on different aspects of it, or on distinct types of dyslexic. It is important to bear in mind the limitations of fixed stereotypes when dealing with a complex subject where researchers from widely different disciplines are constantly exploring new theories and discovering fresh facts. As Farnham-Diggory (1978) points out: 'Definitions are not truth: they merely set up the conditions under which particular actions are to be taken. Some of the experiments may produce results that have bearing on truth. But the definitions themselves simply name the game' (p. 16).

Indeed, the name given to an individual's problem can vary dramatically in moving around the country, whether it is Britain or America. Frye (1968; quoted in Farnham-Diggory, 1978, p. 17) produced a table of 1,000 approximately similar multiple terms which had been used to describe dyslexia. They are displayed in three columns of ten terms each, and are interchangeable, forming a 'do-it-yourself terminology generator'.

The phenomenon of word-blindness was first noted by a German doctor, Kussmaul, in 1877, in connection with aphasics; he was studying the loss of speech/understanding because of head injury (see Critchley, 1970). The word dyslexia was used ten years later to describe the acquired condition (Berlin, 1887). Hinshelwood, who was a Glasgow eye-surgeon, first recorded information about word-blindness in Britain in 1895 with an article linking it to visual memory in aphasics.

The earliest definition comes from the work of Orton (1925, 1937), who put forward

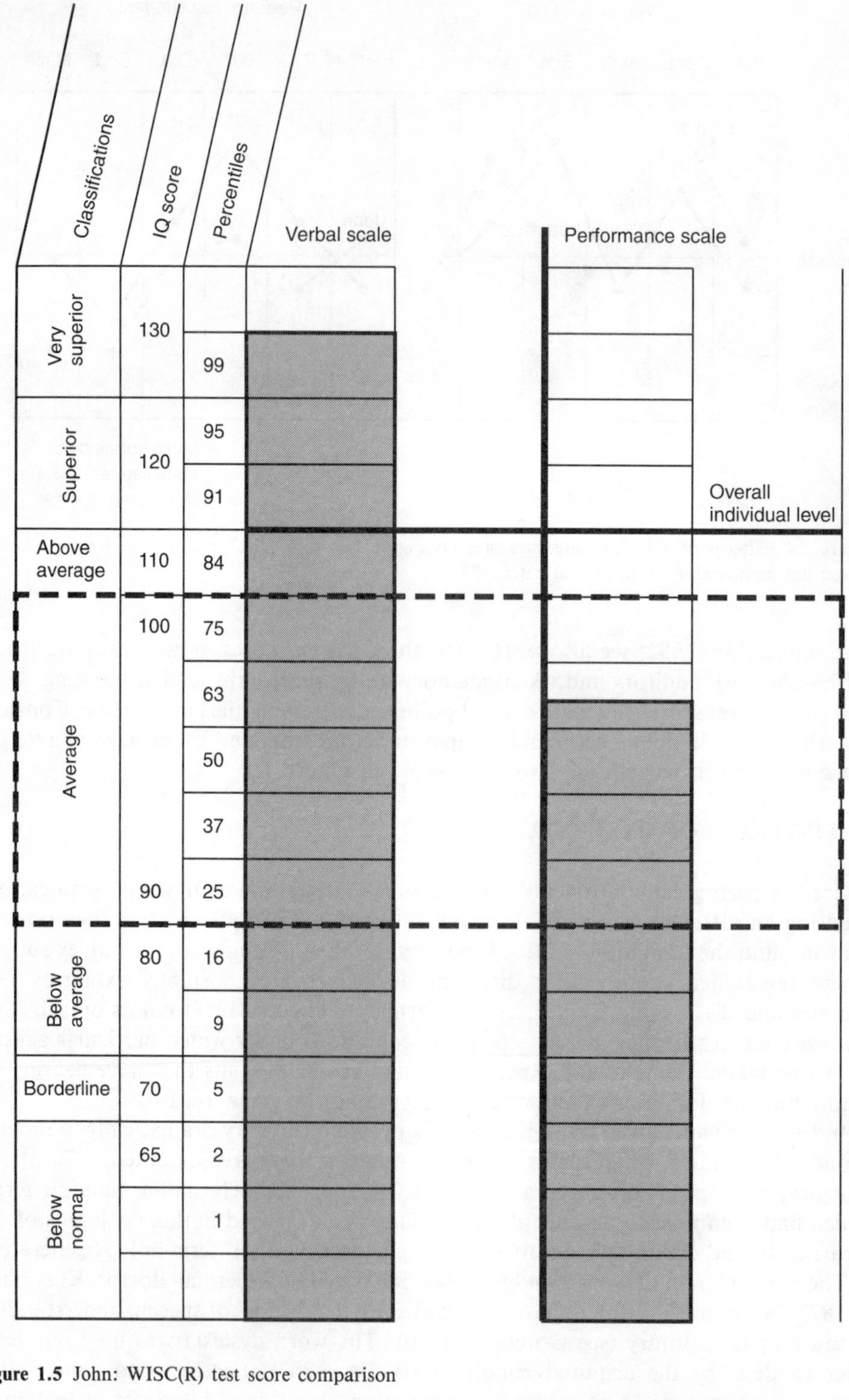

Figure 1.5 John: WISC(R) test score comparison

the theory that for some children reading difficulties were the symptom of a failure of one of the cerebral hemispheres in the brain to become the dominant control centre for speech, language and motor functions. He also identified 'strephosymbolia' or twisted symbols and letter reversals as part of the pattern (1928).

Rabinovitch (1959) considered primary reading delay as 'a characteristic pattern, with much variability from patient to patient'. He regarded primary reading retardation as stemming from biological causes or from within the subject studied. Secondary reading retardation was considered to come from outside the person, from situations such as limited schooling or opportunity, or emotional problems.

Rosenthal (1973) produced this statement for patients and families at his clinic: 'Dyslexia is explained as a specific cognitive dysfunction: the inability to organize graphic symbols "to make sense".'

Kimbrell and Karnes (1975) highlighted the aspect of a specific language disability involving the breakdown of spoken or written communication.

Stoll (1977) put forward the idea that dyslexia was difficult to define owing to the general normality of the subjects, who have an IQ above 90 and a reading sub-score below the lowest 15th percentile.

Badian (1986) pointed out the feature that dyslexics tend to score lower on verbal intelligence and higher on performance tasks.

Chasty (1991) gives the most full and comprehensive analysis of the problem:

> The student with dyslexia or specific learning difficulties shows *some learning skills* developed to an *above average* or *average* standard, but shows organizing or learning difficulties impairing: *motor skills*, organization in laterality, *information skills*, organization in working memory, so limiting the development of curriculum skills in some or all of: speech, reading, spelling, writing, numeracy and behaviour.

Hammill (1990) has tried to establish a consensus view towards an operational definition. He extracts nine conceptual elements which recur:

- Underachievement
- Causes related to central nervous system problems
- Process involvement
- Present through lifespan

Potential learning disabilities in:

- Spoken language
- Academic problems
- Conceptual problems
- Other conditions
- Multi-handicap

Hammill himself prefers the descriptive statement of the National Joint Committee on Learning Disabilities (1988):

> *Learning disabilities* is a general term that refers to a heterogeneous group of disorders manifested by significant difficulties in the acquisition and use of listening, speaking, reading, writing, reasoning, or mathematical abilities. These disorders are intrinsic to the individual, presumed to be due to central nervous system dysfunctions, and may occur across the life span. Problems in self-regulatory behaviours, social perception, and social interaction may exist with learning disabilities but do not themselves constitute a learning

disability. Although learning disabilities may occur concomitantly with other handicapping conditions (for example, sensory impairment, mental retardation, serious emotional disturbances) or with extrinsic influences (such as cultural differences, insufficient or inappropriate instruction), they are not the result of those conditions or influences.

As a working teacher continuously engaged in explaining dyslexia to the general public, however, I still find the brief definition at the start of this chapter from the World Federation of Neurology a useful basic introduction.

TYPES OF DYSLEXIA

The broadest divisions are these:

1. Genetic or hereditary dyslexia. This runs in families, where relatives displaying similar types of problem can often be clearly identified across generations and within the extended family (see De Fries, 1991; Healy and Aram, 1986).
2. Developmental dyslexia. This is congenital, present at birth, and is, therefore, acquired during foetal development and not hereditary. It was first identified by Dr Pringle-Morgan (1896) and James Kerr, a medical officer of health. Research on sub-types in this area is on-going.
3. Acquired dyslexia. This is a problem which develops at birth or later, through some physically adverse situation or injury. A common example is lack of oxygen at birth, or being dropped on the head as a child. Studies have identified four sub-types through head-injury symptoms in adults with traceable damage, who had no literacy problems before their accidents.
4. Emotional dyslexia. This is a highly controversial category put forward by Tomatis (1978), who was convinced that dyslexia was rooted in trauma occurring at the pre-verbal stage and resulting in a specific listening block.

CAUSES OF DYSLEXIA

Understanding of the condition has now moved on from the original concept of word-blindness to examinations of visual deficits, information processing, the asymmetry of the brain, neurological dissection and visual-spatial giftedness.

There is a distinct blurring within much of the literature between definitions or statements about what dyslexia *is* or means, what the signs displayed can be, and what are its root causes. Research has gone in many different directions trying to clarify this complex issue, stemming from different scientific disciplines and operating at various levels within them. Some examples across time follow.

Neurological studies

These have produced some very persuasive evidence.

Geschwind (1983) studied the connection between high pre-birth levels of the male hormone testosterone in the womb, left-handedness and slowing of growth in the left side of the brain. Links with the higher incidence of dyslexia in boys were explored.

Masland (1990) reports that by 1989 Galaburda had carried out nine autopsies on dyslexic brains (two girls and seven boys). Unusual brain structures were noted, including scattered arrangements of brain cells occurring in areas where they are not usually found.

Galaburda *et al.* have found that in all seven male dyslexic brains the planum temporale was symmetrical, which is unusual. Odd features were found in both sides of the brain, but most noticeably in the left side which controls dominance of the right-hand side of the body and contains the language centre. They found ectopias (misplaced neurons), displaced cells and disordered layering; in short, all subjects had differently structured brains to the average person. These features were concentrated in the auditory areas of the male brains, whereas only the two female brains displayed injury scarring from infancy or pre-birth. 'Both types of changes in the male brains are associated with increased numbers of neurons and connections and qualitatively different patterns of cellular architecture and connections' (Galaburda, Rosen and Sherman, 1989, p. 383).

Exciting new technological developments like magnetic resonance imaging (MRI) mean that the living, working brain can be observed as an image on a computer screen. Such methods have confirmed post-mortem findings so far (see Rumsey *et al.*, 1986). Suggesting that the differing brain structures may be unpredictable between individuals means that each cognitive pattern could be original in its variations.

Mapping the functions of the brain shows that advanced processes like reading involve a number of areas and the interactions between them, rather than being located in a specific area or requiring mass activity from the brain (see Euler, Lundberg and Lennerstrand, 1989). This new view of the integrated nature of reading skill diminishes the impact of studies focusing on unusual functioning of the two sides of the brain in dyslexics. It overshadows past studies which have concentrated on dominant laterality, specific processing or perceptual differences as a single root cause for the condition.

Functional deficits have been examined across the established disciplines over time. Nicolson *et al.* (1991) found that in children some specific working memory problems diminish in severity from age 8 to 11, and fade out around age 15, being slowly overcome. Their diagram stressing the complex interaction between automatization, working memory and phonological skill for any task is a useful aid to problem analysis (Figure 1.6). They use it to urge early diagnostic intervention through increased understanding of the wide range of deficits involved in dyslexia, which could be used as a basis for the production of thorough pre-school screening tests.

Visual/ophthalmological research

This has moved through explorations of eye dominance, eye tracking, the uses of specialized lenses and coloured filters to reduce glare from print and assist processing, and the effect of drugs on eye movement. Evidence exists that dyslexics display subtle visual problems which suggest unusual functioning of the transient systems in the brain which convey visual signals and so help process information. Whether this is part of the manifestation of the generally unusual operating system of the dyslexic brain or yet another contributing factor, whether this is a cause or an effect, has not yet been

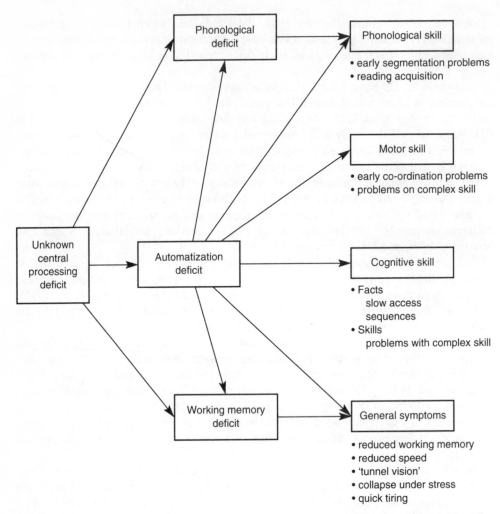

Figure 1.6 A causal analysis of the dyslexic deficits (from R. I. Nicolson, A. J. Fawcett and A. D. Baddeley, *Working Memory and Dyslexia*, Department of Psychology, University of Sheffield, 1991. Reproduced with permission)

established. Studies of timing mechanisms with processing channels in the brain are currently being examined. Lovegrove, Martin and Slaghuis (1986) have reviewed the arguments over the impact of visual deficits in dyslexia. Pumfrey and Reason (1991) sensibly point out that most dyslexic children have well-established visual/spatial ability and conclude that the *link* between the language centre, which holds the 'naming' skill, and the visual centre is problematic. 'Essentially the problem is in the pupil's ability to encode phonologically or decode rather than in their ability to see or visualize the words ... the eyes no longer have the answer' (p. 171). They cite the well-known positive psychological aura of the placebo effect as a probable explanation for gains recorded in reading with the use of coloured filters, as well as regular practice encouragement. This recalls the patients who were originally part of experiments where they were given blank tablets (placebos) but still made improvements. This is now thought to be related to the release of endorphins, chemicals which regulate the experience of stress or pain in animals. Some people have, however, reported great benefits from filters.

Auditory processing theories

These are represented by practitioners like Tomatis, who developed the use of machinery like the Electronic Ear to do thorough audiometric testing. He was a French doctor studying audio-vocal links initially as an ear, nose and throat specialist. He believed in self-conditioning through the use of tapes and music to reintegrate hearing, restore missing frequency sensitivity, and condition a particular muscle in the ear. He has been criticized on several counts.

First, the question of the placebo effect throughout his programme is obvious. Second, on questioning a trained practitioner of the method from Canada who was piloting a programme in a special school, I received no satisfactory answer as to why the same improved listening skills which he claimed could not be gained through an intensive music course. Third, Tomatis related his programme back to a psycho-therapeutic basis, stating that the listening block and left orientation represented a rejection of the father image. He believed in training a left-orientated or crossed-lateral pupil to right orientation, a practice which is dubious. Consider for example the psychologist's report in the case study on Mark in this book, where a forced change to right-handedness was stated as having caused his problems. Finally, the treatment programme was extremely expensive, like the Irlen Filter lenses and training.

Though the views of Tomatis held great sway in France, Canada and parts of the USA where his clinics abounded, his psychotherapy theories cannot be proved correct, and his views on the importance of the ear have not been accepted or taken up by the scientific establishment worldwide. His theories have faded out and been largely overtaken by the international flood of research from neurologists on a wider perspective. Bancroft (1982) explored the Tomatis view.

ADVANCED VISUAL/SPATIAL SKILL IN DYSLEXICS

Examples of severe dyslexics who display unusually well-developed skills in the visual field and in multidimensional tasks have often been noted, both formally and informally. The work of the Arts Dyslexia Trust has recently brought more attention to this phenomenon. The organization was formally set up in 1991 with a wide-ranging opening exhibition at the Julius Gottleib Gallery, Carmel College, Oxfordshire, by 12 successful dyslexic artists/designers who had attended special schools or units. The curricula vitae of this group, with colour illustrations of work, are available from the Trust in catalogue form. Eight professional art and design disciplines are represented. Apart from fine art (sculpture and paintings in various media), the seven other disciplines represented are: silversmithing, set design, model-making, furniture design, graphic work, print-making and product design.

Susan Parkinson, co-founder of the Trust, had been training dyslexic pupils for entry to art college for over twenty years and was the first to suggest that difficulties with literacy skill could be the reverse side of a special gift in the visual/spatial arts,

Table 1.1.   *Students tested on WISC-III (UK) pilot study, 30 May 1992*

Student[†]	WISC(R)			(Random sample)
	Verbal	Performance	Full score	
H.T.	113	104	109	
J.A.	111	138	126	27 point gap[*]
P.R.	98	91	94	
S.T.	142	146	148	
F.M.	120	105	115	
G.M.	106	108	107	
T.B.	88	118	102	30 point gap
D.B.	126	130	126	
A.D.	120	121	123	
T.B.	82	136	108	54 point gap
D.W.	109	138	126	29 point gap
M.G.	105	130	118	25 point gap
M.D.	130	114	125	
A.R.	122	128	127	
S.G.	133	96	118	
Means	113.6	120.2	118.1	

The students were originally referred for assessment because they were failing in the acquisition of literacy and/or numeracy skills in school. Many of them have statements of special educational need. All were receiving some form of specialist teaching aimed to meet their special needs. The date of initial testing varied, from 1989 to 1991.
[†]Five out of 15 pupils positively identified as Visual/Spatially Superior.
[*]Average discrepancy of 33 points between Verbal and Performance IQ scores.
Data from the WISC-III (UK) pilot study are reproduced with permission by the Psychological Corporation, 24–28 Oval Road, London NW1 7DX.

which demand a spatial awareness not so consistently required in the two-dimensional, linear academic subjects. Malcolm, Lord Ritchie of Dundee, a Liberal Democrat spokesman on education, encouraged her to develop A-level art and design courses for talented pupils at the school where he was headmaster. The same type of facility for imaginative/creative writing was noted by the present author, Janice Edwards, an English specialist, and she and Mrs Parkinson on the latter's retirement set about publicizing this creative ability.

Parkinson and Edwards (1992) discuss visual/spatial skill in terms of awareness and control of such elements as colour, flat pattern, three-dimensional skill and texture, focusing on the capacity of the human brain to change response patterns, or to create.

The reports of educational psychologists often reveal superior sub-test skills in the visual/spatial non-verbal performance tasks on WISC assessments. These discrepancies can be quite dramatic. In the case of Trevor, featured in this book, his performance score was a full 18 points above his verbal score. Dr Chasty, when asked to produce an estimate of the approximate number of dyslexics displaying exceptional visual/spatial skill, immediately identified five obvious examples of this pattern from a random sample of 15 dyslexic scores breakdowns prepared for a WISC III pilot study. The average of their performance IQ advantage over their verbal scores was 33 points (Table 1.1). At the simplest level of indication of visual/spatial ability tendencies, then, approximately one third of dyslexic individuals can be expected to have latent giftedness of this specific type.

The history of talented dyslexics is well documented. Perhaps the most famous example is that of Auguste Rodin (1840–1917), who has been called the greatest sculptor of the nineteenth century. One of his favourite themes was human aspiration and creativity, as shown by *The Thinker* and *Balzac*. Yet his father, Jean-Baptise Rodin, had complained bitterly that 'the boy is ineducable'. It was after Rodin that Dr Per Udden, another creative dyslexic and the inventor of the electronic wheelchair, named his International Remediation Academy in order to stimulate scientific research into the condition and communicate the findings to teachers.

Leonardo da Vinci is another master who is thought to have had dyslexic tendencies because of his erratic spelling and facility in mirror-writing code diaries, and because many of his paintings contain reversed images of verified landscapes.

Turner's refusal to write notes for lectures given at the Royal Academy, and his notoriously disorganized approach in terms of brilliant but disjointed comments in a rambling structure also make him a suspect case.

Thompson (1969) gives accounts of dyslexics who were original (and often visual) thinkers, such as Edison, Woodrow Wilson and Hans Christian Andersen.

Stein (1993), well-known for his research in the visual field, comments that many dyslexics report heightened sensory acuity such as observation of visual details which others miss. He notes that difficulty is often experienced in attending to one information channel only, such as focusing on one conversation at a time. In interviewing dyslexic designers, the alternative view of this wider perception is often mentioned: the ability to perform several tasks simultaneously, or participate in multiple conversations. Stein also comments on the frequent dyslexic preference for lateral thinking, with a divergent, holistic cognitive style, and a tendency to think in images as distinct from words.

Einstein himself explained his originality in problem-solving in this way, and he is a notable example of a child who did not talk until he was 4, or learn to read until he was 9 years old. He described his thought-processes as initially non-linguistic, consisting of signs and clear images which could be combined at will. He described the essential feature of productive thought as the associative play of visual and muscular elements. For him, turning these ideas into logical word-based communication was a difficult secondary stage only possible once the primary elements were established and reproducible.

Advanced visual/spatial, mathematical or mechanical skills are often linked to the dyslexic pattern of abilities (see Geschwind and Galaburda, 1985). Baker (1984), of the Orton Society, drew attention to the implications of research by Geschwind, Galaburda and others. She argued that slowing of the left hemispheric language area of the brain facilitated enlargement of the right side, which is more important for aspects of spatial perception and basic skills in art and music. She noted art, architecture, engineering, photography, mechanics and athletics as frequently reported superior skills in dyslexic families as a whole as well as these talents focused on the dyslexic members in a high degree. She puts forward the idea that delay in the development of the left side of the brain 'may have become prevalent in the course of evolution *because* it leads to superior development of the right side. In other words, it may be a means for producing certain kinds of superior talent' (emphasis added). This notion of such genetic design being important in areas of innovation and advancement for the race is most helpful for those trying to draw attention to the wastage of potential talent which these particular pupils can represent if they are not helped in the initial stages of literacy. Vail's (1990) identification of linked dyslexic traits, given in more detail on page 162, also has relevance in this connection.

Thomas West (1991) has examined the effect of learning difficulties on the lives of ten renowned visual thinkers including Einstein, Edison, Faraday, Tesla the electronic engineer, Poincaré the diverse mathematician, Lewis Carroll, Winston Churchill and W.B. Yeats. Recent neurological research connecting visual talents and verbal difficulties is explored, and advances in complex three-dimensional computerized visual information analysis are predicted to give new opportunities to innovative visual thinkers. Particularly interesting is West's thorough study of 'Constellations of Traits, Dyslexia as Diversity' in his book. He also puts forward the proposition that the distinctly linear nature of current educational provision may be actively disbarring those who have the most potential talent in technological and problem-solving areas. 'Different kinds of problems and different kinds of tools may require different talents and favour different kinds of brains' (1991, p. 8). He also points out that people with flexible, eclectic minds capable of handling complex problems could also be those who have difficulty focusing on or recalling single-track rote information in the early stages of education. It is more likely to be the experimental areas of new development that fascinate or obsess these 'global thinkers', rather than learning or repeating passed-down knowledge from books. In such cases, strategies of savage selectivity about reading, targeting effort to the crux of a problem, and looking at it from different perspectives (which a dyslexic often learns to do from sheer desperation) can pare down irrelevant research and lead to success.

Two public schools stand out as providing specialist support for dyslexics and a full range of opportunities for utilizing their visual/spatial strengths through excellent art and design departments. They are Carmel College, Oxfordshire, and Stowe School, Buckinghamshire.

RECOGNIZING DYSLEXIA

Chasty (1988) published a check-list for parents of signs to look for, usefully related to different age-groups. These can be summarized as follows:

1. Under five:
    Delay in initial speech and development.
    Rambling speech, difficulty with sentences.
    Clumsiness, especially pencil control.
    Unusual laterality: no set preference for right or left, e.g. uses left hand and both feet for kicking, or shows ambidexterity.
2. Two years later:
    Problems with: putting things in order/sequence, saying a list;
                   memory, e.g. multiplication tables, names of objects;
                   practical tasks: dressing in order, left/right, tying shoe-laces etc.
3. Further signs:
    School-related problems: reading aloud (poor expression, rhythm, tone);
                   poor memory of story read;
                   gap between written work and good oral skill;
                   messy work, many crossings-out;
                   slow, often wrong copying;

letters out of order;
confusion of letters b/d, p/g, m/w;
excessive tiredness because of problems.

This check-list has been extended in the current Dyslexia Institute leaflet to include as well:

seeming bright in one way but with a 'block' in others
others in the family with similar problems
reversing figures (such as 15 for 51) or words (was for saw)
reading a word once, then losing it next line down
spelling a word several ways
poor concentration span for reading/writing
problems with time and tense
difficulty taking notes
difficulty planning work or organizing personal belongings

There are several diagnostic instruments available to teachers, such as the Bangor Dyslexia Test and the Aston Index.

The Bangor Test, designed by Professor Miles (1983a), requires an interview situation. It covers many basic indicators such as memory for numbers, and then digits in reverse, familial incidence, and copying the correct pronunciation of words like preliminary. It contains varied face-to-face tests of left/right orientation and comes up with positive score indicators towards a diagnosis of dyslexic tendencies. It is fairly short and easy to administer.

The Aston Index, designed by Newton and Thomson (1982), is a very comprehensive analysis. Some items can be adapted for group use, and it contains a traditional reading/spelling age calculation test. It has two levels catering for differentiated age groups, and its use can produce a very full cognitive profile, often complete with age comparisons, on many aspects of academic sub-skills. Individual items can be selected from it. It surveys abilities such as vocabulary level, the analysis of free writing, observation perception and motor co-ordination in the Goodenough Draw-a-man test, copying geometric designs, sound discrimination, auditory sequential memory, and laterality.

Educational psychologists prefer the Wechsler Intelligence Scale for Children (Revised) (WISC(R)) or, sometimes, the British Ability Scale (BAS), neither of which is available to teachers. An example of a WISC profile has been given in Figure 1.2. The 'ACID' test is significant for the dyslexic, where one considers scores on the sub-tests of Arithmetic, Coding, Information and Digit span; these are areas accepted as discriminating against dyslexics, who tend to score below average in these areas.

The BAS was developed by researchers led by Colin Elliott (1983), so it is both the most recent IQ test and designed for Britain. It has 23 scales used in long or short form, ranging over perceptual and cognitive skills grouped according to stimulus mode, process and response mode. It is highly flexible, and Elliott has put the case for training teachers to use it. Many teachers well versed in interpreting WISC results and implications for parents and pupils find the BAS daunting.

RESISTANCE TO THE RECOGNITION OF DYSLEXIA

Opposition to the concept of dyslexia has come from several areas, some of which have vested interests in denying its existence. Some local education authorities do not recognize dyslexia, and employ like-minded psychologists, so saving a great deal of money to be used for other purposes. The findings of Pumfrey and Reason highlight the variability of both recognition and provision for dyslexics across the nation's local education authorities even when they answered direct survey questions about it. Only three-quarters of the authorities responded, and of these only 30 per cent had a written policy on dyslexia. One could therefore deduce that only one quarter of all the local education authorities in Britain had a consistent formal provision of any kind.

Other professionals find the diversity of symptoms listed, and the hotly argued controversies over even such basic principles as what causes it or what it should be entitled diminish its credibility because dyslexia is not a clear-cut, well-defined, traditional disability. These very factors are what make it a fascinating field of study to others – to be at the forefront of knowledge on such a prevalent and complex problem, to discover something fresh, to unravel a relatively new mystery. It is indeed a subtle, hidden handicap, and a very emotive issue both to those who suffer from it and to their families. People who think in fixed stereotypes and black-and-white categories often cannot cope with the grey, unexplored areas connected with dyslexia theory and research, and it can infuriate them to the point of designating it to the academic 'twilight zone'. Even the best way of training/teaching the dyslexic pupil is interpreted in different ways by different organizations. That was one of the main reasons why this book was written – to let dyslexic individuals give their opinions on the matter.

As an analytical problem-solving exercise to some professionals who confidently consider their own particular discipline to have all the answers, the concept of dyslexia can be a vexed issue since it highlights how little we know about important matters such as precisely how the brain and senses co-ordinate in the learning process. It also picks up glaring inadequacies in the British educational system, for which different bodies like to blame each other; for example, the government likes to blame the teachers, the teachers show their disapproval of government policy, and rows ensue over whether vast amounts of cash have been spent pursuing the wrong policies.

If you want to cause an academic riot, just shout 'Let's discuss dyslexia!' to a hall randomly filled with educational psychologists, assorted educational 'experts', politicians, teachers and parents. Then retire gracefully and watch the mayhem commence.

These are just a few of the factors which lead to comments such as that of the late Professor Meredith of the University of Leeds, who referred to dyslexia as 'The unidentified flying object of psychology' (quoted in Pumfrey and Reason, 1991, p. 6). In fact, this is quite a good analogy in some ways, because both phenomena thrive on fear of the unknown. If there is one thing calculated to annoy any group of professionals, it is implying that they are ignorant about something they should know about. It may be precisely this reaction which prompts apparently level-headed professionals to deny the existence of dyslexia without having studied the literature or explored a special facility. The reasoning seems to flow this way: 'I am a professional, and I am good at my job. I don't know about this, and I wasn't told about it at college; therefore it must be a plot by people who wish to make my life difficult and ask me awkward questions, and even worse, possibly blame me for not having done something which

I don't know how to do. This condition cannot possibly exist; it is much too obscure, inconvenient and dangerous to my professional image. My mind is closed: whoever said "I think, therefore I am" was wrong; I work on the principle that "I was not taught about it, therefore it cannot be!"'

As a practising teacher the only practical suggestion I can seriously offer is that people pontificating against the concept should be given first-hand knowledge or experience of dyslexia as it is shown by pupils en masse in a specialist school, across a varied curriculum. Meeting such pupils, examining their work and listening to their experiences soon dispels any doubts about the reality of the condition.

DYSLEXIA OR SPECIFIC LEARNING DIFFICULTY?

The division of opinion over which of these two terms should be used is something I find particularly frustrating. I do not wish to give the subject a thorough discussion here, but would refer the interested reader to Pumfrey and Reason (1991) who analyse the issue in detail.

I am aware of the technical arguments about the terms, but ask many dyslexics about the phrase 'specific learning difficulties' and they find it unclear and incomprehensible to friends. Perhaps it is a little like calling a spade a specific gardening implement – quite a non-specific term for everyday use, in fact. One can obviously explain it at a basic level as specific to language, memory, sequencing, etc., or as an umbrella term focusing on particular symptoms. To me, as an English specialist, the word specific implies the definite; or as the Oxford dictionary puts it, 'distinctly formulated, particular, not general or vague'. Yet dyslexia by its very nature is a wide-ranging and erratic manifestation of cognitive and processing difficulties. The currently fashionable long, complex term still does not imply the variety of effects and sub-types of dyslexic pattern which can emerge from this condition. Dyslexia, the idea of being a non-word-based person, or word-blind, must surely be an easier concept to grasp for the person in the street. The thing many dyslexics actually complain about is being unable to spell the word which describes them!

This term also works against all the sterling work which has been done over the years to publicize the condition of dyslexia by dedicated national charitable organizations such as the Dyslexia Institute and the British Dyslexia Association.

The national inquiry conducted by Pumfrey and Reason (1991) and a team of 11 educational psychologists for the National Foundation for Educational Research (NFER) found that 87 per cent of the psychologists they surveyed preferred the term specific learning difficulties; only 30 per cent felt dyslexia was a helpful term.

The increased confusion brought about by the proliferation of kinder terms for other groups of educationally handicapped children such as the traditional slow learner or educationally sub-normal (ESN) child was brought home to me when I was job-hunting recently. I was looking for dyslexic provision posts (specific learning difficulties in East Sussex). General vague specifications such as 'teacher required for girls with some learning difficulties' abounded. Colleges, universities and comprehensive schools wanted special needs co-ordinators or lecturers, without specifying areas of provision or responsibility. It was necessary to ring each place individually to find out if expertise in my specialist area was relevant. The results were surprising; the blanket term of learning difficulties in the private/charity sector covered establishments specializing in a varied range of problems from epilepsy to slow-learners, from asthma to autism. State schools for moderate learning difficulties could not give any analysis of the type of learning difficulties admitted, or the proportion of dyslexics within them. The colleges and large schools I contacted had not even considered dyslexia as a special need, and had no policy. They were looking for people who had educational experience of the blind, deaf or those in wheelchairs, often stating that the post existed because they were legally obliged to put in wheelchair access provision to buildings by a certain deadline, or were running special courses for the physically handicapped. Are we not in danger of too much generalization, lumping everyone with any handicap as a vague learning difficulty, instead of analysing what specific provision they require, and becoming expert in its effective delivery? I mention this to show how little notice is often taken of a condition which affects 1 in 25 pupils according to the Dyslexia Institute. How is it that their existence in terms of special needs can be totally ignored under provision they are legally entitled to under the 1981 Education Act, classified as handicapped pupils?

SHOULD PEOPLE BE LABELLED DYSLEXIC?

There has been much debate about the problems of labelling children, the ethics, the effects on their confidence and future treatment, being singled out as different, and even the accuracy of the diagnoses implied. Add to this the current controversy over whether an individual should be referred to as having a Specific Learning Difficulty or Dyslexia, and many parents withdraw confused and worried about identifying their child officially in this way. What we should all ask ourselves, perhaps, is how helpful the label is likely to be to the person concerned? Will it help the child to reach a more satisfactory destination educationally? Will it entitle the student to some extra specialist teaching, exam concessions or reduced entry requirements to further education? Will it help the individual to understand their own learning pattern and make some sense of their experiences and perceptions, so improving morale? As the parent of two dyslexics, I feel that the result of this kind of labelling, if it is done with explanation and common-sense counselling to the student, can only be beneficial. I am convinced of this because of the confidence levels which can be rebuilt on the factual framework of a learning profile which has been intelligently explained. I have spent many years communicating to students and parents the meaning and practical implications of reports from educational psychologists on dyslexics. Countless times I have seen amazement cross the faces of students who thought they were stupid, lazy, bad or even crazy when they understood a high score on a sub-test and what it meant. Comments like 'Suddenly my whole life fits into place!' or 'I keep on thinking of things I could never understand about myself, and in a flash it makes sense' come from adults and A-level students after such sessions. 'I wish someone had told me this years ago' is another common response. 'I never dreamt that anyone could call me intelligent, let alone superior' was one sad remark. 'Why couldn't anyone see at school that I had these abilities, that are written here now, locked up inside me? I've wasted my life.'

For a comprehensive description of the opposing opinion, see Pumfrey and Reason (1991) or a brief account by Lowenstein (1988).

DOES DYSLEXIA DEMAND AS MUCH ATTENTION AS OTHER SPECIAL NEEDS?

It is obvious that various groups of children may suffer some failure, emotional disturbance or damage because of variable factors such as physical handicap, home problems, deprivation or illness. A caring school can do much to overcome the problems of these children. Many books have been written on therapeutic matters, such as those of Oakeshott (1973) and Bettelheim (1971). There is ongoing discussion about the advantages and disadvantages of integration for physically handicapped pupils, both politically and at local authority level. The deprivation and decay of inner city areas has been well publicized. With further financial cuts and larger classes, all minority groups in need of special provision are more at risk.

However, the needs of the child who is blind, deaf, behaviourally disturbed or impoverished are obvious to the teacher. The special requirements of these children demand immediate attention and one expects an empathetic professional response. The national support systems and government agencies for dealing with such problems already exist and can be activated. It is the condition of dyslexia, as my study shows, which is often unrecognized, misinterpreted or punished by people who would not consider treating the obviously impaired unsympathetically.

It is the ignorance surrounding this complex condition which causes so many difficulties. It can leave sufferers and their families as well as staff confused, bitter and vulnerable. No nation can afford to waste the potentially educable, or leave untreated any group as large as 1 in 25. Above all, the symptoms of dyslexia can be remediated; literacy, memory and organizational skill can be trained and improved without expensive treatment of the whole family, or resistant social conditions. This makes it one of the more cost-effective areas of school failure to alleviate, especially if intervention occurs early.

Consider also that IQ profiles of dyslexics can reveal high innate Performance and Visuo-spatial powers. If they are neglected, we may overlook potential innovators, scientists and designers.

Recent disturbing evidence has come via televised documentaries about the number of prisoners who have specific learning difficulties. One documentary, shown on Channel 4 in 1992, featured a survey conducted by Dr Chasty of the Dyslexia Institute; his survey, which has not been published, found that over half of the prison population within one establishment was affected.

The figures on suicide or emotional/mental breakdown connected with this particular problem if it goes unrecognized are incalculable, and they demand research. I would echo John Donne's famous quotation that no man is an island; we as educators should be particularly concerned about the rather explosive islands which dyslexics can represent. Not only do any disturbances individuals cause in classrooms affect the educational climate for others, including the teacher, but they are also capable of the sort of self-destruction which can see them sink without trace in the educational system. We should care about the suffering of every individual whose lifetime confidence may have been destroyed by this minority dyslexic situation.

USEFUL ORGANIZATIONS

The Arts Dyslexia Trust
Hon. Sec.: Mrs S. Parkinson, ARCA, Lodge Cottage, Brabourne Lees, Nr Ashford, Kent TN25 6QZ.
Information, newsletters and advice on the creative dyslexic and careers in art/design. Lectures and publications. Exhibitions organized.

British Dyslexia Association
Headquarters: 98 London Road, Reading, Berkshire RG1 5AU.
Many local branches exist, giving extensive information and advice, arranging talks and support groups. Approved teacher lists are kept. Telephone help-line facility.

The Dyslexia Institute
Headquarters: 133 Gresham Road, Staines, Middlesex TW18 2AJ.
Twenty-three centres of the Institute exist nationwide, offering teaching, assessment by teachers and educational psychologists, and part-time teacher training courses. Enquiries welcome.

Adult Dyslexia Organisation
Headquarters: 336 Brixton Road, London SW9 7AA.
Advice, lectures, newsletter. Telephone help-line facility.

Chapter 2

Meet the Students

The boys are very varied, with contrasting backgrounds and skills. Their words are powerful, their experiences shocking or controversial, and the effects on their emotions were dramatic.

JOHN

Picture a stocky, loud 11-year-old with slightly rough manners, an infectious grin and a strong but soft-voiced cockney accent.

He appeared in my class of eight at a boarding special school for dyslexic boys one morning to join the class, new. It was Geography, which consisted of copious coloured diagrams and short facts about coastal erosion, printed on the white board. He answered brief introductory questions about his last schools very frankly and with great confidence. 'I 'ated the first, but the second was a great laugh. Didn't learn nothin' though.'

The cautious, more withdrawn established seven pupils assessed him quietly. He generated a brief discussion with others by way of their experiences, and I told him a bit about the others in the class and what to expect in lessons.

To our surprise, he copied a whole board of writing and diagrams faster than I could write, when my class were struggling and looking at diagrams, and we were all reading the material through. It was perfectly copied, very rare for a dyslexic. I thought to myself, 'Why is he here?' Then I asked him to read the material to me on his own – not a word could he decipher. He had copied it symbol by symbol, eye to paper without being able to process a word. I enquired how he did it and his answer was that his last teacher used to rap him over the knuckles if he wasn't fast enough, or he'd lose all his break and lunch-times copying up. So he developed speed. It took me a long time to cure him of non-reading compulsive copying.

Thus John had entered a special school for dyslexics at the age of 11 years 9 months. At that time his literacy problems were so severe that his reading age was 7.2 (Neale accuracy) and his spelling age (Schonnel) 6 years 9 months. He had an IQ on the WISC(R) of 134 Verbal and 97 Performance.

The general school impression of John was of an extrovert personality with a strong sense of humour and mischief. On arrival he immediately threw himself into every available sports activity – Duke of Edinburgh awards, canoeing, camping, football, tennis, table tennis and gymnastics.

His teacher–pupil relationships were rather erratic, being very friendly in some, and frustrated with others. He had attended a child guidance clinic, and was crossed-lateral (left-handed and right-eyed) with noticeable ambidexterity that was later to devastate opponents in tennis and table tennis.

He had been diagnosed dyslexic at an early age (6 years 11 months) and had received specialist help at regular intervals. At special school he became a prolific potter, and made a startling improvement in reading, gaining 2½ years on the Holborn test in his first year and continuing to improve at a similar rate throughout the rest of his school career (Neale test). He moved into examination sets for five CSEs and three O-levels, gaining acceptable results. A notable achievement was a CSE grade 3 in English Language (above national average).

He stayed on voluntarily for an extra year, and became a memorable, sporting head boy with many responsibilities in a boarding school. Juniors spoke of his kindness when they were upset, providing tea, toast and sympathy in a suitably tough and acceptable way.

John was lucky enough to have been identified early, and given specialist help. He himself describes his special school provision in terms of salvation from thuggery. It is notable that both successful head boys in this study benefited from early identification.

John's mother had been very supportive as she was dyslexic herself. He was also very lucky to have been able to take refuge in sporting achievement. John's literacy problems had been very severe, yet he left school able to read and discuss Shakespeare.

Negative experiences

Violence from teachers

John started off his free recollections with memories of violence connected with school, and at a surprisingly young age. These incidents occurred at a private prep school which he attended for his first four years of education. He got very hot and bothered when he first told me about that school, had to loosen his collar, and doodled someone running:

> I used to hate most of the kids, just a few of them were alright. The teachers I really hated. One of them hit me over the head with the thick end of a broom. Right across the side of the head, I had a whacking great bruise on the corner, and a long, thin bruise right across the back of my head. I never told my mum. I used to keep it quiet. I don't think the teacher meant to hit me as hard as she did. I was about six or seven; needlework teacher she was, Mrs F. her name was. You can imagine how needlework and me got on! That was the school where I learnt to bounce, I think. There was a teacher there called Mrs T. who used to hit me over the knuckles very hard with a ruler every time I messed

about. (I threw things, skived off work.) Feeling went in the knuckles eventually, you get used to it.

Mind you, from what I can make out I was a right sod then, from all accounts. That Mrs T. hit me really hard once – she asked me to do a piece of work and I just couldn't, so she said I was stupid. I said if she was so bleedin' clever let her do it herself. So she hit me. I used to spend all day at her desk. I was always saying things like that.

It's the only school I've never been back to, even to walk past; I sort of dread it.

Humiliation

John was quite bitter about his first primary school, even after so much time had passed:

> It was a private school and I used to hate it there because they were all bloody clever and I was stupid. They all passed their 11-plus and I couldn't even read the bloody questions. I hated all of them.

Teasing/persecution

John had unhappy relations with other children in private school, and his school records confirm this. In a pilot interview for a reading study he told me he had been teased and bullied by other children, though he had one good friend he saw at breaktimes. He said he had been asked to leave because he wouldn't pass his 11-plus and remembered having been put in a class with 'older, bigger, posh kids'. He also said, 'It's as simple as this. If you get the mick taken out of you 24 hours a day, you go crackers' (comment at age 14½).

John's reactions to this sort of treatment were strong and long-lasting, even though he had been identified early and given some specialist help, as well as removal to a special secondary boarding school at the onset of senior education.

John managed to get off school even at infant level – police were regularly called because he had run off to the canal. Then at his state primary school truancy became habitual: 'Afternoons we never used to turn up after lunch. No one used to bother. We used to muck about in the yard with a load of cardboard boxes.'

Inadequate help/neglect

A worrying picture of the inadequacy of some of the help given formed. John went to a state school for 2¼ years, after he was asked to leave the prep school as he stood no chance of passing the 11-plus exam. John's comments on his primary school teacher were scathing:

> I read *Roderick the Red* [Pirates series] six times in two years. It was the easiest in the school. I knew it off by heart. I chose it – the only easy one there. She didn't give a toss; when I finished she used to start again. You know what state teachers are like. Also she had the worst class in the school and was fresh out of college. I had her for all my time there, two or three years.

Assistance given was extremely superficial:

> Mr Z. [Head] used to take me for five minutes' extra reading in the corridor, twice. Then he could say to the parents of three or four boys he teaches remedials. It really used to pee me off.

His school claimed in reports that he had remedial help every afternoon, when he had in fact truanted (see p. 27). His lack of improvement in scores during the two and a quarter years at this school corroborate his neglect. Nor are his memories of a famous special unit particularly warm, though his reading improved from unscorable to 7 years 2 months (Neale accuracy) and spelling reached 6.9 years (Schonnel). (When I charted his progress, he had only ever improved scores during individual teaching.)

> I used to have a day off school a week to go to Unit E for an hour remedial with some American woman. She was a right stupid cow. She used to freak me out. She used to make me do all these exercises like lay on the floor face down and pull myself along by my fingers to help my writing muscles. She made me draw some man without any clothes. I remember drawing a very basic man, then when I left I had to do the same, but it had hair, eyes and everything. I had one of them who wrote the book, just once. Really nice house and garden – got lost in it for a day . . . Mum and me always had Cornish pasties/pie shop treat, that was the best thing about it.

The running man sketch in Figure 2.1 was a recurrent motif during John's preliminary interview, a pilot for the main study, when he was aged 14½. In all, the figure occurred six times, in varied forms and different sizes, usually being wounded or pursued by some war machine (Figures 2.2 and 2.3). He was noticeably doodling at tense moments, when relating particularly unhappy episodes from his primary school life, such as the violence from a woman teacher. He also drew a rather vicious-looking toothed logo of his initials (Figure 2.4). He got physically hot under the collar and had to loosen his shirt neck, commenting 'Is it hot in here, or is it just me?' and asking to open a window. The room temperature, however, was average.

Associative reactions

Lack of communication

John had a tendency not to tell anyone about his suffering, even his parents. He said about being hit with the broom at the age of 6 or 7, 'I never told me mum. I used to keep quiet.' The same applied to fights later.

Lack of confidence

John's most noticeable lack of confidence occurred when confronted with the written word, especially in public. When asked how he felt about exams he said, 'I feel more worried when I have to read out the register.'

This was his duty at assemblies as head boy, and involved reading 110 names in front of the same number of boys and all the staff (truly a dyslexic's nightmare). He practised with me a lot, and memorized the register totally to avoid embarrassing mistakes. This is similar to his mother's account of him reciting a Bible story to an audience

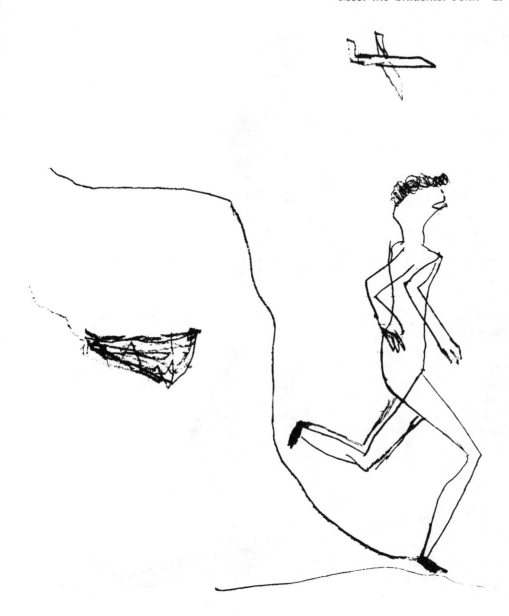

Figure 2.1

of parents at junior school when required to read aloud. He was word perfect; but unhappily he held the book upside down, so he got laughed at anyway.

In her parental interview John's mother commented that he was never unhappy except when paper was put in front of him – even the *TV Times*. She used to ask him, after he had left school for three years, to write down what he wanted in his lunch-box as a shopping list and he refused, saying 'I can't spell 'em.' Yet his mother is also dyslexic. In fact, as already mentioned, he has a CSE grade 3 in English Language (above national average). He also took O-level English Literature (with an amanuensis).

Figure 2.2

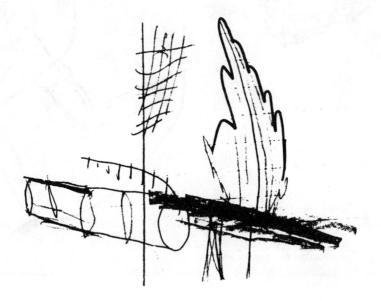

Figure 2.3

Another example of his residual feeling of literacy inadequacy was shown over his driving test. He asked, 'Do I have to fill in any forms?' When he was told no, he said, 'Then I'll pass.' He sailed through the test first time.

John actually used to score higher consistently on the Neale reading test with me than with his county psychologist. It seems that this was the result of a lack of confidence and a feeling of panic.

One of John's psychological reports says he is incapable of learning in anything but

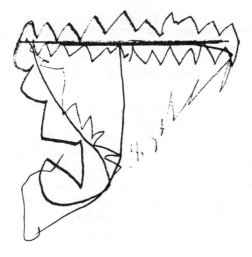

Figure 2.4

an individual situation. He had to feel very secure before he would work with any teacher. When he was 15 we had long individual staff/parent discussions at open day (including the games staff) about how he had to feel exceptionally liked before he would co-operate or work for any teacher. He did overcome this eventually, and pass public exams for varied class-teachers.

Self-doubt/denigration

John felt out of place at his prep school, but his low opinion of himself as a child showed in his free interview: 'D was a state school. We was all thick and stupid together, it was a great laugh.' His comment about staying on for an extra year reflected this to a certain extent: 'We're all the same – you're a bit scared of work, though you want the money.'

When asked about his work and his intelligence he consistently answered 'average'. Yet he had a verbal IQ of 134 (WISC(R)), which he knew about. His full score was 117, which put him in the bright normal range of intellectual potential, in the top 16.1 per cent of the population.

Competitiveness disorders

No particular question was asked, but evidence emerged via records. John's tendency to give up prematurely on difficult tasks and situations was commented on throughout his school career, even being noticed at primary level. A report strongly recommending residential placement states:

> A large comprehensive will swallow John and this will only strengthen his tendency to withdraw from a failure situation instead of persisting. . .
> John is a likeable boy, gets on well with adults. Has a lot of energy and determination

and good intelligence but is very quick to avoid 'the failure situation'. I can only conclude that a large school would swallow John and lead to a continuous failure situation.

His SE2 medical advice form reads in a similar way: 'His concentration is limited by his withdrawing it from a difficult situation. He has no difficulty in concentrating on what interests him.'

However, I did not find this concentration problem made him withdraw from his English remedials, but he needed a great deal of convincing that he should go for classes aiming at public exams, English Literature in particular. He tended to opt out. When convinced he was as good as or better than others in the group he became a 'star' for that particular teacher, whereas before she saw his work for me and his IQ details she felt he was fairly vague mentally, purely because he would not participate.

This manifested itself even on the games field, where he was an all-round brilliant performer. When he was 15 there was protracted discussion at school about his unwillingness to participate unless he felt he would win even in sport. He would give up before attempting to reach the goal.

As captain of a very impressive football team he was heavily criticized by a keen player on one occasion for giving up when the opposing team scored rapid goals early on. This keen player said John would not even try after that, so the whole team lost heart. The early stages were crucial with John, and he found it difficult to rally and fight back once he felt he had slid down. I also recall going through John's reports with him as his tutor. He received the usual batch of As for effort and Cs for achievement. He looked less than elated and I asked what was wrong:

> It's always the bloody same. It really guts me off. 'Tries hard but don't get nowhere', that's what it means! I wish just once I could get it the other way round for something in school, saying I didn't put meself out but did well anyway. Just once! Like all those other buggers! It ain't fair.

With that he left, quite politely but obviously disappointed.

Sensitivity to criticism

John's mother commented on this in her questionnaire answers about her son's temperament: 'His personality is outgoing, but he has a short fuse. Doesn't like to be told he is doing something wrong – shouts and hollers! You have to be careful *how* you tell him.'

This touchiness syndrome seems to come into play quite early. Mrs J. recalled that even as a young child John would become exceptionally huffy if told off, and sulk at the bottom of the garden, or up a tree. On return from boarding school he would cook and leave a mess, and the same reaction would occur in a more sophisticated form. Though this is typical of adolescent behaviour generally, in combination with the other identified reactions John displayed, it is relevant. The conflict was alleviated by distancing and careful management. Mrs J. highlights the problem effectively in her accounts when she comments that she had been worried about spoiling John in order to compensate for his literacy difficulties and setbacks. It is very hard for parents who are deprived of their children for long periods of time in special boarding school provision to maintain a balanced relationship and consistent discipline. The boys themselves report some resentment at missing home life and feeling jealous of children left at home.

These are not families with an accepted tradition of boarding school, and they may not be in harmony with discrepant special school attitudes and regimes. Communication needs to be very good between home and school, and dyslexics tend not to be communicative, as shown in my results. Some emotional reaction problems can be brought about by the boarding school situation.

Behaviour problems

John's own account of his behaviour is fairly startling, once he went to state primary school. He seemed to feel he had a running vendetta with the staff: 'I got my own back though, it was only fair – sneaked in and blocked the staff loos. I remember feeling really chuffed – they was all women, I couldn't see them using the men's.' At special school he merely got up to some normal boyish pranks like dorm-raids and midnight walks in the park.

The previous report from his last school commented, 'Tends to disrupt. There are some problems handling him in a large class but in a small group he is quite amenable.'

He was considered to be somewhat aggressive, and also cheeky to adults. John felt his behaviour could have gone dramatically astray if he had not been sent to a specialist boarding school. He also mentions the idea of coming away from the home area and fights as useful, finding the special school a sort of country refuge:

> If I hadn't come here I'd have been a skinhead or Mohican. Worse than that, I'd have probably left home by now. All the crowd I used to hang about with are really bad.
>
> Anyway, it's a relief to get back sometimes. Things cool down. You think twice before you get involved again. I know others think the extra year helped them calm down; think they'd be in a lot of bother, else.

When asked what he felt was the worst thing a school could do to a dyslexic, his answer was immediate: 'Taking all their confidence away.'

Appendix

Public examination results

Summer 1984	CSE	Arithmetic	5
		Metalwork	4
	GCE	Art	E
Summer 1985	CSE	Arithmetic	4
		English Language	3
		History	5
	GCE	English Literature	E
		Woodwork	E

John

A walk in Brick wall park
Wun night I could not sleep so I whent far a walk in Brick wall park I whent
out the frunt dour and thrue the side gate. the gate was old and
rotted a bit from the wind rain and all the boys how whent thro
it cicking and pulling it about.

When I was about a hundrin yards from the old gate
i saw a Brark in the wall So i whent thro it in to the wall gardens.
it was very scary and I saw an big bird fly out to an tree it
must of Been an owl. then I that Davis patting the prevch to Ded. So i
hid Behide a tree so he did not see me and when he whent I hed
along over a wall and in to Bladkig main park. I walked up to
the pvyilyon and in to thers not Ainyone. it was all mudey from
where horse rides have Been. so i cepted to the side. when i get
to the wood I whent in a bit But it was not very light and
I was getting colud and a lost I tride to fide my way
out But I get deeper and deeper in to the wood and got more and
more lost. all of a sudon I saw a Dond it was the lilypond.
so i whent to it and saw the allomnes paynt and a gray hed
put up par the gross cunty canse. So I made up my minde to
fotod the corse Because avenchiy thay would leed me home.
So I did. I whent in to the wood agane and follded the
allomnes croos aloes That wanoked out a Bit. But ater a whole
I got lost Agan. and I stoded to wunder about and all of a
sudon I saw a light it was a car hed light so I New
there was a rode. I warked over to it and stoded warking I whent
along past a cuple of house and over a stile. By nowe I was
ouitet ticvad and I was getting cortable and tirlk tiled so
i stoded runing noing that i would nave to get sume where and
I did I whent in a staft line and whchd about ten san
mine's I came to a brick wall I whent around it and fovnd my
gou way past it. I looked up and I saw the house it was
silente and qiet

good when night
my muns say good by to mot Davis. So I whated par about
five miniss and whent up sters got chaved got in to Bet and
fell fast asleep the next night day mort Davis came in and
sed had a good night, well what else code I say But yes.

Figure 2.5 John: sample of free writing

Career/occupation

John did training for bricklaying/heavy blockwork on leaving school. He is now a successful bricklayer, working on a sub-contract basis and as self-employed. His sister does his bookwork.

Work samples

The following poem by John expresses his feelings about his hobby of pottery with great sensitivity and humour. It shows how fluent a communicator he could be with a familiar amanuensis/scribe to record his thoughts on paper. Compare this with Figure 2.5, a sample of his free writing. It took years to overcome the frustrating inhibitions about getting spellings wrong which used to prevent him communicating in the written form at all. One boy described this sort of literary constipation as 'scriptophobia'. Contrast Figure 2.5 with the earlier sample of his work in Figure 1.1 and it will be seen that there is greater confidence and complexity, although dyslexic spelling patterns still persist. Despite this, it is an effective, atmospheric communication which is far more phonetically logical and reliable.

Pottery

I walked in to the small room,
Where the wheel is kept,
The room looks a mess,
With bits of half-squashed pots
stuck to the wall,
And big buckets
filled to the brim with
horribly slashy clay.
The floor is covered withh
a thick layer of dust,
And dirty towels
For cleaning the wheel off.
Finished pots sit allround the
room on shelves and
in the kiln which is
up in one cornner of the room.
The air is dry and
Thick with dust,
In the winter.
But in the summer,
You open all the windows
And the sun shines in
And lights the place up.
I spend a lot of time there,

To avoid boredom,
There is always somethig to do
People around drawing,
Or doing disign work on the computer.
A kettle and coffee stand in one cornner.

The place has an atmosphere
Cought from many boys
Spending thier time there
Though the years.
A worm, frendly, chaotic
Atmosphere
Homely, a refuge.
The wheel churns over,
Making a noise like it is
Breathing and humming.
When you press harder
On the clay, the wheel
Makes a noise likeit is
Yawning or growling,

Until you have made
the pot.
Then you take the pot off carefully
And put iton the shelf
And everything goes quiet
And peaceful.
So you turn the lights out,
Lock the door,

The pottery room goes
All dull again,
And you leave,
back to Civilization.

TREVOR

I first became aware of Trevor as a pale, withdrawn presence around the school; rather a ghostly shadow of a boy, usually complete with a frown or downcast gaze. He was often hurrying somewhere, sitting apart, or on the edge of things, looking slightly alarmed or nervous. He wore the air of a martyr, and a large crucifix around his neck invited comment from other boys. He held his head stiffly, tilted slightly back, and dark blue eyes gazed out from behind a very long black fringe with suspicion, some touch of superiority blending with definite suffering and defiance. He arrived at special school at the age of 12, fully statemented.

At that time he had a reading age of 7 years 4 months. He had a verbal IQ of 119 and performance IQ of 137 on the WISC(R) intelligence test. His behaviour at school was excellent, and from our own impressions and those of past school reports it was evident that his personality was complex, sensitive and deep. He had attended a child guidance clinic. He displayed some ambidexterity and some confusion in dominant auditory laterality. His mother had been particularly supportive towards him.

His dyslexic symptoms had been identified early, and he had been given remedial help. His degree of dyslexia remained severe for spelling. He became a responsible prefect, deputy head boy for the smaller boarding house, and went on to do A-levels at a further education college in preparation for teacher training. His public examination results were admirable (see list on page 44). Special talents were revealed in Art, Creative Writing and Drama.

Negative experiences

Inadequate help/neglect

Trevor's free interview started off with a grim account of his first encounter with remedial education at the age of 7, when he was first diagnosed as dyslexic. His aversion was compounded by being removed from his favourite teacher for the lessons. He was also in conflict with his remedial teacher, with whom he felt he made no progress:

> He was an old man, not very understanding, rather rough and harsh ... I did not like the bloke at all. He saw me as just a job that had to be done. When I left the school it was a relief to get rid of him. That's how much I hated the guy. We used the Languagemaster tapes. He even used to do me for being late when it wasn't my fault.

The sense of resentment and unfair discrimination that Trevor felt even at the early age of 7 highlights the problems of withdrawal systems for extra help. Pupils need to be consulted, and negotiation should take place over timetabling.

It was at middle school that things really began to go to pieces for Trevor. Remedial provision again proved unhelpful: 'I had remedials in a group of four with an English teacher, Mrs K. She was absolutely useless, used to rant and rave, and I used to rebel against her.' Trevor reacted against what he called 'the remedial attitude', which he described as 'patronising and two-faced'.

Humiliation

Trevor felt especially humiliated in middle school. He was regularly insulted by a staff member and began to feel isolated. This had a very adverse effect on his morale:

> I didn't like many of the teachers. Mr L. had a Hitler moustache and was always telling me I was useless and no good and would never get anywhere in History. I'm waiting for my 'O'-level results now, and I'd love to show it to him – 'Remember me?'

Unfair treatment/discrimination

Trevor felt very strongly about being left out of plays and losing his turn for performing as a result of literacy difficulties:

> I enjoyed drama, but never got major parts as the teacher thought I wouldn't be capable of learning the lines. I suspected it then, I'm sure now. It was a rotary thing – every child in class had a turn at the main part, but not me. Same with assemblies. It peed me off. I wanted to know why, but never asked anyone; it wasn't my style.

This boy had a lot of dramatic talent; he was a 'natural', judging from the performances I have seen him give at school and what I have heard drama teachers there say about him. Fortunately, his parents had earlier found him an improvisation-based drama club outside his previous school. I saw his performance as Nerissa in *The Merchant of Venice* and he always took part enthusiastically in all our school modern drama.

Again, one is left with an immense feeling of past teachers neglecting this dyslexic pupil and letting him go to waste. This affects social development and can make a child a loner, as Trevor experienced for a long time.

He was very bitter about being downgraded generally in another subject because of his literacy at the middle school he attended from age 9 onward:

> When I moved up to the seniors I went from the bottom to middle maths groups. The last year there I went from bottom to middle and was top of it instantly. I did very well. Mr L. I greatly respected and looked up to. Last test, we were graded before being moved to the next school. I got 86 per cent, top; next was 23 per cent behind me. I got a grade C, yet all my other friends got Bs. That totally shattered me – I just couldn't see *why*. I really looked up to him. He never moved me to the top group and told me later he thought I couldn't cope with the reading.
>
> My parents and I think I was downgraded by the head as I was having trouble getting extra help. I got it, and it was that old geezer again, which I hated. It didn't last for very long.
>
> (The 'old geezer' was the man from his primary school, a peripatetic member of staff.)

Teasing/persecution

Trevor suffered particularly from this at middle school, where he felt his lack of literacy caused persecution:

> This school is where the teasing started and people used to take the mickey. I used to have quite regular fights. There was a group of boys, about eleven or twelve of them, headed by a girl, all chanting round me.
>
> I enjoyed games there, especially rugby, but *not* running ... Mr P. was very enthusiastic, a good bloke. In running everyone used to cheer people on – nobody ever did for me, so I never ran.

In the end he snapped, and retaliated to the chanting group (quite bravely since there were about thirteen of them):

> I laid into the first boy. He had a couple of black eyes, a broken tooth. It took four to pull me off him. Next day the same thing happened. I got taken up to one of the teachers, but it was dropped quite quickly.

Trevor at first welcomed special schooling, but found that it too could have social difficulties, if not academic ones:

> I never got homesick until two days before we were due to go home. It seemed good to start with because all the boys had the same problems so there was no mickey-taking. However, in a small community you get various scrapes, and people form groups. It seems to be good sport to bait, annoy, mickey-take, wind up and generally make a person's life hell. You are in a set environment and you cannot get away from a person, especially if you're in a dormitory with them. Centred on one person who incited everyone else. . .
>
> About a year and a half ago, Oliver was making my life purgatory/pure hell. Shared a dorm, and in my classes. When he was quiet he was worst – scheming how to wind people up. He turned me into the person I am – I thank him. I got to see the other side, mickey, 24 hours a day; sick practical jokes, picked on, wound up constantly. (Being so

much younger than everyone else.) Clothes, family, prevention of doing things. Got others to join in. Art room episodes.

Associative reactions

Truancy/school refusal

Trevor stoically resisted the temptation to truant: 'I've been reluctant, but I've always gone. I've thought about it, but it never seemed the thing to do. It would have repercussions, and was pointless anyway. Escapism.'

Psychosomatic pain

At the most miserable stage of his career at middle school, aged 12, Trevor's unhappiness manifested itself in a physical form:

> While there I developed a pain in the right leg – went to hospital. Later it was diagnosed to be psychosomatic. At the time I thought it was a rare disease, but I didn't care as I got off school.

This is supported by records, and he spent some time on crutches. A doctor described it thus:

> Essentially the problem appears to be:
> 1. He is dyslexic but intelligent.
> 2. He is therefore frustrated.
> 3. The frustration is expressed as pain in the right thigh which occurs about once every six months and may last ten days at a time.

Isolation/alienation

Trevor's educational psychologist expressed concern early on that because of his high IQ (137 Performance; very superior, WISC(R)) and lack of comparative competence with classmates he might feel alienated owing to frustration and anxiety. Our interview bore out that this fear was justified:

> I was always the ringleader with other pupils. Always on top, until I went to middle school. There I started to withdraw, be by myself. I was being diagnosed at the time.
>
> There were gangs at school – trendies, mods, and it's where I started to withdraw from groups. I was never in a gang, though I wanted to be.
> [Middle school; approximate age 11]

> I wanted a black jacket with checks inside it, like them. I wanted to be a part, but yet different. I lived apart, so I didn't see them outside, so I was basically on my own, though I had friends at school . . .
>
> I was so often by myself. I didn't allow them to get close, I didn't want to know, I was too scared of getting hurt, especially with girls . . .
>
> I had trouble with the girls – a group of them were evil, taking the mickey all the time. I found and find it difficult to talk to girls, be interested. I knew I was intelligent, but in what I just didn't know at the time.
> [approximate age 11]

I was the oddity of the class – a girl I really liked in a year lower just didn't want to know. Homework took me half the night. I spent all my time in at home, or rode my bike alone. My parents were worried – they tried to get me to do more swimming because I was supposed to be good. I enjoyed it and it was relaxing, but I packed it in.

I eventually reluctantly joined Boys' Brigade and Scouts, but I was very nervous of meeting outside boys, I didn't know what they'd make of me. I enjoyed it because they took me for what they saw I was, not in school. I was never asked to read in church or anything. I enjoyed Scouts because of the countryside, you could get away from everything. I learnt recently that my parents were really worried because I never laughed, I was never happy. I went to America and I did laugh a lot there, I remember giving a talk about it [family holiday to Los Angeles]. My parents commented.

Trevor gave a very clear picture of how a child comes to feel so isolated by his answer to Q35 *What do you think is the worst thing a school can do to a dyslexic person?*:

Treat them differently to the rest of the class, especially if the rest of the class is not dyslexic. If they are treated as different, inferior, stupid, less valuable – then the rest of the class will pick up on that and the child will submerge into himself, never to be seen again. You are basically outcast.

Lack of communication

It can be very lonely. I can cut people off, be wary of them. There are not many people I can talk to like this. You are the only one I've ever really spoken to. I don't know why, perhaps it's the way you teach. Perhaps it's something about you. You're easy to talk to.

It can be scary to have someone understand you . . .

People you meet change you, you develop. I think what's wrong with the world could really be the barriers people put up – they can't open up.

Lack of confidence

Trevor's mother observed her son changing in his levels of self-assurance, as she comments in her questionnaire manuscript.

Q3: At what ages, if any, did you notice any severe lack of confidence or unhappiness in your son?

From quite young at nursery school his teacher described him as different from other children. From 7 years he was rarely seen very happy and I remember being so pleased to see him relaxed and happy on a holiday in America at 10 years old.

Trevor has always felt that his sister outshone him but at last he is beginning to realize that he is an individual in his own right and can excel at different things, e.g. poetry and art, and photography . . .

I feel Trevor's confidence grew when he realized there were others in the same boat as him and he wasn't singled out. In the final year at school and since being at college he has gained confidence as he has made good relationships with people and had academic success.

Q8: *What do you feel has been the most important factor overall in helping your child cope with dyslexia, and why?*

Success, because it has helped him grow in confidence and believe in himself.

His records were riddled with comments about his lack of confidence and low self-esteem. For example, his middle school head described temperamental behaviour as 'an attempt to hide his lack of self-confidence'. After three years at special school, Trevor's educational psychologist stated in a review:

> Although still lacking confidence with regard to his literacy skills in particular, Trevor remains well motivated to succeed. He explained that he feels he must do well in order to justify the money that is being spent on him.

This is despite having been promoted to the senior examination group (selection by merit rather than age then) and being the youngest boy in the senior school.

Self-doubt/denigration

A striking example of Trevor's insecure opinion of his ability to cope came when he was in his last term before going to sixth-form college. He had always been aware of his intelligence, and already had several successful examination results behind him, taken early at O-level and CSE. Yet he had a real panic about whether he would be able to keep up in a 'normal' college, or get on with the people. I had a hard job convincing him of his true ability even with population-based statistics. (He was very successful when he got there, both socially and academically.)

Competitiveness disorders

Trevor's early tendency to withdraw in fear not only from competition, but also socially has already been mentioned.

He also felt very strongly in competition with his sister: 'Very gifted, can do anything she wants to do if she puts her mind to it. Effortless, strolls along – I have to work so hard – she's so gifted and doesn't use it. It's not fair.'

His mother also commented on this. Trevor's account of his school life is full of references to his rank-order position in subjects – it is something which matters to him very much. The occasions when he was second top in Maths, best at Mental Arithmetic, and lead in the school play were glowingly reported and obviously vital vindications of his worth and self-esteem in a painful school career.

His reports show how obviously hard his inability to compete in literary areas must have hit him:

> Despite the early identification of his difficulties Trevor's progress has been merely marginal and he is becoming increasingly aware of his own disability and disturbed by his inability to work at a level which is in keeping with the other boys in his class.
> (Age 11 years 5 months)

When asked about foreseeing future difficulties Trevor said:

No, because I don't think about it. I suppose I should. I didn't put it on the form. College knows. I must stand on my own two feet. I'm going to succeed, I *will* succeed, I've no intention of being a failure.

It is very gratifying to know that Trevor has competed now and taken A-levels at the age of 18, winning a place at a top-grade teacher training college.

Sensitivity to criticism

Reports mention this effect, as different teachers at the special school comment:

Trevor always performs well, but he finds it difficult to cope with defeat on a personal level. If he is caught in the wrong he will not accept a reprimand. He must learn to accept advice and criticism.
(Mr I.)

Trevor appeared to overcome this tendency during his stay:

A good term's work. Trevor has accepted criticism in an increasingly mature manner. The scope of his work has expanded and he has recently come to realize that planning and close observation can go a long way towards producing satisfying work.
(Mr T.)

On relationships with adults, his middle school reports display the same comments:

Sometimes appears to be quite mature but finds difficulty in accepting criticism of any sort . . .
   He is easily upset and when this happens his manner can become a little aggressive. This, however, can be overcome by a calm but firm 'no nonsense' approach. His over-reaction and sometimes aggressive attitude is, I think, an attempt to hide his lack of self-confidence.
(Head)

I found him very amenable to suggestion, though he could get frustrated with other boys not concentrating in class when he was very interested. I would sum this up as an artistic, sensitive temperament 'not suffering fools gladly'. However, I was fortunate to deal with Trevor in a sphere where we discovered he excelled (creative writing), as well as English Literature, and we had joint enthusiasm on our side. I would say he demanded mutual respect from his teachers.

Behaviour problems

Given his withdrawn period, one does not automatically think of Trevor as having behaviour problems, but there were some indications at his very first school:

I was the class leader. I was the troublemaker, who used to tie girls' pigtails together, cause rubber-bit fights with biro blowpipes. I used to have a lot of fights, mainly play. I got on very well with everyone.

He used to be a hopscotch whiz-kid. The same boy tripped him up three times and then got his head cracked. Blood and tears, and Trevor said to a mouthy girl, 'Who's laughing now?' He also smashed up a drum kit. At middle school he retaliated to severe mockery by fighting. He also liked rugby, saying it was the only way he could let his anger out.

The alienation of middle school seems to have been his worst period, and records show real concern about his state of mind and sensitivity at this stage. His educational psychologist reported this:

> Indeed, his own awareness of the difficulties he is encountering seems to have begun to have an adverse effect on his general adjustment . . .
>
> He appeared to me to be painfully over-anxious about reading and in the light of his relatively good command of the sub-skills of reading and spelling I can only come to the conclusion that the underlying cause of his reading difficulty at the moment is an emotional one rather than being perceptual in nature . . .
>
> This would appear to be another case, therefore, of a boy who could be labelled mildly maladjusted and who will need to be educated in a school which will cater for his emotional as well as for his scholastic needs.

Trevor coped excellently with boarding school, despite some persecution as the clever youngest of the senior school. In his final year especially he was a witty, colourful 'star' to whom boys went with problems. He was valued by staff.

Boarding school

Trevor made some positive comments about specialist boarding school provision, while showing up some of the inherent difficulties:

> In my last term at my last school I knew I was coming to boarding school. I'd looked at lots – we came in and saw boys walking round in jeans and the atmosphere seemed good.
>
> The teaching was good, on a one-to-one basis – smaller classes, caring and interested teachers – the head was friendly, the main thing was that the staff cared about what was going on. There was no need for care staff. It seems to be becoming a school for kids with problems rather than learning problems. Whilst I was at the school I felt there was no way of getting out and relaxing [junior section of school]. Now I'm in the top year I find I can.
>
> I felt the school had broadened my outlook, a different experience – a merging of different backgrounds. Unfortunately, it broke down the social life – the three weeks away broke down relationships which just peter out. I felt very alone and sometimes felt it a relief when I did go back. The school built up my individuality and was positive. There were still people trying to be a 'lad'. After a year the head changed and the feeling at the school seemed to change. It was not quite as free; new staff, changes.
>
> At the start I found remedial teachers very understanding and caring, someone to talk to; but when older, starting to find them patronizing and two-faced. Found new interests – art flowered more, enabled me to broaden my outlooks. Photography, poetry [this year]. Creative writing this year.
>
> I'm starting to stand up for what I think more.
>
> My boarding special school and the people in it have made me what I am. I think I would be a less understanding, more selfish person, otherwise.
>
> I thank it for making me what I am – even though it's been painful at times. I don't think anywhere else I looked at could have done much for me.

This boy finally came away from Roehampton College with an honours degree in Art and Education, and is becoming a successful artist in his own right in terms of commissions, national competitions and exhibitions. Yet his first introduction to art was not auspicious according to his questionnaire answer.

Q6: *What is your earliest memory of school?*

Being told to paint a picture of rain. Being told I'd got to paint it going in one direction. I painted it going in all different directions. She gave me a mass rollicking and we had a row over it, and then she confiscated my cars.

His answer to another question is also significant, and shows how important academic success is for many dyslexics in the process of proving oneself.

Q7: *What is your best memory of school?*

Getting a B for my English Lit. There are other memories, but that just about crowns it. Some of the plays and things.

I would like to close this study of Trevor with the comment he gave about his school career from the questionnaire transcript.

Q29: *How would you describe your school life on the whole, looking back?*

Different! Like a cat in a tumble-drier – a lot of ups and downs! A lot of noise. Coming out a different shape and colour than what you went in. Or a guinea-pig, or a lemming!

Appendix

Public examination results

Summer 1985	CSE	Geography	3
		Science	1
	GCE	English Literature	E
		History	U
		Maths	D
	Cambridge	Certificate of Arithmetic (Pass)	
Autumn 1985	GCE	Art	C
		English Literature	B
		History	D
		Maths	D
Summer 1986	CSE	Biology	1
		English Language	2
		Technical Graphics	3
	GCE	Geography	C
		Maths	C
		Technical Drawing	E
Summer 1987	GCE	Photography	B
1988		A-level Art	
		A-level Photography	

Career/occupation

Trevor is temporarily involved in care work for the handicapped, and is considering training as an art therapist.

Work samples

Trevor himself typed out his poems for the manuscript of this book; he also drew the illustrations (Figures 2.6–2.10). I started him writing poetry as part of his English CSE course, and it flourished from there, becoming a full part of his creative repertoire after leaving school. I was also encouraging him to take English Speaking Board examinations, which he passed very successfully. I felt that a boy with his obvious intelligence and creative talent, who was under a lot of pressure, needed as many outlets for self-expression as could be provided for him.

I have provided some general analytical comments on Trevor's work, of which the eight poems reproduced are a very small sample.

Themes

1. A strong sense of the cruelty of mankind is conveyed:
    'the harsh realities of man' ('Cross Roads', line 3)
    'she is the one who will stand there
    And watch me as I bleed' ('She', lines 3 and 4)

2. Corruption and pressure from society feature in his work, accompanied by a sense of helplessness, of being swamped:
    – A thought bubble 'worps, twists/And comes out maimed,/By the flickering tongues of the masses' ('Cross Roads', lines 9–11)
    'a concrete gray, desert,
    Of isolation and insanity' ('Cross Roads', lines 6 and 7)
    'a soul/That silently screams . . .
    as I watch paralysed . . .
    Drowned in the industrial waste of man,
    Possessed by the thoughts and impressions of the multitudes' ('Silent Scream,' lines 3–4, 7 and 14–15)

3. Disguise of the inner self, the mask and pretence is repeated ('Pierrot', and 'Cross Roads', line 12).

4. Sadness and vulnerability are seen in 'The Poet' and 'Pierrot'.

5. Escape and the desire for refuge is an interwoven thread:
    – Walking in a 'fantasy land' ('Cross Roads', line 1)
    'my chameleon self' ('Cross Roads', line 16)
    'like an unborn child in its mother's womb' ('Cross Roads', line 17)

6. The transience of pure happiness – catching a moment in time – is described in 'Summer'.

7. Romance is displayed in the intense teenage interest in the interplay of male–female relationships. Danger and disillusionment are portrayed in 'She' and 'Possessed', seen from the perspective of each gender. He can also write with humour, as shown in 'The Grope'.

Imagery

Trevor can produce powerful images: 'chameleon self', with its associations of change, uncertain identity, being controlled by one's environment and hiding through camouflage ('Cross Roads', line 16). The sustained target imagery in 'The Poet' has great impact, and works on several levels – danger, violence, collusion in self-destruction and self-sacrifice in an attempt to change society a little.

Rhyme and rhythm

Trevor uses irregular erratic rhyme which follows his thought pattern scheme and so sounds like comment, or some unconventional song words. The rhyme is just enough to give a lyrical quality to the words but not enough to make a piece sound tight and structured.

Diction

Trevor uses sophisticated vocabulary like 'isolation' and 'oblivious' ('Cross Roads, lines 7 and 18) and 'intertwine' ('She', line 8).

She

She is what I want
She is what I need
And she is the one who will stand there
And watch me as I bleed.

She is the one I want
To be held by
And to hear the beeting of her heart
Beside mine as our souls intertwine
And then depart.

Possessed

Man plagued and possessed
With his passion for lust
And all he touches, with his priests hands
And his devil's heart,
Turns to dust

And his dreams are shattered
Like a gust of wind
Scattering the chared remains of his love.

Figure 2.6

Reflective words recur:
  'endlessly searching' ('Summer', line 8)
  'thoughts and ideals' ('Cross Roads', line 5)
  'lost and forgotten' ('Pierrot', line 5)
  'thoughts and impressions' ('Silent Scream', line 15)
A religious register of words is used, such as 'souls' ('She', line 8), 'soul' ('Silent Scream', line 3), 'priests hands' ('Possessed', line 3), and 'prophet . . . saviour' ('The Poet', line 12).
  Trevor uses an extensive vocabulary of pain:
  'worps', 'twists' and 'maimed' ('Cross Roads', lines 9, 9 and 10)
  'bleed' ('She', line 4)
  'plagued', 'shattered' and 'charred' ('Possessed', lines 1, 6 and 8)
  'poke', 'prod', 'lifts the gun to his temple', and 'madness' ('The Poet', lines 4, 4, 7 and 9)
  'black . . . tear' – 'fragile' and 'broken' ('Pierrot', lines 3, 9 and 10)
  'screams', 'paralysed', 'twisted' and 'drowned' ('Silent Scream', lines 4, 7, 10 and 14)

Summary

Trevor's poetry at this period tended to be personal, self-exploratory and expressing a feeling of the hurt soul. Knowing Trevor, I feel he achieved exactly what he was aiming at. He had an idealistic, imaginative quality which was faintly mystic and so provided strong contrasts: 'his priests hands/And his devil's heart' and 'dreams are shattered/Like a gust of wind' ('Possessed', lines 3–4 and 6–7)

His hallmark is a subtle sensitivity which could range from great gentleness to bitter cynicism. There is a strongly judgemental sense of society's uncaring injustice. Quite apart from being interesting poetry and worthwhile in its own right, I feel that this was a valuable outlet for an intense, deep-feeling young man, who had in the past tended to bottle up his emotions, withdraw and feel depressed (see his own comments in the case study).

Pierrot

The sad porcelaine pierrot doll
With its pale complexion and its
Black painted tear
Sits on the high dusty shelf
Lost and forgotten –
Its clown's suit faded by time –
But his face is painted
And he wears a dignified smile;
But like me he is fragile
And if treated too harshly, broken.

Figure 2.7

Silent Scream

Swimming in the madness
Of a suburban maze
There is a soul
That silently screams
As it is aimlessly swept down-stream
And out of sight
And as I watch paralysed
To the bridge, unable to move,
Unable to utter a sound,
To help this poor twisted fellow creature.
I saw him disappear under the surface
Immersed in the bubbling, swelling mass of the river
That was the last I saw of him
Drowned in the industrial waste of man,
Possessed by the thoughts and impressions of the multitudes.

Figure 2.8

Summer

Sumer
Lying on the bank of a river in the long grass
The smell of pollen and the sounds of nature
Fill the air.
The river –
The bees
Going from flower to flower
End lessly searching for nectar,
Their golden life blood.
And then there is me
Lying on the bank in total peace
At one with nature
Content yet sad
For I know that this moment will not last for ever
And that it will fade
And turn into one of those blissful memories
Of when I was happy.

Figure 2.9

The Poet

The poet puts a piece of himself
In each word, each letter –
A thought, an action, a deed, a will;
For some reader to see, poke, prod and pry.
The poet puts himself with each word
Further onto the target range,
He takes your hand, lifts the gun to his temple
And asks you to pull the trigger,
And what for? For some insane thought that his words
   may cool the madness.
The fruitless insanity of man.
The fetish, feeding ground
Of the prophet, poet, saviour.

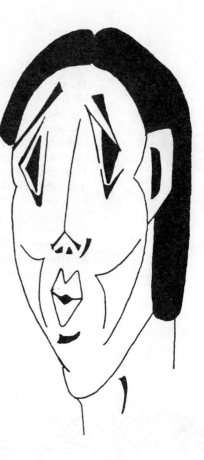

Figure 2.10

Cross Roads

Walking in a fantasy land,
Which has been proved by another's hand.
To protect me from the harsh realities of man.

But I burst the bubble,
With my own thoughts and ideals
And walk out into a concrete gray, desert,
Of isolation and insanity.

I then try to form a thought
But the bubble worps, twists
And comes out maimed,
By the flickering tongues of the masses.

So I grab a mask
From off the shelf,
And throw it on

And now in the silence
Of my chameleon self I feel safe.
Like an unborn child in its mothers womb,
Oblivious of the harsh realities again.

The Grope

The room is dark the atmosphere is right
I think I'm going to get laid tonight.

There's the girl for me!
She looks so nice,
She looks just right.
To kill the fear I'll have another beer
Then I'll prove I'm not queer.

I'll ask her to dance
And get her a drink
And then we'll get down
On the sofa I think.

We start to kiss.
O'god this is bliss.
Then I start to grope
And now her hands are at my throat.

O my god what have I done?
I must have lost my mind!
Was I so blind that I could not see
That she had feelings as well as me!

The work samples in this collection attempt to show Trevor's great range of creative skill. I tried to encourage diverse outlets for his abilities, so increasing success and confidence. It is particularly important for the intellectually advanced dyslexic to be challenged and well occupied, and given enough opportunities to develop his or her talents. To focus only on the difficulties can be highly destructive and depressing for an individual and create a dangerously negative self-image. Identifying a child's special talent and developing it to maximum potential is the key to the difficult transition into a successful adult for many dyslexics I have interviewed.

The puppet teacher in Figure 2.11 is a particular favourite of mine because it can be seen from two perspectives. From the pupil's point of view it expresses the punitive stereotype, a faceless representative of the establishment, the system which is trying to process him through it just like all the other pupils. From the teacher's point of view it accurately represents how helpless one can feel when stifled by the limitations inflicted by the educational system. Factors such as lack of finance, large class sizes, sudden poorly-researched government changes, and outrageously increased work-loads pull our strings.

There are two of Trevor's photographs (Figures 2.12 and 2.14), which featured in the school magazine.

Figure 2.13 shows a sample page of his free writing produced under CSE mock exam conditions. In addition, I have included an entire translation of 'The Tower' because it is an outstanding piece of work for a dyslexic student, and shows how well Trevor had overcome exam nerves to be able to achieve this. I wanted readers to enjoy the full flow of his story freed from the distraction of spelling errors. The descriptions have a multisensory vividness which is very intense. This is exactly the sort of essay which in its original form might have been slashed with punitive red ink by a teacher focusing only on technical matters.

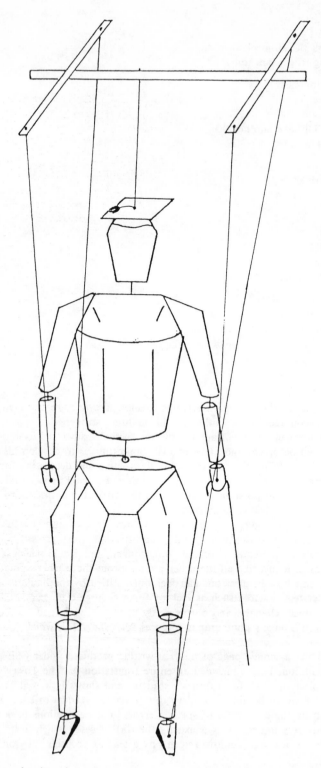

Figure 2.11 Trevor: drawing of a puppet teacher

Figure 2.12 Photograph by Trevor

1

Trevor   Age 16

3, <u>The Tower</u>

I clim the stone stairs. There
wet & slipery the gard pushes
me from behihd, & again. the air
is damp & cold. The stairs
spirale up words, ever up words
avenchaly we, the card & I,
reach the top, a solating
wooden door confunds use.
T here the ratle of the
keys, which the gard hade
conseld on him, Then the
hevy dunk of the old
iron lock, The gard push
the old door open it is
ruluctent at first it grows,
and then gives in and
open's. A wind hit's my face
it comes from the solato
bard window, the gard untise
my hands pushes me forward
I hite the old stone &
strone with a grash, & breath
hurd at last released to
have my hands, free from
the biting rope. Then I hear
the thud & clunk of the
door & lock, and the
footsteps of the card die
a way into the distents.

Figure 2.13 Trevor: sample of free writing

Figure 2.14 Photograph by Trevor

The Tower

I climb the stone stairs. They are wet and slippery – the guard pushes me from behind
again. The air is damp and cold. The stairs spiral upwards, ever upwards. Eventually we,
the guard and I, reach the top. A solitary wooden door confronts us. I hear the rattle of
the keys which the guard had concealed on him. Then the heavy clunk of the old iron
lock.

The guard pushes the old door open; it is reluctant at first – it groans and then gives in
and opens. A wind hits my face. It comes from the single barred window. The guard
unties my hands and pushes me forward. I hit the old rotting stairs with a crash, and
breathe hard, relieved to have my hands free from the biting rope at last. Then I hear the
thud and clunk of the door and lock, and the footsteps of the guard die away into the
distance.

I now survey my new surroundings; they are harsh, bleak, all stone and festering straw.
Then I go to the long barred window, look out at the free world, the hating world, the
world that put me here – and what for? My beliefs, speaking my mind, but that world
looks so peaceful and calm from up here, in your tower of my fate.

I press my hands against the bars wishing they were not there, and as I do so one comes loose from its mooring deep in the stone. It has been weathered away by the long years. I pull at it, it comes away in my hand. Now there is a gap, a small gap, a small chance! I push my head out and look down, it is a long way down, but there's a moat, a small moat. Now it comes to mind – shall I jump? It's a hell of a long way down – how deep is the moat? It might only be shallow. It's a chance I am going to have to take.

I push my head out, then my shoulder, then I back my legs out holding on to the ledge. Now I am hanging there high up on the side of the tower. Well here goes! I push out with my legs away from the stone and let go. I'm falling faster and faster, I want to scream but I cannot. Then, as suddenly as it started, it finishes. The experience changes from one of falling to one of being submerged and enveloped in water, cold water. Where's the bottom? I can't feel it – swim up, up for air. Any longer and I'll drown! My lungs feel as if they are going to burst, then at the last possible moment, I break the surface gasping and spluttering, pleased to be alive and best of all out, out of the tower and free!

For how long though? I'll live each day as it comes and take my chances like the rest; one thing is for sure, I'm not going back there, I'd rather die than be subject to the loneliness and boredom of that cell.

GARETH

Gareth was a tall young man, built on the grand scale, who suffered from teasing about his weight. In manner he reminded us of a big, affable bear who was unaware of his own strength, power or intimidating proportions. He would lope around the school, like a playful St Bernard, telling northern jokes and looking for a quiet place to smoke.

He came to special school late, at the age of 14. His reading age on entry was 8.7 (Neale test). He had an IQ of 104 (Verbal) and 112 (Performance) on the WISC(R) intelligence test. Gareth's degree of dyslexia was average by special school standards. He gave the impression of a strong-willed individual who was naturally quiet, genial and bluff. He had minor difficulties relating to staff and was a heavy smoker.

He had been identified early as having difficulties, but dyslexia had not been recognized by his local authority at the time. Consequently, he had been sent to a special school for mixed handicaps at middle school age.

At boarding school he became an under-prefect, and stayed on for an extra year to obtain CSEs and O-levels. His results can be seen in the list on page 63. He went on to further education college. His special talents were in mechanics and practical skills.

Negative experiences

Violence from teachers

Violence inflicted on Gareth only came to light during the questionnaire, in response to Q14 *Was there any particular age you felt really bad about school?* The violence occurred before corporal punishment was banned nationally.

> Yes, the, the worst ages were, say, the age of about twelve, twelve to fifteen; they were the worst ages, they were at G-Comprehensive and I hated it. Like, the idiot in the class,

used to get up to trouble and you used to end up with the oh, with the thong, the thong or the cane. I mean, and then there's just no point, after a while you just got so used to it that hands goes numb and the teacher trying to hit, and he's even broken canes on people's hands and stuff. 'Cos they're so, getting so used to it; it's just the way, the way life goes.

Sometimes the lads, we used to fall asleep. I remember once when he came round to me, I . . . one of these, like, bendy meter plastic rulers I have and they're a bit flimsy 'cos they easily break; comes round and belts me about the back of the head and I just woke up and the thing went flying, each part of it went flying off to each end of the classroom, and I thought, 'Oh, what's the matter?' (Free interview)

Unfair treatment/discrimination

It seems to be particularly unfair for a council to send a dyslexic boy to a special school for the handicapped where many pupils are in wheelchairs (two-thirds spastic). Gareth was placed at one for five years, though he was actually happier there than at his comprehensive. However, I feel it could have affected his self-image and confidence – he was certainly poverty-stricken in both areas when he first came to us. Also, there appeared to be some carelessness in supplying evidence, under the 1981 Education Act for special provision:

> There was a scandal when they were trying to get the council to pay for me, 'cos all my English books from G-Comprehensive disappeared into thin air. They said, 'Oh, we don't know where they've gone, they must have got lost or something.' One or two teachers asked us to hand them in, then the next time they were asked about them, they just said they lost them or they got filed away somewhere.

Inadequate help/neglect

Gareth developed a deep aversion to any form of remedial provision:

> School remedials, I always find you get stupid books and stuff, little boxes of words to help you, and I find that pathetic. I mean, how many; all you do is empty the box and use it for something else, or . . . they give you a stupid book and you know you can do it, what's the point in doing it? I mean, there's no more thing to doing that than there is to being stupid; 'cos having remedials, after a while I used to hate; I still hate them, these days I don't turn up for them. Last remedial I went to was two terms ago and that was it.

He also had a lot to say about the disadvantages of having remedials in a comprehensive school:

> Um, no, an ordinary comprehensive school, remedial help, no way would it help a dyslexic person. Because an ordinary school will be alright, a comprehensive would be, would be maybe alright for them but if they start having remedials the mickey-taking starts going on; you start hating it, trying to avoid it. Then there's. . .then it comes to bunking off school and stuff like that starts. For some reason, lucky for me, I've never had remedials at comprehensive. I mean I've always been put down with the farmers, farmers' kids who don't really want to do anything.

Humiliation

Gareth's comment about school revealed the deepest frustration and humiliation. He summed up the whole situation thus:

> I never really liked it. I mean, I've never liked school full stop since the day I first started. Never bothered. Used to always be sat in English lessons; sit there doing nowt. 'Do that, do this, copy off the board *this*.' I just felt; boring, nothing to do. The school system's not good. I mean, then, nobody ever noticed the word dyslexic – it was like a disease, you could say, it set you out – instead of saying, 'He had a learning problem,' they were saying, 'He's slow, he's dumb, he's thick.' They're never really saying, 'He's got a problem,' or anything. 'He's just stupid,' it's no good saying he *can* do it. But he can't. The problem is he can't. I was never *able* to do it. Never was. I just used to try and get past. *Every time I tried, they just knocked me down again, so I just stopped bothering.*

He had a lot of insults from teachers too at secondary level:

> They just wanted to give us some remedials and stick us away somewhere . . . some of them used to say I was as thick as two short planks and then the next lesson they had, I beat all the rest of them in their subject, just to prove it wrong . . . Because the teacher says, 'You can do this every week,' then I didn't bother, 'cos he knew I could do it. Then he just, after a while, I was forgotten about and he started calling me thick and I thought, 'I'm not going to try every so often, why should I if he's just going to carry on, carry on calling us an idiot, why should I bother?'

Also, consider the teacher who told him he was not dyslexic once he had been officially diagnosed (in response to Q4, *What do you think makes a bad teacher?*). I was quite disgusted to hear how his work was treated by this teacher. No wonder he had an aversion to English teachers when he first came to special school:

> Once I was off, sometimes I used to get homework and once I mean, I really tried my hardest and got this full essay, it was about two and a half pages of foolscap, and of course I was off. I'd been off on Monday for some reason so I wasn't able to hand it in, so when I came in on Tuesday, first thing I went, I went and told her about it, and she, all she did was tear it up and say, 'Oh, it wasn't handed in on time.' I mean . . . I used to get into trouble a bit for foul language 'cos . . . they always used to *get at me*. They just kept on bickering at me. At comprehensive I used to get a lot of tormenting, I just didn't really bother. After the teachers started off with it. I mean, I didn't mind about the boys, I just ignored them; but when the *teachers* started off with them, what's the point in doing anything?

His answer to Q34 about teachers' opinions also revealed how staff had degraded him, and showed his corresponding frustration:

> Definitely at G-Comprehensive. I think I'd be, to put it one way, seen as an idiot, as a thick old twit; sits back of the classroom, doesn't do anything except disturbs lessons. I mean, that's how I expect teachers to see me at G. 'Cos sometimes used to sit down and they used to call me thick on purpose, they used to try and wind me up and then they'd start calling me stupid and thick and I'd just turn round, once or twice. Instead of hitting a teacher, I just picked the side of the desk up and chucked the, . . . turned the whole desk upside down, just missing them. I mean, I'm definitely not stupid, but that's how things went. I mean, teachers maybe thought of me as a, . . . a big idiot, whatever.

Teasing/persecution

Gareth avoided teasing by becoming the class clown (in response to Q15 about embarrassing experiences through being dyslexic): 'I just used to make a laugh of it or make some stupid comment and end up with everybody rolling in laughter.'

He also found with his own friends that his practical abilities helped – he was good at mending all sorts of things, so people needed him and did not fire insults at him.

He spent many years at a special school for the disabled, and I feel this has made him realize his disability could have been a lot worse than just educational (see interview comments).

However, he felt quite bad at comprehensive:

'It was a state, yeah; 'cos after a year up there I went up to the fourth form and there they says, 'Oh, no way you'll be doing exams, nothing. The only exam you'll be able to do is woodwork,' and that was it really. I mean, they put me in for the English CSE and the first time I was there, they put me in for the English exam and I got 2 per cent out of the whole thing, the whole exam, and after that I used to get the mickey taken out of me all the time. Really didn't bother. And every time I could get off, I was off school.

Associative reactions

Truancy/school refusal

Gareth's truancy occurred in comprehensive school:

Skive school; never really any point. Used to get caught and used to get sent back. And I stopped doing that 'cos they threatened to see my parents and get hold of my parents, so I just stopped it. (Free interview)

This worsened in the fourth year after exam teasing:

I used to fake all kinds of things just to stay off . . . Oh, morning, Monday morning sickness and stuff like that. 'Cos my mother was . . . she gets migraines and I used to wake up in the morning and say I had a bad headache and didn't feel too well and stuff. 'Cos she has them herself she used to know what they were really like, so she used to sympathize with me.

In answer to the specific question on truancy, Gareth said more about his motives in avoiding lessons:

I've played truant a bit 'cos, lessons, English lessons and stuff; I mean, lessons where you really need to read a lot and spell a lot, I used to say no way I was going to them. And I found lessons that teachers were getting at me, never turned up for those either . . .
  Um, on average about three to four times a week . . . The only day of the week I never really bunked off was a Wednesday. Um, Mr F. . . . metalwork teacher . . . big fellow he was. I mean, . . . he was a bit loony, he used to wear sweatshirts and T-shirts with stuff like 'I'm a member of the mushroom club,' and during Christmas he fixed up, . . . things of mistletoe to hang up between his eyes . . . He was . . . one of these loony teachers; and we had this other, . . . he was a science teacher but . . . he was nice. I mean, everybody liked him unless you got really on his bad side, he'd just tell you off, and that's it; except you really got on his nerves and I mean, he used to go wild, I mean, he would really turn round and punch you one, belt you one. So he was hard.

Q: *But on the whole you stayed on a Wednesday because of the people rather than the subject matter?*

Yeah. I mean, I had rural studies all afternoon, used to feed the pigs and mess around in the fields and the teacher we had for rural studies, he wasn't . . . he was all right, 'cos most of the time we were doing, doing this, doing things . . . but um, used to sit in his classroom and we used to end up, started talking, started talking about pigs and stuff and you went on to subjects like smoking, sex, religion, politics and then you used to go back to pigs or cows or something in the conversation.

Gareth revealed the extreme and painful lengths he went to in order to ensure injuries of a scale which would successfully achieve time off school:

No, I've never really refused to go to school but I used to, used to get up to my old tricks like fake tummy stuff, tummy bugs, um, migraines, um, sore arms, oh, used to get infected bruises.

Q: *How did you manage that?*

I just used to bang myself up, go out the night before and get into a fight on purpose.

Q: *Really? Just so you didn't have to go to school?*

Yeah, and the other reason was, you want . . . you get a boy and belt, and if we both kick the other person's head in or he kicks mine in, average about two or three days off school each so . . . never really done it in anger but we'd do each other for the sake of it.

Lack of confidence

Gareth's mother believed he gained confidence being an able-bodied child amidst spastic and wheelchair children at his first special school. Then it worsened again, however – even his metalwork teacher at secondary level commented on his lack of self-confidence. His mother reported:

At 13 years he was sent to comprehensive school where his confidence dropped and he became aggressive towards me and unhappy. At 16 years he went to a special dyslexic school for two years, where after a slow start he gained confidence. He still lacks confidence socially.

He went off to agricultural college for a year and after a tentative start, she felt: 'The work is mainly practical and it has been a boost for him to realize he can do it . . .' and 'if he passes this exam [City & Guilds] I think he will be "launched".'

She felt that the impact of being in a community with other dyslexics had been very beneficial for him:

His progress was more marked because he was at last with boys with normal or high IQs yet with problems like his own; he was no longer *alone*. He also formed good relationships with one or two of the teachers. He would never have considered college were it not for the influence of the special school.

She also reported a cover-up style of behaviour:

He has an underlying lack of confidence which is sometimes covered up with brashness, and is reluctant to join social events unless going with someone he knows really well. He is shy, though interested in the opposite sex which he covers up with a sort of pretend chauvinism. He is sensitive to people less fortunate and immediately becomes confident in their company, i.e. small children, old people or handicapped . . . Passing his driving test before his brother was an enormous boost to his self-confidence.

She described the appalling fight she had to get dyslexic special-school help for her son:

I honestly believe that if he had not gone, his self-respect and future life would have been totally different and he would certainly not have gone to college, which has given him a totally different outlook on life. He now really believes in himself.

Self-doubt/denigration

Gareth again sums up the feelings of all the boys on this topic: 'Um, I would put it; intelligence – before I came to the special school I didn't think I had any at all!'

Yet this is a competent and practical young man with advanced skills in mechanics. His Performance score on WISC(R) was 112 (above average ability). However, it should be remembered he was 15 points higher on Performance. This discrepancy is telling. As Gareth put it:

'Cos, the thing is, if it wasn't for my mother I'd never be anywhere at the moment. I mean, I'd still be going on with the system, I'd be . . . on the dole now, more likely. At G-Comprehensive they were always going on, he'll never pass exams on paper, he's a thick lad, there's no other way you can put about it.

Competitiveness disorders

During the two years when I taught Gareth as part of a very small group for lessons on six days of the week, I noticed he was often loath to enter into competition.

He would rather opt out and play the clown, trying to avoid competitive situations with humour. This did improve, however, with his growing confidence. He finally passed the CSE English Language that he had once got the dreaded 2 per cent in. Nevertheless, he had to be very sure of his good standard before making himself vulnerable again.

His PE report is interesting: 'Gareth only tries hard if he thinks he can win, if not he merely gives up.' Extremes of this non-participation through lack of confidence are recurrent characteristics of the dyslexic.

Sensitivity to criticism

Gareth's outbursts tended to be reserved for home. At school all his reports remark on his tendency to act the clown and fool around. Yet at home his mother saw the tension and frustration burst out in touchiness. She reports about his dyslexia: 'It made me more protective, perhaps too much and for the two years he spent at comprehensive he was difficult and took it out on me.'

Behaviour problems

Gareth's exploits were mainly reactions to persecution at secondary school. Witness the desk-turning-over incident already discussed (see page 58). Bear in mind that Gareth is a very tall, broad young man who could have been extremely effective and frightening if his easy-going temperament had been different. At special school we had to point out to him how unintentionally intimidating his size could be. He picked his remedial teacher up once and refused to put her down. Then he came up behind me one day in a corridor and put a half-nelson round my neck. I was distressed and said I would kick him somewhere essential if he did not desist. Poor Gareth was very offended as he was only playing about. He genuinely was not used to dealing with female staff and treated them like other boys. He very quickly remedied this 'over the top' rough and tumble, discovering what was appropriate, but initially we often had to remind him about acceptable comment and where to draw the line.

The disabled school he went to summed him up like this:

> He shines verbally and offers a ready stream of quips and repartee which might be construed as impertinence – except that he is very easily reduced and set down – or could be interpreted as stemming from basic insecurity and the need to prove himself . . .
>
> In science – when not deliberately acting the fool and playing up – Gareth has shown average ability in class. Again, it is felt that he possesses a good brain, if he would use it . . .

It was also pointed out: 'Generally speaking, Gareth is found to be a large, likeable extrovert, friendly and extremely helpful in most circumstances.'

However, listening to Gareth describe how he and his friend used to batter each other to get wounds to keep them off secondary school, one is very relieved Gareth is basically kind. I am sure his mother's love and security and also the much-needed help he gave at the disabled school are largely responsible for this. Nevertheless, he seems to have been fairly disruptive at comprehensive:

Q23: *Have you ever directly disrupted a class?*

Yes, often. Used to do it *all* the time.

Q: *Deliberately?*

Yeah, I mean, there were classes, used to, used to get things like um, Swiss army knives have got a saw on them; you'd saw halfway through the teacher's chair legs and stuff so as soon as they sit down one end just goes . . .

I used to have um, Geography lessons, great big map come right above the blackboard. We used to fix it with two little pegs in at each end and we used to rig it up to a bit, to fishing lines going down 'cos you couldn't really see them, and soon, soon as he starts off, soon as he starts going off about geography in southern Asia and India, and it gets too boring all you do is pull the fishing lines and the maps used to go everywhere . . .

He couldn't do anything, 'cos if something fell on the back of your head what do you expect?

Earlier his behaviour had taken the predictable course for many dyslexics; his mother commented:

> Soon after he started school he became difficult in class, which I found strange at the time because he had been an easy child at home; this was when the others started to read and he didn't . . .

He becomes angry and retreats if pushed, though has matured considerably since starting college. The funny thing is that overall I feel he has overcome so many problems and obstacles in his early life ...

Although going to the special school was important and also the constancy and security of my love for him, and willingness to be used as his own private 'punch bag' through the more difficult times, I feel I must isolate Miss M.B. of the B-Dyslexia Centre as the key to the turning point.

Appendix

Public examination results

Summer 1984	CSE	Arithmetic	3
		Metalwork	4
		Woodwork	5
Summer 1985	CSE	Arithmetic	2
		English Language	4
		Woodwork	5

Career/occupation

Gareth studied and worked in agricultural engineering. At FE college he was studying for City & Guilds in Forestry.

Work sample

> The Dance
>
> It was one of the normal dances.
> There was a lot of music drink and girls.
> The dance was going well until a load of punks came in. The fight really started than.
> The punks wanted their stupid music on and the grides wanted the heavy meal music on. The grides did not want a fight so the leader of the grides Bill tolled the punk leader Turd-face to get lost. The punks could not start a fight becaus the grides out numbered them 20 to 1. Nothing waize herd of them untill the end of the dance.

Figure 2.15 Gareth: extract from a CSE essay. The essay contained a 12 per cent spelling error rate and had been self-corrected already; the errors were initially underlined by the teacher.

CLARK

Clark's reputation preceded him to the school in the form of two very thick blue folders full of accounts of disruptive behaviour and evidence such as packets from false blood capsules. A small, stocky teenager with a wicked grin and a very strong will, he also had wit and a vulnerable side.

He entered special school provision, statemented as dyslexic by his local education authority, at the age of 14. He had a reading age of 7 years 8 months (Neale test) and a residual spelling problem. It was unusual to have a more severe reading than spelling problem – the majority of pupils had a spelling age retarded by at least two years in comparison to their reading age. Clark's spelling was commensurate with his reading age (Schonnel test). He was crossed-lateral, being left-handed, right-eyed and right-footed. He had a fascinating IQ profile on the WISC(R) intelligence test of 97 on the Verbal scale and 139 on Performance.

His behaviour was often a cause for complaint by certain staff, and he had a history of this kind of problem. His personality was extrovert, and his teacher–pupil relationships were erratic and extreme, ranging from excellent to dangerous. He was a responsible fire-prefect, and stayed on for an extra year. He had attended a child guidance clinic. He had never had the benefit of either early identification or early help with literacy. He did not enter further education.

He was described by the specialist art consultant, Mrs Susan Parkinson, as the most natural artist she had come across, and he was considered full of potential but difficult to deal with. He also had great talent in creative writing and wood-turning. He finally became a craftsman in wood, preparing to run his own business.

Negative experiences

Violence from teachers

Even at primary level Clark had some very bad experiences. The following account is from when he was aged 10:

> The headmaster didn't really like me very much. They used to just mess me about. I mean I couldn't play a recorder because I couldn't read the notes properly. I used to pretend I was playing along with the notes and one time he came over to me and thumped me in the face hard, with his fist 'cos I wasn't doing it properly. This was one of the teachers. So I lobbed my recorder at him and legged it away.
>
> By the time when me mum and dad went down there they'd got the teacher sorted out an alibi, they just said he hadn't even hit me, I'd just run off. My dad said he didn't believe his son would lie to him like that, 'so someone isn't telling the truth here.' My dad said to ask the others in the class, but they said, 'That won't actually be necessary.' Then the headmaster backed down a bit and said, 'He might have slapped your son, but certainly not thumped him.'

This unfortunate incident set a pattern for Clark, who developed a strong anti-authoritarian attitude, and a determination to see justice done, even confronting teachers on behalf of his peers.

At secondary level Clark encountered violence with inconsistency as well, and – he felt – a teacher who drove him to the very edge of sanity. I have found it impossible to summarize Clark's words without losing the depth and poignancy of his description. No précis could adequately convey the experiences that remained so vivid to him that he gave a blow-by-blow account of a gradual emotional breakdown. We had indeed had children at special school who had suffered full mental breakdown during comprehensive schooling as early as 11 years old, though thankfully Clark was not amongst them. It seems no research has been done on this particular area with specific reference to dyslexics.

> Then I got into, then I went into the dunce class, um, which was taught by Mrs, um, forget her name, Mrs, er . . .

> Oh, that was first year and the other the second year, and er, she used to drive me insane. In the end that's what she did, 'cos I used to run off from school and I really was depressed and all that lot, and I'd dread going to school and having to see her, she was such an old bag . . .

This clash resulted in bizarre confrontations over treatment which Clark felt patronizing and demeaning: 'Any time English, I had her: I used to dread those lessons all week.'
The worst incident occurred in a music lesson:

> I walked over there and she goes, 'Arms up in the air,' I went like that, 'No, no,' then she goes, 'Arms down to the ground,' and she goes, 'Now I want you to put your arms up in the air,' and I wouldn't, and I wouldn't do it and er, so she grabbed, so she grabbed 'em and lobbed 'em up in the air, put 'em up in the air and she smacked me across the face and I just told her to piss off or whatever, like that, and er, and then she chased me round the room and that lot, round all the tables and then I ran out the door and er, ran home.

It was on one such occasion that Clark used in his mouth the stage blood capsules mentioned on page 64, before the teacher hit him.

Unfortunately, Clark also got aggressively handled at boarding school, though the incidents were reported to the head and dealt with. The teacher eventually left.

> Oh, oh, well, yeah, Mr I., Mr I. The one who I hate most in the world.

> Prompt: *What, as bad as that?*

> Yeah, I'd kill him. I tell you I'd kill him if I had the chance; I wouldn't . . . I'd have no trouble in that. If I was walking along the street and I saw him I'd . . . put it like this, if you was allowed to shoot somebody in the world and you wouldn't get done for it, I'd shoot him and I wouldn't regret it.

> Q: *Why? Can you put your finger on exactly why? Be a bit more specific. What is it about him that makes you so mad?*

> Well, there's loads of things, it's not just one; how he is, I dunno, he thinks himself such a man, when he acts like a little kid and when he's, he's got the mind of a child and he acts like a child, then he . . . You know, he can call you a child and how he says like, . . . oh, you know, well, you know what he does to me, don't you? He comes and man, hits me and that and him he's big enough, I can't hit him back and he just messes me about all the time.

He related a long account of an incident when he was hit on a minibus trip, which he deeply resented as it was in his free time. He seemed to accept that being hit was part of his role in life within school hours. Clark's physical stature was small, and he stated that this teacher only pushed around such pupils and 'crept round' the macho weight-trainers.

Q: *And that's it, really, it's just those two, Mr H. and him?*

Yeah, Mr H. is just a . . . has to show he's a man like anybody, and he craps himself and goes away. But now, with me, I just, when he pushes me I push him back and if he hits me I'd hit him back. I haven't had a chance yet, but I'm hoping to get a chance.

Q: *Get your own back at last?*

Yeah.

It should be noted that this man was smaller in physique than the other master, but of course anyone who cannot control their temper and is prone to violence, even if provoked, should not be in teaching.

Unfair treatment/discrimination

Clark felt very strongly about grammar school selection and provision in his local area – as already stated, he had an IQ of 139 on Performance (WISC(R)), a very superior range of intellectual ability, which put him well within the grammar school band of 120 upwards on intellect alone.

There is no way a dyslexic will ever get to grammar, there's no way at all; don't believe in it up there, they still don't. They didn't recognize dyslexics, they thought you was just thick up there, and that's the way it's going to stay for a while, I reckon.

He described an incident when his sister found grammar school permission slips (naming who passed) in the classroom bin, and a system favouring the rich or local dignitaries.

He got his first taste of corruption earlier on in his school career, however, with the cover-up over teacher violence towards him in the recorder incident (see p. 64).

Inadequate help/neglect

It was obvious that Clark was badly treated and neglected at primary school:

I just used to sit there and draw. I drew what they wrote [handwriting styles]. It was like drawing a flower. I couldn't read it. I didn't know what it meant. I couldn't read none of it. I hadn't got any idea what it was all about. I hated it; just write on the board and copy it, that's what people did. I'd just used to write it off and I didn't know what I'd written 'cos I didn't get any help or anything.

In answer to Q32, about what sort of teaching provision is best for dyslexics, he stressed the importance of having a teacher you got on with:

Depends. Specialist remedial help in a comprehensive would be good if it was done well, though the other kids might say, 'Ugh, you need remedials,' and that might put them off. It depends on the teacher really. Mrs M. [remedial] didn't teach me nothing, it was you really. You need a really good English teacher. Class English was best – I never really had a remedial teacher I liked, and that makes a difference.

Humiliation

At primary level Clark's problems only fully came to light when serious testing started to select who went to grammar school. Up to then he was so bright he managed to hide his literacy difficulties:

> I didn't make too good a start [at primary school] but it was all right. Then with working for exams they found out I couldn't read and write ... and they just reckoned, said I was skiving. I didn't read 'em because I couldn't read 'em. Then as I went on I just didn't do too well. When they said I was thick my parents said, 'Well, *I* don't think he's thick because I *know* he's quite bright.'

Tests ensued, and he was told he was dyslexic:

> But all I got from the headmaster was I'd be lucky to be a dustman, so I didn't get on too well with 'em. They just said I was thick, that's all. They classed me as thick and that's what my parents didn't like. For about eight years ... they were trying to say I was dyslexic ... I just used to sit and pretend to do it and draw. I wasn't really bothered. I was in the lowest set for whatever was happening. No one really helped, none of 'em.

At secondary level Clark found some of his remedial help humiliating in the extreme. He had this to say about dyslexic pupils:

> I mean, they're not stupid, they want to learn. I mean, like trying to tell them the word cat and draw a little pussy cat on a thing, you know. Just put it to them different ways, I think.
>
> Q: *How old were you when you were asked to draw things like this?*
>
> I think I was 16 years old ... Sixteen years old and I was to draw George the Giant Giraffe. And um, I mean, you resent that, I tell you, the more you resent it so you mess them about, the teachers and that lot, it's not gonna get you anywhere. Treat them like adults.

Clark reveals how insulted and degraded a young person can feel because of juvenile teaching methods inflicted upon him. Many teachers treat dyslexics as if they are dealing with inferior beings, and present primary level materials to sophisticated and mature brains simply because the student has a primary reading age level. This is not logical or justifiable since many dyslexics excel in areas specific teachers may not be aware of – art, sport, mechanics, drama, technical drawing, oral work or creativity, woodwork or pottery (see Hampshire, 1990).

Teasing/persecution

Clark found comment worsened once he was identified as dyslexic:

> At the start, when I was there, it was all alright. I never got into trouble and that lot and er, er, it was more when the blokes came, started coming in and seeing me about my reading and that lot, ... 'cos I just forgot about it and like nobody had known, 'cos I'd've just gone through life not reading anything in lessons and that lot; so, you know, soon as these blokes started coming in and I was trying to read and that lot, people found

out that I couldn't read and by then, you know, they were pretty childish and that lot, 'cos you know, they called me dunce and that lot near the end. Just messing about you know, . . . my mates doing that. But it didn't bother me too much. You know, I let them have their little laugh.

Q: *How did you feel about coming away from there?*

Well, that was more when they started calling me dunce, 'cos they said, 'You're going to a dunce school, a school for dunces' and that lot.

Associative reactions

Truancy/school refusal

I have already given an example of Clark running away from primary school (see p. 64). It worsened considerably at secondary school with his encounters with the hated Mrs G.:

I got, got so, you know, if I didn't come back from, after dinner or something . . . used to ring up, school used to ring up and say, you know, 'Did you send Clark off this morning,' and I used to run off from school.

In response to Q22A about truancy he said more about this:

Yeah, like I say, I used to run off; I used to run off from school and I'd go down the Willows and roar my eyes out, roar till I couldn't roar any more. Used to roar till I ran out of tears and er, and I just used to roar and want to die, 'I want to die, please let me die!' and all this stuff. I tell you, I used to roar and roar, I dunno why, it's just silly, you know? Roar, or I used to cry a lot. I never used to cry when I was little, then I went through this stage of crying and that lot, I used to cry and that and er . . .

Prompt: *Probably did you a lot of good at the time.*

Probably did, get it out of me. Nowadays, you know, if I'm really wound up, you know, I have to cry to get it out . . .
 The Willows: it was, um, it was a bank, 'cos all the areas were flat and there was a bank to, like, protect them, and down one side of the bank there was willow trees, loads of them all round the side of the bank. I used to sit in there. 'Cos that was the only wooded area round, round where I was. Used to sit in there. Was only about as wide as this room. A wooded area as wide as this room on the edge of this bank for about twenty miles, something like that. I used to sit there, I used to sit by the end of the passage to my house and, er, . . . elderberry bushes, used to sit in them right, dead quiet and, you know, commando style. Sit in there and then when, soon as I saw (there was a passage, right, going to the back of my house) soon as I saw the first school-kid going past, used to go in the house. 'Hello mum,' you know, 'Everything all right?' and she'd go, 'Clark, we know!' . . .
 I did it pretty often 'cos I remember, I didn't turn up after dinner for school or something; used to have to ring and check with my parents . . .

Q: *Would you say about two or three times a week?*

Well, whenever a teacher really bollocked me and I couldn't handle it so I'd run off, you know, try to get away from it, you know; that's all I could think of, getting away from it, was running away.

Q: *What did the teachers do when you went back?*

Give me the work again. No, they used to let me off, basically; so I thought, you know, it's a good idea, it's working, so I kept doing it.

Q: *Have you ever refused to go to school?*

Yeah, loads of times . . . you know . . . You can roar, you can stick your fingers down your throat, you can be sick, I could do anything, but oh, 'Off to school with you!' You know, my old man used to make me go. I used to have to go to school. The only way I used to get off school was if I run off once I got there.

Psychosomatic pain

Clark at age 10 was investigated by the doctor for severe cramps in the abdomen. No cause was found. (Records consulted.)

Isolation/alienation

Consider Clark, aged 11, alone all day in the Willows, in floods of tears and wanting to die (see p. 68).

Lack of communication

There is no evidence of this problem in Clark's character profile, though I did get the impression from facial expression, pauses, repetitions and hand gesture during his interviews that it was quite a struggle to clarify his inner turmoil into words, though his reflections upon it were very clear.

Lack of confidence

Clark's mother noticed the lowest ebb of self-confidence at age 9 or 10 and feels it is still a pronounced feature: 'Clark needs a lot of encouragement, even now he will not fill in forms or ring up to find out something; he will ask me to do it.' She says of his personality: 'He is wary, not sure of himself.'
  She also considered that the crucial factor was:

> finding something he was very good at and showing him he was not thick in other people's eyes. The frustration at 13 on reading Jack and Jill type books was as much as he could bear – he hated it.

Clark himself felt very strongly about reading, that he wanted the skills to survive on his own, independently – to acquire confidence in his own competence:

> I don't want nobody helping me. That's my main thing, I want to become independent, you know, do things on my own; that's all I want to know how to do, 'cos you know, I've made it and I don't need anybody else.

He also suffered a distinct lack of confidence when he was diagnosed as dyslexic.

Q: *Any particular point which was worse than others?*

> Um, in the third year, when I was looking, probably when I . . . I really thought I was dense; in the third year when I thought I was dense, you know. I was looking for a school 'cos I thought then a spacky [spastic] school, I thought I was going away because I couldn't read and was dense and that's what I thought. You know, I thought, 'cos everybody was telling me I was dense, I was in the densest class; 'I'm dense, I'm going away' and that lot.

The reason he thought people should know about their own dyslexia was quite enlightening also:

> To tell people, so if someone says 'You're dense 'cos you can't read,' . . . 'What's wrong with you then?' and you say, 'Oh, I'm dyslexic,' and they say, 'Oh, yeah, what an excuse!' They can explain it to somebody else, what dyslexia is, then it's alright.

Clark's mother seemed to suggest that he used his entertainment value to distract people from his true low confidence level. Also, she said of two women teachers: 'They could see through his anger and clowning and feel his frustrations. Women's intuition.'

Self-doubt/denigration

Clark, with his quicksilver creative intellect and the highest IQ of all, had this to say:

> It was only my parents kept me going, I'd have just sat down under it as thick 'cos I'd have just gone with the ones who were thick and got lobbed out like them, started acting like them, stealing. It was my parents trying to get me out that did it.

Competitiveness disorders

I would define Clark's attitude as an extreme ability to opt out of competition and avoid it altogether. He had all the strategies of teacher-baiting developed into an advanced art form, if the majority of his teachers' reports are to be believed. He felt he had no alternative, however:

> By then I was with er, people that messed about a lot, 'cos you know, I couldn't read. I couldn't read and then I just messed about and er, sort of, I even started other people messing about so I got done as a bad influence; and I was probably the worst person in the school 'cos I couldn't read it, so I used to distract everybody else, 'cos I got bored fiddling with my pencils and then I'd soon start a riot, and then, like I'd start flicking plasticine at people then they'd all start.

With us, he liked to come first in being the centre of attention, but if *given* adequate attention, he could work brilliantly (see his poetry on pages 75–6). He won our school creative writing competition with ease and the teacher judging said it was amongst the best writing she had seen in twenty years of experience at both special and private boarding schools.

Sensitivity to criticism

Clark's own comments shed a little light on the problem:

> If there's any pressure put on a dyslexic child, I mean, he'll just freak. I mean, he can't take it, 'cos you know, he don't know how to read and that . . . you know, dyslexic kids just can't take that.

Once Clark had left school, his father commented on how his son got on with various employers:

> You know, Clark, if he likes you and feels you're on his side he'd do anything for you. But he won't be 'put down' by anybody and he will have his say and sometimes he can overdo it a bit and be a bit touchy like. He doesn't like to be told he's wrong, and you can't go head-on with him. 'Cos he won't back down. He's a bit suspicious at first. If you can just get him on your side he'll work damn hard and well. But he's not easy, he won't get on with just anybody.

Behaviour problems

Clark's past school records make entertaining reading. Perhaps the most notorious incidents within the file were these two. The hated Miss G. who was prone to slap Clark round the face/head quite forcefully did so one day to find him collapsing to the floor covered with blood from his mouth and moaning. She was horrified, begged his forgiveness, and called an ambulance. Clark only got caught out when a girl ratted on him, showing the teacher the plastic wrapper for a fake blood-capsule he had held in his cheek. (The wrapper is preserved in his school files as evidence.) Another incident involved a mouse and a female pupil. I believe there was another occasion in Science when a live frog was deposited in a girl's undergarment. Girls featured large in Clark's catalogue of incidents:

> And I ran off one time and I, um, this girl was really messing me about and that lot, pushing me about; so I punched her straight in the face, gave her a blue nose and she started roaring and, 'The teachers are gonna kill you, gonna kill you,' so I started roaring. She ran off home and then they said, 'The headmaster's coming to bollock you, 'cos the teacher went to get the headmaster.' Oh, I didn't want to get into trouble, so I ran off as well. So we both ran off, this old girl had run off 'cos I'd hit her and then I ran off. It was very funny.

Clark also had a fairly stormy career at special school in confrontation with some of the male staff who did not care for his remarks. This led in 1984 to his educational psychologist levelling the charge that:

> Clark, in a nutshell, is presently treating special school as a retirement home for disenchanted dyslexics. It was necessary to remind him that the education authority was footing quite a considerable bill for the maintenance of Clark's special education.

A member of staff had complained about Clark's disruptive influence and use of 'any opportunity to demonstrate how adept he is at making any remotely serious discussion pointless. He does this through asides, jokes, ridiculing the content and purpose of his learning.'

Clark, however, when involved in art or practical skills of any kind and English or creative/imaginative tasks was above average because he felt respected. He is a classic example of a disruptive pupil whose teachers often did not bother to find out what lay behind his behaviour. It was not until he gave his interview that the underlying tragedy and waste this mischievous attitude covered up became clear. When dealt with sympathetically and treated like an adult, Clark could be very reasonable.

His headmaster's report in summer 1983 stated:

> These reports are a great improvement on the comments his teachers made to me at half-term. I talked to Clark then very seriously – and it seems to have had an effect. Now please will he manage for himself without external pressure? Start with History.

Clark's greatest contribution here is his account of how someone is made disruptive by the school system. He charts the rake's progress very clearly, especially related to remedial streaming.

When asked how many of the pupils in that class were actually dyslexics, he stated

> one other, but the rest were just dense and we got put in with them

and

> Once they, um, were in there they didn't even wanna work, they just were, you know, the bad lot they were, so they just messed about.

> Q: *How did they get treated by the rest of the school?*

> Not too bad. If you was in that class you sort of led the rest of the school 'cos you had to; I dunno, you had to be like that, you were dense and you did all the messing about, so people looked up to you, you know ... and you had to hit somebody and that, you know, make yourself so you was the biggest in the school and that a lot. Nobody used to mess you about.

He makes some relevant comment about teaching methods, degree of sheltering, and difficulties dyslexics find even when helped:

> I mean, be nice to them and that lot, and if they mess you about, I mean, you know, being about to make them work 'cos if ... most dyslexics, before they've come here they've probably been to a school, ... they've been skiving all their lives and you've gotta make them, stop them skiving. You've gotta find ways of stopping them skiving ...
> If a dyslexic kid does not have his say, you know, I mean, if he can't speak I mean, he's gonna get wound up and wound up, and wound up and they're easily, *easily* wound up, you don't have to make him wound up. Yeah, I mean, they don't want coddling; I dunno, colly-moddling or whatever you call it. I mean, wrap them in cotton wool or anything, you know, they've got to um, have a bit ... of a hard time 'cos you know, they're gonna have to go in the big wide world you know? Don't want them to be frightened when someone tells them to piss off or something. Yeah, but most of them, when they *get* dyslexic schools they've um, they've been at the back of the class, you know, they're with the dense ones anyway, and they've all got into trouble ...
> I supposed I could've worked harder er, but I'd skived all my life at other schools and er, my excuse is I found it difficult, you know? I'd always skived, it was still in me and er, you know, I just found it quite difficult, difficult not to skive and it weren't at all bad, but now near the end it's well dragging on.

He explains some of the pressures the peer group places on someone once he has a reputation as 'the lad'. Examine his account of confrontation with Miss G. about whom he used to have nightmares and daydream-nightmares.

> Q: *Did any of the others react like that to her?*

Um, yeah. But they didn't have the bottle to do anything. Like, I usually had the bottle, I'd come out and tell her to sod off, or whatever, like that, I had the bottle to do it. Like, I was, you know, I had to be the lad then, you know, I led the class into disruption you know, 'cos I couldn't do the work so I had to be the lad that, . . . you know. I used to sit there and get bored waiting for something to do; trouble, that's all you could get into, trouble, so I used to make trouble and I used to get everybody else into trouble. I mean, if you can't read, pretending you don't read, instead of doing homework you had to be, 'Oh, I don't have to do that, I'm, you know, skiving,' you know. 'I'm the lad, the class,' and you *had* to be the lad of the class, and then you didn't have to read if you was messing about. I mean, nobody thought you couldn't read, just, 'Oh, he can write, just dosses about; he's just a lad, I mean, he's a great laugh, he.' If you sit there and you can't read . . . you sit there, then you might as well die, so you have to be the lad of the class and mess about.

He also sees very clearly his own behaviour tendencies:

I just go into a stupid mood and I just do some really silly things. Otherwise quite a nice personality when you get to know me. But if I don't know somebody very well, they've got to really, . . . I mean, someone like A., I mean he's really, really dense, . . . he's like a cabbage, you know, and I start; I take the mickey out of people a lot, a hell of a lot, . . . I take the mickey out of people probably too much, and at my other school I was a bit of a bully, you know. You know, not so much here, . . . and if I'm wound up I don't show it but now and again if I do show it I really show it . . . I'm just that sort of person, I suppose.

Q: *When you say bully; you mean physically, or mentally, or both?*

Both. I mean, I can . . . wind up someone so easily . . . Comes easily to me, I don't know why.

Prompt: *You've got the advantage.*

Would you believe I'd have been a real bad bully if I hadn't come here? I used to smack my brother about something awful. He was always running down the road barefoot and me chasing him to kill him. He used to take refuge with the neighbours. I used to really batter him.

In a comprehensive school you've got to make a name for yourself when you first get there, then people leave you alone. It's worse if you're small. I remember one day they were stuffing this kid down a drain. He was really roaring, really upset. I felt quite sorry for him, it was awful. But when he got out, it was me he went for, though I wasn't doing anything, just 'cos I was there and small. Actually, if you're small it's still worth hitting someone if they pick on you, even if they're much bigger than you. You get battered at the time, but they know they're going to get smacked if they have a go at you, so they don't bother next time.'

Q: *Have you ever deliberately disrupted a class?*

Er, every class I went into.

Q: *At that school?*

Yeah, every class. I always deliberately did it. Well, it depends what you call deliberately. I couldn't do the work so I deliberately wrecked the class. I deliberately didn't want to not do the work. I mean if I *could've* done the work I would've done it, but as I couldn't do the work I'd deliberately wreck the class.

Q: *So you had no choice really?*

Yes.

He had this to say in response to the staff criticism about his ruinous classroom comments:

> Mr U. reckons he's so clever. He gives you things that are not necessary to do. He writes on the board and doesn't read it out to you. It was a waste of time and I'd done the work before at my last school. So I wouldn't do it and sat there making smart comments, which he didn't like because they were smarter than his, and he thinks he's the smartest in the world. I used to embarrass him in front of the class, and he tried to do that to me, but nine out of ten times it didn't work and he ended up looking the fool. He couldn't handle that, so he lobbed me out, which I was very pleased about.

He seems to have had an irrepressible character and strong determination to get his own back. For example, after he was hit over the recorder incident at primary school:

> Yeah, then I did some things myself. Used to play a game, last one on the wall, where you had to leg it across, you know, you had to be the first one there and my mate was in front of me. I was legging it after him and I kicked my shoe off um, to get there first, you know, and it went straight through the headmaster's window, smashed the chandelier, and put a big dirty mark on the wall behind. And I got done for that.

However, he saw very clearly the delinquency danger he was in – he felt it just as John and George did.

> Q: *So you think your exam courses were worth it then, do you?*
>
> Oh, yeah, they were worth it. Really good, you know, 'cos you know, I suppose, like I wouldn't have done any exams, I mean, I wouldn't have got any exams and stuff . . . I skived, I were so bad in English and that lot, I never went to school, . . . skive straight out of school . . . and I was on the way. I was, you know, like, . . . if you're out on the street more, or, and that lot . . . it's just, one thing leads onto another. I mean, if you ain't stopped and you can't read, you know, you might as well, . . . you think you're dumb yourself, you think, 'Oh, I'm dense, I might as well go and nick something, have a laugh,' you know?
>
> You just go, you just go, down and down and down, nobody'll listen to you, you know, . . . nobody's prepared to teach you 'cos you're dyslexic, you just go down; I was going downhill all the time . . . but you know, I wouldn't have got any exams at another school. I think the exam course was a good idea.

Appendix

Public examination results

Summer 1984	CSE	Woodwork	3	Summer 1985	CSE	English Language 3
					GCE	Art	B
						Woodwork	E

Career/occupation

Clark has tried varied work, such as stonemasonry and building. At present he is happy as a skilled wood-turner for hand-made staircases, and is hoping to open his own business.

He has also tried coach-building, and making rocking-horses individually. The latter he enjoyed, and it developed into his current occupation.

References and job application

There follow some references which Clark gained before leaving school, and Figure 2.17 (overleaf) reproduces his curriculum vitae in the form of a letter.

Report: Leaver's reference
Subject: Woodwork
'Clark has reached the stage of good joinery capability, he has attempted CSE and 'O' Level (Cambridge), and I expect the results to be good.
   'Clark has had considerable Turning experience and reached a high standard in Design and Finish.
   'Within craftwork, he is a good worker, showing initiative and considerable ability.'

Art: Leaver's reference
'Clark . . . has been known to me since September 1984. During that time I have been his art teacher at school. Clark is capable of good, well-observed drawing and is gaining an understanding of design and layout. He has worked sensibly and with maturity to assemble a portfolio. He has also done work to a high standard in glass engraving, woodwork and metalwork.'

Tutor's reference
'I have known Clark since September 1982, and have spent a great deal of time with him in the course of his daily English lessons. He has a powerful creative mind, and has worked hard for me on a course which he has not always found easy. I also supervised an Industrial Studies course last year, in which Clark showed a deep interest. I have been with Clark in many free-time extra-curricular situations, and I am his personal tutor. He has always impressed me with his intelligence and artistic flair, which has the unusual quality of being totally practically orientated. I have always found him to have a good sense of humour, and he can be very good company.'
J.R. (Tutor)

Work samples

Two poems by Clark which appeared in the school magazine are included. A poetry illustration appears in Figure 2.16 as well as an illustration he did for the school magazine (Figure 2.19). A sample of his free writing appears in Figure 2.18.

Hidden Treasure

As I drew near the pond
I spotted the smooth green lily leaves
Like plates floating on a murky green tablecloth
And the reeds that fringed the pond in small clumps,
Some standing up tall and strong,
Others dipping their heads into the water like willow trees.
Then suddenly from deep among the thickly growing reeds and lilies
A black flash
As a moorhen drove itself deep into the murky water.

The balloon-like bubbles floated gently to the surface:
I climbed along a moss-covered log as far as I dared
And looked into the place from which the moorhen had fled.
There, in a cocoon of reeds,
Warm and safe, were its two brown speckled eggs
Like beautifully glazed pots.
I stood and gazed at the sight for a few moments,
Then edged my way back along the log.
I had stayed long enough.
I must let the moorhen go back to her nest
And guard her precious clutch.

Figure 2.16 Clark: poetry illustration

The Glass Engraver

Once the molten mass oozed out to lie on a mercury bed
A smooth, still rippleless sheet waiting to be cooled into a solid state,
Like water waiting to be frozen
And now cool and strong.

I use my diamond tool,
The strong, hard diamond cutting into the surface sharply,
Bringing life into the smooth expanse,
Transforming it into many pieces like fractured ice,
Each engraved piece, like an island in a deep, transparent sea.
The sparkling, hard granite of the frosting tool
Shades, patterns, tones,
Bringing out the picture from nothing.
So real you can almost feel it with your eyes:

Two kingfishers, suspended, imprisoned in a sheet of glass
Wait to be set free to return to the safety of the reeds they knew,
Before the eye of the engraver captured them.
The reflection of the light upon them
Suggests every colour of the spectrum –
The deepness of turquoise,
The shiny, brightness of orange,
The glazed blackness of their eyes.

Box 2568 Peterborough Standard
11,13 Crow Street,
Peterborough,

Dear Sir,

This is my curriculum vitae, as requested. I wish to apply for the recently-advertised job as a trainee greetings-card artist.

I have been to two schools, the first being a large comprehensive school in Lincolnshire until I was thirteen. Here I found my favourite subjects were art, woodwork and metalwork.

I found these were also the subjects I was best at when I moved to . . . . a boarding school at . . . . where I have studied for "O" level art which I am taking this year and I have C.S.E woodwork at grade three. I am also taking C.S.E. English and Technical Drawing, with "O" level woodwork this year.

I am taking a St. John's Ambulance certificate in First Aid this year, and have passed English Speaking Board exams at Introductory and Grade 1 Senior level, achieving "very good" passes. This involved giving a one minute reading, two minutes learnt piece and three-minute talk to an audience about natural history and glass-engraving.

I have as free-time interests, glass engraving, pottery, wood turning and metalwork. I will be leaving after I have taken my exams, but I could start work at any time and return for the exam dates only.

I hold the position of elected senior representative on the school council and am a fire prefect responsible for the safety of my dormitory. I have also been helping the younger seniors with their art metalwork and woodwork.

I will be available if you want to consider me for an interview and would appreciate any further details you could give me. I have a portfolio ready.

Yours faithfully,

Clark .....

Figure 2.17 Clark: curriculum vitae in form of a letter

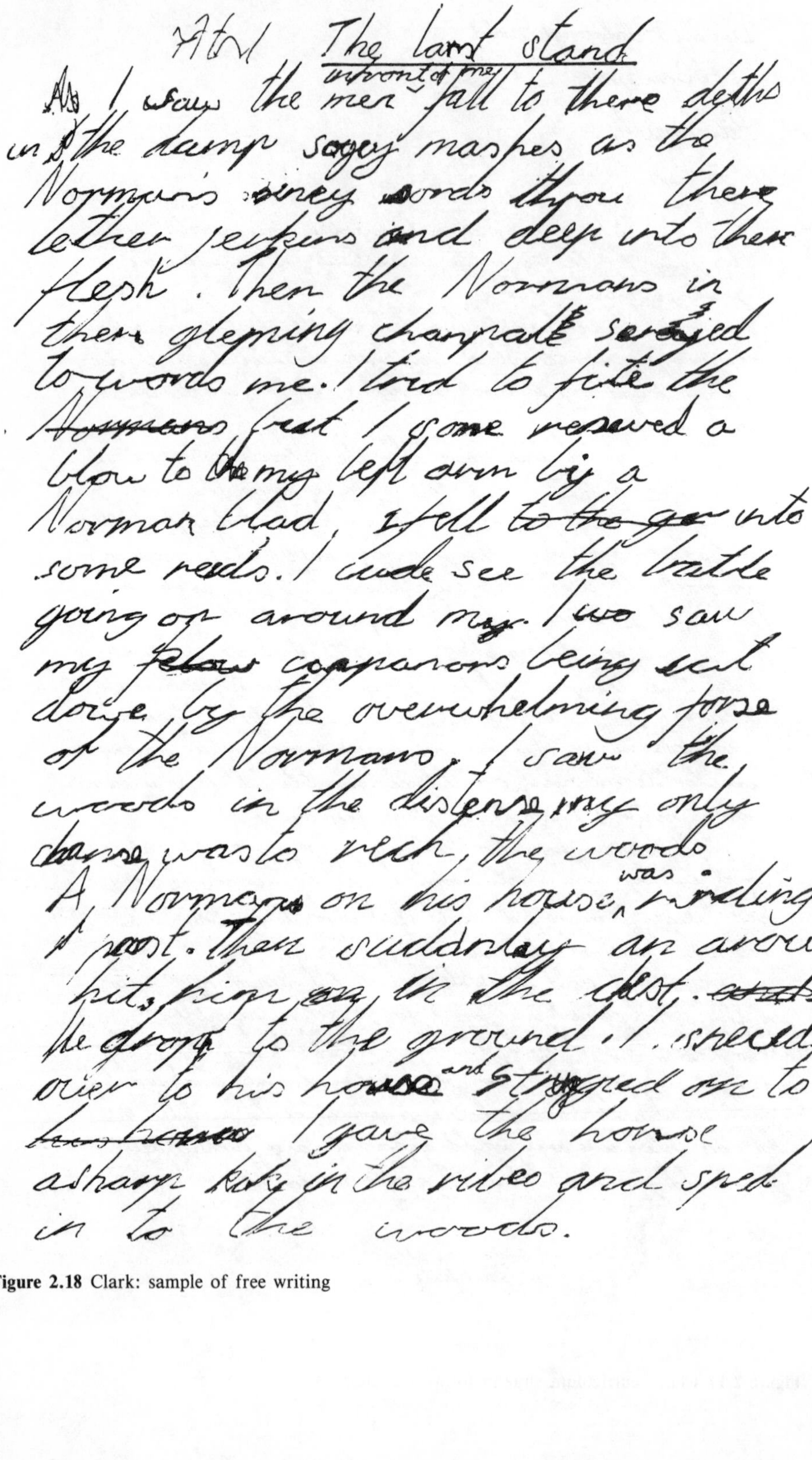

The last stand

As I saw the men (in front of me) fall to there depths in the damp soggy mashes as the Normans piercy words threw there lether jerkens and deep into there flesh. Then the Normans in there gleeming chanmale serged towords me. I tried to fite the Normans but I some reseived a blow to my left arm by a Norman blad, I fell to the go into some reeds. I coude see the battle going on around me. I wo saw my fellow companions being sent doune by the overwhelming force of the Normans. I saw the woods in the distense my only chanse was to reeh, the woods A Norman on his house, was winding it poost. Then suddenlay an arrow hits him in the dust. and he drops to the ground. I sreeed over to his house and strugged on to his house I gave the house a sharp kik in the ribes and sped in to the woods.

Figure 2.18 Clark: sample of free writing

Figure 2.19 Clark: illustration for school magazine

GEORGE

George at first seemed painfully shy, and was continuously asking staff how long it was before he was 'cured' and could go back home. The first term he was with us he was in trouble quite often and on the edge of many forbidden activities, though he was never caught. He was extremely fit and sporty, muscular and strong, came from a tough area, and had a reputation for being the hard man of the school. Tall and dark, he rarely spoke to adults unless directly questioned. He very soon mellowed and relaxed, however, and developed a profound interest in country pursuits, walking, fishing and watersports. He had a powerful presence; difficult boys causing riot calmed down the moment he glanced at them.

George was statemented for special schooling for dyslexia at the age of 14½. His reading age on entry was 7 years 9 months (Neale test), a deficit of 6 years 9 months. He had an IQ of 102 + (average range) on WISC(R), though English was not his first language. He had *not* been identified as dyslexic at an early age nor had he received adequate help. His degree of dyslexia was very severe for both reading and spelling, even by special school standards. He had attended a child guidance clinic for behaviour problems. The special school almost refused him on the grounds of his reports, which mentioned aggression to peers and behaviour problems, but on interview with his parents he presented well, and the headmaster at that time gave him a chance. His mother had been particularly supportive to him.

George often had letters sent home about being on the edge of trouble, but was never actually caught. There were incidents involving groups of boys in a minor theft, 'borrowing' a steam-roller and damage to a cricket pavilion. Mr Lushington, the headmaster for whom George had a lot of respect, gave him a stern interview. In a letter to his home in November 1982, the head wrote:

> I talked to George separately today and told him that the school had much to offer him, but if this was the sort of behaviour thought acceptable by his peers in London, it was not acceptable here. I very much hope that he has learnt his lesson, which is a serious one.

George soon became interested in weight-lifting (in which he was a national championship finalist), weight-training and karate, and was very successful in these areas. An early report read that 'he should be heartily congratulated' (housemaster, May 1983), and describes him as having become 'a powerful influence within the senior school' and as being 'adept at keeping out of trouble'.

He was eventually made an under-prefect, then a full prefect, which meant a very responsible semi-adult role in organizing the boarding house. He was extremely efficient, liked and respected by juniors, and helped female staff out by instantaneously stopping any fight which broke out amongst the oldest boys. He was the perfect gentleman. He also became a star at English Speaking Board exams, talking about weight-training, his country of origin, and sharks. His artwork posters for these performances were impressive. He came to enjoy and write poetry, and his approach to reading changed greatly. His senior educational psychologist states: 'Previously he refused to attempt unknown words but now he makes a real effort to use his phonic skills and is much more confident.'

His relationship with his father had improved, and the council were pleased with his application to work, happiness and progress. His education authority granted him an extra year to work on basic skills. This information is drawn from an LEA document of September 1983. He is now successfully involved in the family textiles business.

It emerged from George's interview that school life had been particularly frustrating, painful and embarrassing for him. His first memorably adverse experience occurred at age 9, when he was moved to a city school which had a special class for children with difficulties.

Negative experiences

Violence from teachers

George recounted the following about his primary school:

> We had Mrs H. and Mr V. – the old grandad. I didn't like him. He gave all the attention to one young girl. I had an argument with him, and he pushed me in a corner and banged my head. There was me and a white girl, the rest were coloured.

Unfair treatment/discrimination

George did not express any opinion about being treated unfairly, and no direct question was asked. In fact, his apparent acceptance of the way he was treated is in itself disturbing. He comments in his free interview: 'I put up with it.' Even then, the primary school never even informed his secondary school that he had problems, and he was thus caused further embarrassment.

Inadequate help/neglect

In George's free interview and questionnaire manuscript, an over-riding feeling of having been ignored and overlooked is communicated. He is very sensitive to attitude and opinion and suffered whilst labelled 'remedial':

> The teacher wouldn't take any notice, he'd like have a favourite person in the class and he would just like boost him up to help him a lot and all the others like, he would look at them as scum and he just wouldn't want to know.

He seems to have been subjected to some very unimaginative and boring teaching: 'Those Peter and Jane books, ten to eleven! The only thing I cared about was getting home and going out.'

Remedial help at secondary school was only a little better, and the first quotation below was said with real feeling – the remedial stream seemed to have connotations of being relegated to a position of deep misery:

> Thin books, three times a week; ten kids, one and a half hours. Then I was lucky 'cos I came out before we got divided up into the remedial stream.'

> I got caught by my teacher, she caught my friend writing it for me (he offered, like); nothing in my book. I had a special English class with [Language Centre] tapes. 'I have a hat, I have a ball.' I could do all that, but I couldn't write an essay like I can now. You're in a class with all the dense people. I wanted to be with all my mates, and gave hassle.

George pinpoints how fruitless and futile remedial help can be if the teachers are not really interested in bettering the lot of each and every individual in the class. He also shows the predicament of outwardly tough and sophisticated teenagers who need specialist help but resent simplistic and patronizing childish materials and methods, and the social stigma of the 'special' class. It might be expected that such a pupil would be equally set against a special school for dyslexics. However, the desire for help and the proximity to others with the same difficulty overcame this, along with the chance to excel in extra-curricular activities.

Humiliation

George immediately recalled humiliating episodes in his primary school remedial class in response to Q8 about the worst memory of school:

> Mrs H. helped, but Mr V. was always on about gold stars. All he ever yelled at me was, 'Get in the corner!' Mrs H. didn't do anything, she said forget it. They took my shoes

and socks off at playtime so I couldn't get out. I gave him mouth. All lunch-time standing there, face to the wall.

Extremes of embarrassment over his difficulties dogged him at secondary school. George is the most eloquent of the boys on this theme, in that he manages to convey the painful state of the dyslexic whose disability is used to degrade him publicly. I therefore feel justified in quoting his account in full. His experience is not that of a typical self-conscious adolescent, but is entirely focused on his dyslexia-caused illiteracy:

> I was embarrassed. The school never told secondary about it. You don't know, you think everyone can't read, equal, the same. When I went to the other school and I thought, 'God, I can't do it!' I saw they could all read and I got frightened, like every day you think, 'What's going to happen, who's going to laugh at me today?'

About special school he said:

> The first term I was worried, I thought, 'Ah no, I'm gonna be embarrassed and everyone'll laugh at me.' I know, here, someone's got the same kind of difficulties as me. We know the mistakes we do, but we don't bother laughing at each other. Or we might laugh at each other, but we don't actually like mean it, we've both got the same problem. So it don't worry me at all here. Till you go home and they don't know you that well, and you don't know them that well, and you like read somethink or somethink like that and they look at you, and pretend they didn't hear you, and they look at you like this; that's when you feel a bit of an idiot.

This is from an answer about exams.

> Q26: *Have you ever felt very angry about school?*
>
> Well, yeah. Like you're in your room and I've got a whole load of comics what I used to collect, but I couldn't read them, I'd just look at the picture. That used to really wind me up, school. I'd try and read and I'd just think, 'Why am I going? You know? Why am I going? It ain't worth it, I ain't learning anything.' ... The third year was when it really got hold of me, why was everyone else reading except me?
>
> Q27: *What is the worst thing about being dyslexic?*
>
> The actual worst thing? It's like if you're going out with a girl and like you want to say something, you've got to read something and you can't actually say anything, and you don't want to just ignore it. And, you know, in the paper or something, 'Oh, read this.' You don't know, you just pretend. You say, 'Oh, can you read this for me, I can't ... a bit of a hassle, just read.'
>
> Q28: *What is the best thing about being dyslexic?*
>
> I don't know ... you get treated different, don't you, than other schools? Like you feel sorry for some other people in comprehensive schools, the way they get treated. It's different. You get treated a lot different. Well, some people treat you a lot different; some people just treat you like normal. And you don't get, you know they don't laugh at you. Teachers know what's wrong with you and can't laugh at you. Like some other teachers would try and not say anythink, but then you look up and you know what's going on in their head. 'Oh God, he can't read.'

George said emphatically that the worst thing a teacher can do to a dyslexic is: 'Embarrass them in front of other students and make their life miserable. Then they'll just turn, turn bad. And not bother helping them, ignoring them.'

Q: *Do you think that happens at special school?*

Some of the lessons, yeah. But you expect it to happen a bit, you can't have like a perfect school all the time, can you? Yeah, but this school is alright. I seen some schools really bad. Always getting . . . a teacher's like just bored.

Like I had to put a case in science [in my last school], we were doing acids and all that and I couldn't read them. I was alright just mucking about with chemicals, but I couldn't like . . . CO something and all that! And when the teacher asked me he'd know I couldn't read it, one of the teachers would have told him, like, 'Give him easy work,' and then you'd just stand there and you'd like have to try and say something, try to think to yourself what to say and the teacher'd say, 'What's up [Surname], can't you read it? You thick or something?' And everyone'd be laughing. And you just stand there and go red. You just stand there with your mouth open. It's like someone traps you like that, you can't say anything; you get more embarrassed and more worked up and more people laugh, the more it just stirs up.'

Prompt: *What did you do?*

I'd just walk out of the lesson. Just stand, and that's it.

Q: *Did you ever get your own back?*

Yeah. Let his tyres down. I ___ his tyres.

In the response to the embarrassing situations question (Q15), George felt awful about being shown up in front of his foreign relatives over literacy.

Teasing/persecution

George did not get teased badly once he began to get a reputation for being hard. As he put it: 'People used to take the mick at first, then I started throwing my weight. about and it didn't bother me so much.'

Another boy who attended the same comprehensive school told me he remembered George as being covered in blood all over from continual fights on the first day he met him.

His reports from this school were full of references to playground trouble, probing why, and directly blaming his severe dyslexia and reactions to it as the cause (see section on 'Behaviour problems', pp. 87–9).

Associative reactions

Truancy/school refusal

George's miserable time at age 9 in his special class (already described) prompted him to truant for a month. He gave an account of imitating his mother's signal to the school bus drivers not to wait for him as he was ill. The bus would sound its horn, and George would stick his hand out under the curtain to wave them on. His mother was out at work and he got away with it until the school telephoned home requesting official confirmation of absence.

At secondary level George got into worse trouble over absconding. He had an efficient system operating whereby his cousin's sister would write absence notes, and they also had an undated dentist's card. In view of George's answer to Q16 (*What do your friends think about you being dyslexic?*), the number of possible dyslexics and illiterates amongst groups of truants should give teachers pause for thought:

> Some of them don't know, . . . some of my friends can't read and write. I think some of them are dyslexic. Some of them ain't had the right teaching.

George was subjected to physical punishment as a form of discipline and truancy deterrent from his concerned family, but he preferred to risk this hazard rather than undergo the mental torment of the classroom: 'My dad done me over – then my brother, then my other brother, . . . slapped me about a bit you know. Gave me a good hiding. First year. Then I got to know some [bad] people.'

In the third year he used to 'bunk off' school and got arrested for petty crime in the middle of the city. Relatives abroad and at home were most upset and George felt this very badly.

Psychosomatic pain; isolation/alienation

These do not apply to George directly. No question was asked. However, he did suffer stomach cramps over speech exams. His alienation from his father was attributed directly to dyslexic difficulties which his father could not cope with. It was felt he should be removed 'from the orbit of his father's disappointment' (Form SE3, educational psychologist's statement for special education). Mrs G. confirmed that this polarization of father and son continued even after George had left school for several years.

Lack of communication

George commented on his tape that he had never told anybody most of the things he described in his interview. At boarding school he had a reputation with the other boys of saying very little and was often silent in class. It was partly because of this that he was encouraged to prepare public speech exams on topics which interested him.

He made a comment to John when they were both leaving at the end of their extra year which indicated how much he would have liked the ability to chat easily to staff members and get on well in a light social manner: 'I try really hard. I do everything right. And you just chat away and joke and they all love ya. It really pisses me off. It makes me sick.' George's mother mentioned this factor in her interview, saying George could never sit down and talk with the family at home although he seemed alright with his friends, and could talk to her.

Lack of confidence

George was very successful with English Speaking Board speech exams involving a visual aid, 3-minute speech, 2-minute learnt piece, and 1-minute reading, with open exchange of questions. He actually took three exams very successfully. Before the first one, however, he was so nervous the boys were worried and came to find me. He was shaking, his stomach was knotted, and he felt sick. The audience was eight of his friends, also taking the test. I had to sit outside with him for a long time and calm him down. I had put him in for it because I felt it would help his confidence, so I felt very guilty. In fact, he was easily the best in the group when he did it, the examiner was very impressed, and George enjoyed it. Yet I had not expected such worry from a tough prefect, used to controlling other boys. Work experience was another area which gave George cause for anxiety. He worried whether the people would like him, whether he would get on all right, whether he would fit in, and whether he would do it right. His friends told me how much he was panicking the night before. He got very good references and report answers, but the builder mentioned to me how shy and quiet he had been at first. In fact, the employer liked that because he felt it was good to work with a youngster who was not cocky or thought he knew it all.

His educational psychologist mentioned an improvement in confidence while George was at special school that led to a great change in his attitude to reading: 'Previously he refused to attempt unknown words, but now he makes a real effort to use his phonic skills and is much more confident.'

George told me during a reading session that he could read the Underground signs fine when no one was waiting there. However, in rush hour with lots of people he panicked and could make sense of nothing. Yet he could read to me very competently. He was another who tested badly for relatively unknown adults.

Encounters with professionals who were strangers seemed to be the worst for George. On entry to the school he had felt like this: 'Remedials and all that – you're a bit shooken up, and you don't want to let it out that you can't read. Couple of days then it got better.'

A certain lack of confidence also came out in discussion about CSE exams.

> That didn't bother me doing it, it's just some of it I didn't understand [instructions]. And T. [staff], he wouldn't help me. The others I got on alright. I weren't nervous. Now they don't bother me that much, I ain't in the state I was in then. Well, a bit. Like, inside I'd be like shakin', then I, you know, I won't show it . . . No, I couldn't have done that before . . . Yeah, that first one [speech exam] I remember, my voice kept goin'.

> Q: *I think you could take on anything now, any audience for a talk, without any worries.*

> Yeah.

George's mother felt his lack of confidence was worst at age 7, and had improved, being okay with other people, but not in a family setting.

He himself had this to say about the whole process:

> It was like at first you think, 'I can't read! I won't be able to read for like such and such a time.' If you've got like someone to boost you up, then you just, you know, like get confident, then you read it. But like if they don't, you just go down and down and like, don't want to know.

Self-doubt/denigration

George thought for many years that his lack of progress was his own fault. When he found out about dyslexia between the ages of 14 and 15½, he was surprised: 'Well, at first I thought it was like me being lazy, but then after, when I came here I looked around . . . and there was lots of other people had difficulty but were getting help here.' (All school assessments record him as intelligent (102 WISC(R)), but he felt himself to be at fault and blamed himself for his problems.)

George had no dizzy heights of academic ambition – all he ever wanted was to learn to read and write, 'to get by' without being embarrassed all the time. He was prepared to stay on a whole extra year at school to achieve this.

Competitiveness disorders

This idea of wanting to avoid failure, not to compete, not to try, not to be shown up, features in the account given by George's mother after he left school:

> He *can* read and write; it does upset him still, it makes him unhappy. He don't want to know. He doesn't want to read anything.
>   Special school . . . it helped – he can read and write; his ego, doesn't *want* to – but when he has to, can.

It is implied by George that the desire not to compete or try is due to pressures built up during the day:

> By the time you think 'I don't want to, I don't want to do it', it's like every time you go home, 'Aren't you going to sit down and read the newspaper? Aren't you going to do this?' And like after, you just can't handle it any more.

Sensitivity to criticism

George's mother related a sensitivity to criticism in the world of adult work: 'If there is no shouting, telling off, he is a very good worker. Then he gets very upset. He has got to go.'

His school seems to imply the same thing:

> George is quite open and friendly . . . [in description of special characteristics]. George has a fragile temper and can be moody and sullen when things do not go his way. When upset he can be very aggressive and show obvious signs of frustration.

One cannot help reflecting that very little *had* gone George's way in his short life at this stage when he was 13, so this is hardly surprising.

It is important to remember that he became the top prefect in his year, competent, capable and reliable, totally in control of younger boys. This was quite in contrast to his vulnerability in new situations.

Behaviour problems

George's truancy eventually led him into trouble with the police at a famous store as a juvenile, which really upset him: 'Bad name, all round relatives abroad. Knew they were looking at you behind your back and thinking "Bad!" though they were good to you at your face. Real bad thing.'

The report from his educational psychologist clearly blames dyslexia for his problems:

> He is often disruptive in class and this is felt to be largely due to his great difficulty with all written work or work requiring reading. George is intelligent enough to perceive his 'failure' and does not care to settle for silent compliance.

The psychologist goes on to say that when George was particularly disruptive he was suffering from poor concentration in a large class and 'usually being confronted with work which he cannot read'. George's head of year and teachers obviously liked him: 'George is a happy, friendly boy.' His difficulties were sympathized with:

> He finds it difficult to concentrate for any length of time and needs much personal attention. He generally mixes well with other members of the class without having formed any close friendships. However, I feel he is often led astray by others which inevitably leads him to being involved in many disturbances in the classroom.

Actually, George's friends were in the year above him – 'the hardest loonies in the second year'. Some of these ended up in prison while others formed a successful reggae band.

His secondary school gives a very clear analysis of how and why George got into behavioural trouble:

> During his first year . . . it became clear that George also had serious problems in connection with his relationships with other pupils. He found himself on several occasions in situations which could, and sometimes did, lead to injury to himself or to other people.
>
> A lively and rather dangerous game in the playground resulted in George receiving such a violent blow on his nose that he had to take two weeks leave from school and undergo a small operation. Although in this case George was the recipient of the attack it later seemed clear that his pent-up frustrations combined with a fragile temper lead him to want to establish himself near the top of the playground pecking order. He tries to succeed as a 'tough guy' where he feels he cannot succeed in the classroom with his work. Thus his 'friendships' often seem to involve very physical play which can quickly turn into fights. He is tempted to seek attention in the classroom through argument and disruption when it is difficult for him to approach the work.
>
> There have been several fights and a nasty accident involving a broken window where George cut his hand and needed several stitches.
>
> To my mind these incidents are all symptomatic of the central problem – an intelligent boy who is becoming increasingly frustrated by his inability to learn.

There was also the tyre incident after a teacher utterly humiliated him in class (see page 83). George gives a vivid description of how tensions built up and exploded into fights at school. Another boy who had broken a window playing football lied that George had done it. George tried to explain, but the teacher, whom he hated, blamed him. He felt inarticulate: 'And I couldn't say no, and my parents got a bill and then I got hassled at home; you know, "You're gonna work, you're gonna pay for it." You know, you try and explain to all of them and they just won't listen. So you feel like

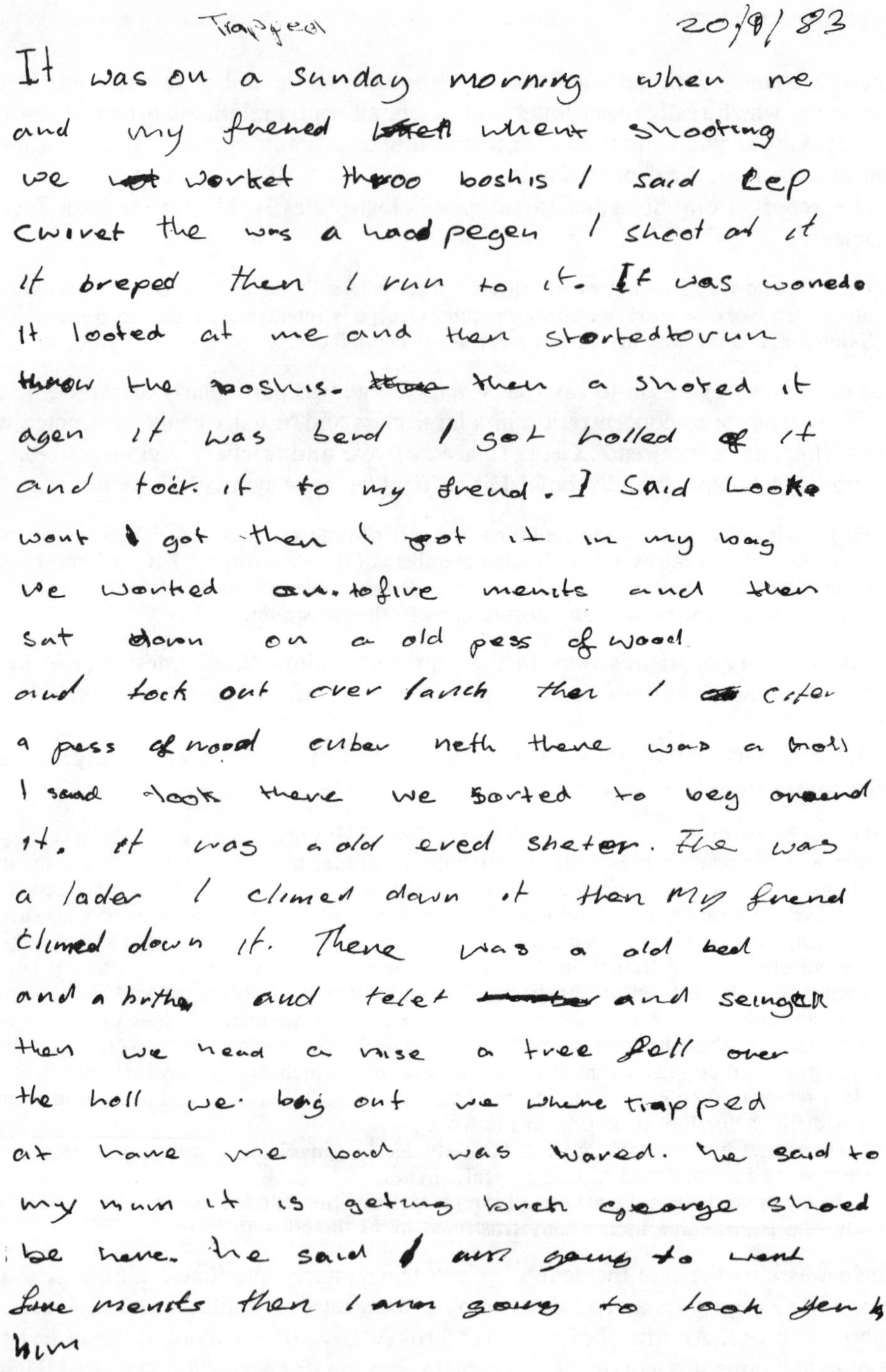

Trapped   20/9/83

It was on a sunday morning when me
and my frened ~~late~~ whent shooting
we ~~wet~~ worket throo boshis I said Rep
cwiret the was a haad pegen I shoot at it
it breped then I run to it. It was woned
it looted at me and then storted to run
~~throw~~ the boshis. ~~then~~ then a shoted it
agen it was berd I got holled of it
and tock it to my frend. I said Looke
wont I got then I got it in my bag
we wonted on. to five menits and then
sat down on a old pess of wood
and took out over larch then I ~~cut~~ citer
a pess of wood enber neth there was a troll
I said look there we sorted to beg oraand
it. it was a old eved shater. The was
a lader I climed dawn it then my frend
climed down it. There was a old bed
and a brthr and telet ~~water~~ and seingatt
then we head a vise a tree fell over
the holl we bang out we whene trapped
at hawe me bad was waved. he said to
my mum it is getung brch george shoed
be here. he said I am gouing to went
five menits then I am gouing to look yen h
him

Figure 2.20 George: sample of free writing

ences

eachers

flicted by a teacher occurred first for Mark at secondary school when
.

r I had this Geography teacher, I can't remember his name; I didn't want
... There was a form sent round saying I could not read or write (bits of
w, it stopped teachers getting me up to read.) The Geography teacher had
head. My dad in the end said I wasn't going to the class of *him* as he said
on it ... I was not worse than the others ... just not trying.
phy teacher in the first year wound me up; I wanted to cry all the time,
stick on the desk, poking me between the shoulders. He hit me a couple
ked the back of my head with the stick; a walking stick it was, with a rubber
ump on the head. Brand new, I wanted to do well. Half-crying, always;
afraid of school – *him* and tests. Two terms; Dad rowed with him. His old
I'll never forget his face, I always had to call him 'Sir'. He had asthma,
rrible noise at times. Why I wanted to leave – I thought I might come across
ke him. I have a real fear if teachers stand or sit on my left. I hate it. Even
w I sit in the middle of my parents. My brain gets nervous. I get cautious,
at they're doing ... Can't stand teachers talking to me even from that side.
quick reactions enough to stop anything coming along. I can't do much at
eft now. Doctors even make me nervous that side.

er his books to correct his spelling, it was noticeable that Mark was
me being on his left. He would get twitchy, swivel round in the chair,
get cheeky and persuade me to do it from the other side. I accepted
nds to with individual foibles, but it did not occur to me to find out
re he would not have told me in a full class anyway. It emerged that
lst he was sitting at his desk by the teacher with the stick, from the
ection.

nt

relate any incident. No specific question was asked.

p/neglect

had one very helpful private remedial teacher for a short period.
riticized remedial provision in comprehensive schools in response to
t do you think is the best way to provide help for a dyslexic child?:

and remedials don't work] because you're splitting up lessons from remedials
oo different. Boarding school it's remedials and then small classes so it's
dials with a few more people. I went to lots of remedials – I used to get
use they taught things different ways and confused you (endings, for exam-
up worse than what you started off with. I used to end up arguing with
over the way I'd been taught [Remedial teacher versus class]. Here, I get
sh and remedial and everyone does the same. That's what makes the dif-
never break the pattern.

freakin' out on someone.' After school the other boy got knocked out and left a tooth embedded in George's knuckle. It had to be removed in hospital, requiring six stitches. Next day, the boy confessed.

We never had any real problems with George at special school, which was a small community, though he tended to be on the edge of trouble or suspiciously close by when it began to occur. He valued his chance to be 'cured' as he put it, and ended up our most responsible and effective prefect, which then amounted to a full staff-assistant in some duties.

In George's words:

Weird, 'cos used to getting away with it; you couldn't here, like walk out. Like living two lives, put a mask on. I'm glad I came, I keep out of trouble. You don't muck about, teachers get to know what's in your head and you get on better because of that. They get to know how you act. Yeah and no – they know who causes what.

Appendix

Public examination results

Summer 1985	CSE	English Language	5
		Woodwork	5
	GCE	Art	D

Career/occupation

George is now helping to run the family textiles business, with driving and delivery of products.

Work samples

There are two poems by George while Figure 2.20 shows a sample of his free writing.

A Cold Fish

We sit and wait
The frosty wind blows
the float is blown across the pond
A bite?
The cold is un-noticed
The float bobs and runs
My heart beats wildly
What is it?
I strike,
The rod bends over
Nothing happens
I reel in slowly
I think I've lost the fish
Then I feel a welcome jerk

I shout for help
My friend comes running,
The excitement builds up,
He dips the net to bring the fish to the bank.
A 5 lb roach?
I must go home to weigh it,
Mum gets out the scales
It weighs 2½ lbs,
It looked like 5 lbs!

The Return

From the air it looks like a tiny model –
Unreal.
You see the whole island,
Light brown all over,
The sea sky-blue and see-through.
Then the plane sweeps round.
You see the mountains,
Light brown, chalky, with low bushes.
Small churches cling to the slopes,
Villages spread out from a thick centre
To far-off Horgha.
We get closer to the run-way,
You can see dry bushes on one side,
The run-way and parked planes.
The Greeks on board are shouting,
Back to their country!
Saying what a long time it has been,
Excited!
The air hits you as you get off the plane,
It feels like an oven.
It seems like a dream.
Lots of our relatives are here to greet us;
Me trying not to mix my Greek with English.
Some of my friends have forgotten their Greek
And feel embarrassed.
Everyone round you,
Amazed to see you grown up,
Making a fuss.
You feel really weird,
Half-forgotten people all around you,
A big family get-together in the evening.
The next day I rent a bike –
Travel round the backstreets,
Remembering pictures in my head,
Knowing I've been here before,
Stopping and looking at places I know.

MARK

Mark came across as a confident, cheeky,
appreciator of girls. He was often seen b
making witty remarks, taking the mickey
laughing around. He conveyed a great sens
He had two inseparable mates who formed
he got on well with groups of other pupils.
bold and hostile if he felt unfair treatment
This came out particularly when he was a

However, one was also aware of strong m
not achieving enough, and of depression.
periods of days when he would not speak to
cloud. When dealing with him on duty or in
that the tensions evident were to do with mis
school and encountering it at a late stage in
relative had paid for him to attend a specia
Mark a great sense of responsibility for h
wanting to waste opportunities or money. He
work hard whether there was any point him

His interviews amazed me by the hidden
and the backlog of bitterness at the core of s
practical exterior was a sensitive and generous
not realized was the extreme cynicism which
root of many of his decisions. His experiences

Mark entered special school at the age of
He had a very erratic IQ score on BAS which
sub-test scores on reasoning. His degree of d
behaviour was also erratic, while pupil-teach
of loyalty or dislike. His personality was felt
and he had attended a child guidance centr
handed (forced to change to this), right-eared
benefit of early identification or sustained ea
reading simple print before he went to infant
laterality was altered on entering school. He w
clinical psychologist, producing puzzling repor
gence was shown by his comprehension level be
ability (Neale test).

He achieved the status and responsibility of
for an extra year, and tried a term at technical
the theory paperwork though he scored high on
defunct apprenticeship system would have bee
practical, done on the job, and often on a one-t
from a school situation, paid something and
interest was football, at which he displayed so
witted in conversation and argument, lively an

Negative expe

Violence from

Physical pain
he was aged

In the first y
to know him
the school k
a row with t
I was playin

The Geog
slamming hi
of times, wh
bit; I had a
that made n
wrinkly fac
wheezing, a
another one
at an interv
I can't see w
I don't have
all with my

If I leant
unhappy abo
joke about it
this, as one
why – I am
he was hit w
behind-left c

Unfair treat

Mark did n

Inadequate

Mark actua
However, h
Q32B/33 *W*

I think [u
to class.
just like
peed off
ple); you
the teach
you for
ference.

Humiliation

At junior school a serious trauma occurred in Mark's life connected with a teacher's determined insistence that he change to the right hand for writing. Mark was to the extreme on the left-handedness scale and it confused him utterly. His educational psychologist's report confirms this. Mark recalled:

> Halfway through the junior school my mum realized my reading and spelling was going wrong and my reports were getting bad. I was called lazy all the time and I said I wasn't to my parents. I thought, right, they say I'm lazy; I bloody well will be!
>
> Football and maths was alright (I was never bottom of the class). If we had tests I'd put my hand down my throat, or eat cotton wool sandwiches, anything to get out of it. I thought, 'Teachers are right bastards, I'm always getting shown up.' They always took the mick if I got the easy ones wrong. I was eight or nine.

At secondary school Mark's reaction after that distressing first year was to employ battle tactics with teachers because he had been so degraded before. He wanted to get his own back:

> The only thing I got out of that school was a thick ear. You only learnt the bits here and there you were interested in; if not you thought, 'Right, how can I get him?' Women got the worst. One [subject] teacher was solid, like a man, strict. At the pictures we photographed her with a boyfriend [she was married]. If she went too far we said, 'You remember . . .' 'Does that mean I don't have to read?' I wouldn't try, she had the idea: gave me verbal. Then she made the rest of my schooling enjoyable – something to look forward to, winding her up – I *had* something over a teacher! Never told my parents.

He would resort to negative behaviour in order to avoid humiliation:

> 'Couldn't read it' – I said to one English teacher about the work four times; I got told off, bollocked, got a pink slip, and sent to the head, who said, 'No, he *has* a reading problem.' I was red raw. She said I should have told her about it. I said, 'Why should I?' I said it was private, my business.

Here Mark told me he was not going to explain all about his reading in front of the whole class:

> I shut myself off from everything. Shouted abuse at teachers when I knew I was leaving. Daft, looking back – they could have helped me, though they didn't know how to teach dyslexics. The head could have seen people about it, advertised it. Most, when told, thought it was just a posh word for thick kids who can't read and write.

Mark hated most having to stand up and read at his comprehensive school. In his response to Q15 *Have you ever had any embarrassing experiences through being dyslexic?*, he said: 'I used to make a joke out of it and say, "I ain't reading this, it's a load of rubbish!" '

Teasing/persecution

Mark's mother clearly remembers his suffering:

> Because Mark would not mix with other children he was always indoors which meant we never had any time to ourselves which we needed, to deal with the upsetting times in the day when we had to often take time off work to get Mark into school as he was tormented by other children who called him thick and dummy, etc. as well as teachers who said he was useless and lazy.

Mark found at comprehensive school friends all stuck together against the teachers. If he did get any teasing he dealt with it personally, resorting to blows when necessary. His response to Q24, *Have you ever smashed anything up on purpose, because you were upset about school?* was that he hit a boy who was 'mouthing off and being a smart-arse' while Mark was being told off.

Associative reactions

Truancy/school refusal

Mark 'wagged it' in the first year at secondary school for geography because of the hated master mentioned above (see page 91–2). He said about being sent to boarding school: 'You dropped down a level; because you wagged it they get hold of you and send you somewhere else because you couldn't handle the normal school.'

In response to the specific question about truancy Mark elaborated further on the methods he had used. He had a very wide and versatile repertoire of school avoidance techniques. He had a network of friends covering for him and writing forged notes; he used to slip out after morning registration and return for lunch-time registration only or keep watch to see whether he was missed. If so, he would stroll in with an excuse. Mostly, he felt 'teachers didn't care a toss'. He got great joy from out-foxing teachers who were out to give him trouble over something. He would make himself sick by sticking his fingers down his throat and actually demand medication from the doctor for false headaches/sicknesses/stomach pains. He stopped short of trying this on the dentist, he said!

In the second year he tried 'wagging it' to go fishing. In the third year he attended more, but 'didn't care and did nothing'. Mark had a 'bunking' spell over third-year exams at comprehensive. He went fishing – his friend's elder brother forged notes for them, and various other dodges were employed.

Mark also went through spells of school refusal, especially in the first year with the hated geography teacher:

> I used to hang on to the bannisters at home, when sussed out as not sick. Mum had to get Dad out of work. (I got hit.) They didn't know what to do. Ripped blazer, everything. I went to a doctor and got hypnotized, for fear of school. Small green tablets they put me on. (I used to eat cat's food to be sick.) Three or four times I went. Really scared. Dad joked, snapped me out of it ... If I had tests, even at junior school, I'd put my hand down my throat to chuck up, or a cotton-wool sandwich ... I used to wag it every time we had a test at school – save me being bottom of the class. Feels like you're empty inside, but it goes.

Isolation/alienation

As has already been noted, Mark's mother commented on the inconvenience of the fact that he would not mix with other children and he was always indoors.

Lack of communication

Mark informed me that he seldom told his parents what happened at school. For example, over his making himself sick to avoid school at age 8 or 9 by sticking his fingers down his throat, he told me, 'Mum doesn't know.' The same theme recurred over behaviour at comprehensive: 'They still don't know, though.'

Mark also related how he threw away a medal for being in the football finals as he felt he didn't deserve it since they didn't *win*: 'I didn't tell my old girl and Dad – told them we lost and they said, "There's always next year".' Yet he had always desperately wanted a winner's medal.

Lack of confidence

Mark's parents felt lack of confidence entered into almost every aspect of his life. Six of their questionnaire answers specifically mentioned lack of confidence.

Q3: *At what ages, if any, did you notice any severe lack of confidence or unhappiness in your son?*

The most noticeable time Mark showed lack of confidence and unhappiness must have been between the ages of 11 and 13 before starting special school.

Q4: *If so, have you any reason for thinking it still persists in any area?*

Mark still lacks confidence in many ways such as reading a book because he thinks he will not be able to read it all without help, so he would rather not try to read at all; therefore his reading is getting worse because he is not reading regularly. This also applies to writing. Also a general lack of confidence in his self, which can sometimes be overcome, because if it means going out he will take someone with him.

Q5: *When did you feel your son made most progress in school work or happiness?*

Q6: *Why do you think this was?*

The most progress made by Mark must be in the years spent at special school [1982–5] which helped not only his school work but gave him back a lot of his confidence. He became the happy, cheeky son we used to know years ago. This was due to the fact that teachers spent time with him on his school work and hobbies, showing him he could be as good as anyone else; where his last school disregarded him as a waste of time, telling him so. He still puts his self down even now but not as much. Although I must admit it helped being with other children with the same problems, the teachers must take most of the praise for their time, patience and dedication to their job.

Q7: *How do you feel dyslexia has affected your son's outlook on life and personality?*

Dyslexia affected Mark's outlook on life, towards other people he meets, as he is inclined not to trust them as readily as he used to and because he feels he is not as good as other people. With regards to personality I don't think he is as carefree as he would have been (or seemed) before the problem arose, but I think it has made him more caring and loving towards people as he hates to see anyone hurt, especially by something he might say.

Q8: *What do you feel has been the most important factor overall in helping your child cope with dyslexia, and why?*

The most important factor in helping Mark cope with dyslexia must be the teachers at the special school I mentioned before. This is due to the fact that they cared enough to give their own time to show the children that they could excel in many ways and not only in school work, giving the children the confidence they needed to be able to learn. Without these people Mark would by now be a frustrated hermit.

At age 21, Mark still lacked confidence in his ability, often saying he wished he could train as a PE instructor but would never be able to pass the written exams to do so. At this stage he had tried many different jobs and found none of them particularly satisfying, only doing them for the money.

Self-doubt/denigration

Mark's view of himself was very negative and lasting, in spite of strong parental support and some school success: 'I just thought I was thick. Then I was told about dyslexia and I thought, "Oh, that's why I'm thick." ' (Variable score on IQ; above average on innate concepts and pure reasoning.)

Competitiveness disorders

Mark applied harsh perfectionist standards to himself and could not feel a sense of achievement being on exam courses or gaining a good average CSE in English, because he had help (see results on p. 98):

> I don't feel very successful . . . Here they work round you, instead of you working round them. It's like football when you drop down a league. It would've been an achievement if I'd stuck it out at the other place and got exams. But I don't think I've achieved nothing.

At that stage, when leaving school was on the horizon, he obviously felt a very poor bet in the occupational rat-race:

> People who are dyslexic always work hard because they have to and they think they won't get another chance. Other people who can read and spell better can get promoted through an office if they need that stage, then go back outside. You never get there if you're dyslexic, you stay at that level.

He was very clear and matter-of-fact about it.

> There's three types of people – top, middle and us. There's always going to be some word you can't read and someone who *can* read it. That interview [careers] brought it home to me, it's always going to be dragging behind me as far as I go in life. Like a chain round your neck pulling you down . . . Lacking communication – you've *got* trouble reading and writing. Concern that teachers will meet you and treat you like an animal in a cage; well you're *not*, you're just like anyone else. But it's all on your records and it'll always follow me; I can't never get rid of it, can I?

He seemed to feel it was like a permanent debilitating black mark against him on the job market. I explained about successful dyslexics and profitable practical careers, but he was not convinced.

Sensitivity to criticism

I taught Mark for English and remedial work for over two years and I felt his reaction to correction and suggestion was one of extreme sadness. He was deeply convinced that nothing he did was ever going to be good enough, despite praise for his considerable effort and some definite talent in creative writing. I would say he put at least double weighting in importance on any mistakes found and was very reluctant to accept compliments. He almost disregarded the latter pessimistically as sheer fluke that he had done something right, or felt you were being too kind. It was hard to encourage improvement without getting him disheartened. He worked hard and set himself perfectionist standards, willingly working in his free time. He often destroyed essays he had worked hard on because he felt they were not good enough. He hated including drafts which had small errors in them in his files, getting upset even when assured that they showed his improvement and hard work compared with the final copy.

Behaviour problems

Mark had a fairly riotous primary school career. The first thing he mentioned in his free interview about it was a girl who called him thick. He hit her and she pulled his hair. He felt 'well shamed up, hitting a girl! Friends didn't care – they hated her.'

Mark was in the A team for football, and remembered trying to break a boy's nose with his foot, intentionally and aggressively applying extra power and pressure to the boy's nose with his boot whilst playing rugby. He recalled: 'Rugby and football, cricket – throwing my weight around.'

He was also involved in throwing food at paintings and setting up other children, sneaking two lunch sittings, collapsing trestle-tables, etc.

As regards Mark's general behaviour at his comprehensive, there are accounts of Coke rings spinning and hitting the teacher's face as well as of exercise books 'nicked' from store cupboards and paving the playground with them as graffiti. He would go to the sick bay with headaches and spit the aspirin into teachers' waiting drinks. He felt war had been declared after the way he had been treated. He relates a story about applying for a grant for special school when an official tried to put him off, telling him he wouldn't like it. His reply was:

> Well, *you* stay here if it's so good and I'll go. I don't really want to go and leave all my mates, but I ain't prepared to put up with all the shit I'm getting here.

Finally the official swore and shouted, Mark's father came in and a row ensued with the result: 'That's it! No grant!' Fortunately, a relative eventually stepped in to pay the fees.

He never went back to his secondary school once he had left – 'hated it'. He felt the school was 'only good if you're brainy, if not they don't care. Other teachers turn up and write something down, thinking okay – flop if you want to.' He shouted abuse at the teachers when he knew he was leaving. He does say this in mitigation of his secondary school;

> It wasn't their fault they couldn't help me. It started in the junior school and I took it out on them. They were like Nazis in the war sat up there. Really, I see now, they couldn't come to me all the time, and help in class. It wasn't fair trying to sell them laxative chocolates and things like that. It was a personal war.

He said of his streamed remedial class:

> You had a choice to make every lesson – how you could get chucked out, or be quiet and take it – gauge the mood of the teacher and level of danger. They was out to get you, so you tried to get them first.

Mark said there was a fear of him getting into trouble with the police, and so that was why his relative paid the fees for special education: 'I wanted to learn, I didn't think there'd be much hope for me ... My attitude to teachers *here* changed, you don't have to call them Sir, you could be more open.'

Again, after a few initial difficulties and run-ins with male staff, Mark became a popular and much-respected prefect as well as a capable games assistant.

Appendix

Public examination results

Summer 1984	CSE	Arithmetic	4
		English Language	4
		Technical Drawing	5
Summer 1985	CSE	Arithmetic	3
		English Language	4
		Science	4

Career/occupation

Mark has tried varied work – builder, floor-layer, hospital porter. He is currently operating a car valet service for a national company.

Work samples

There follow a poem by Mark (spelling self-corrected) and two stories which appeared in the school magazine. Figure 2.21 shows a draft and neat copy of his free writing.

Speedway

The atmosphere is tense in the pits,
Before the rides start their bickes.
People waiting excitedly,
As the revs get louder,
It sounds like thunder in the night sky.
The first four riders come up fast
Slowing down forwards the tape.
Pushing against the tape anxions to start.

Lights go off around the stadium,
Leaving only the spotlights shining on the track,
Lights shine down, like a space-ship
To the dark black, night sky.
Tapes up! riders let go of the clutch,
and they're away!
People shout, a deafening noise,
Yelling for the rider they want to win.
As they slide arourd the bend
The brown gravel goes fiying
Into the night sky.

On the last lap
The two back riders are close together,
Battling it out for third place.
Their wheels click on the last bend.
They crached strayight into the safety fence.
The crowed shout out in disappointment.
The riders get up safely,
And shake hands.
They pick up their bikers
And walk off to the pits.

The Shipwreck

It was the year 1519. I was on a warship in the middle of the ocean. Everyone was asleep when I heard a shout from the man on watch. 'All hands on deck!'

There was a big rush to the cannons. When we got there we saw there was another warship which had started firing. We returned fire, but a cannon ball hit the stern of our ship and it began to sink. All the lifeboats were let down into the sea. There was a lot of pushing and shoving. I stayed on the ship till the last moment and then jumped. When I hit the water I shouted because the cold winter sea was biting into my back. Then the ship went down.

There were a few screams as the ones that had stayed on the ship drowned. As the boat finally disappeared the suction of it nearly drew me down. I panicked and started to wave my arms and legs. I finally managed to get to the surface of the water choking and coughing and found a piece of wood from the wreck to hold on to.

By this time my legs were so numb with cold I could not feel them and it was difficult to swim to a life boat. When I finally managed to get to one I tried to get on but the men on it said, 'There's not enough room on this boat,' and hit me with their oars. I lost consciousness.

The next thing I remember was a nice sandy beach and a girl stroking my hair.

'Where am I?' I asked her.

'I'll tell you all I know about this place,' she replied, 'but first let's have something to eat.'

After dinner she told me about the island and how she had been shipwrecked there too some years before. 'You never can leave the island,' she added. 'I've tried.'

For weeks I tried to get off, but it was no good. One day I sat on the beach as the sun was going down and thought, 'I'm never going to leave this island so I might as well enjoy it.' And I did.

Speedway

I first got interested in speedway when my dad took me to see the Crayford team. I was about ten years old. My dad likes speedway as well and has been going to events for about seventeen years.

Speedway is where two teams of seven motor cyclists race against each other. There are four riders racing at one time, two from each side. Numbers 1, 3 and 5 are what they called heat leaders in that side. These riders have five rides each. Numbers 2 and 4 are the next best riders. They also have five rides each. 6 and 7 are what they call reserved rides and they have three rides each. Speedway can be a dangerous sport if a rider falls off for he is quite likely to be run into, but more especially because the bikes have no brakes and there is no way of stopping or slowing down, unless you use the clutch. When the riders stop they disengage their engines quickly.

There is now a safety device which has saved hundreds of lives. It can cut off the engine when a rider falls off. Before the rider used to fall off and the back wheel used to kick. This has only been out two or three years.

Speedway tracks are oval shaped. When the riders are on the straight sections they go faster. Though they lose speed on the beginning of a bend they accelerate coming out of it. Speeds going round the bends can be as high as 70 mph.

The riders have to do four laps of the track to finish a race. You get 3 points for a win, two points for a second, one point for third and for fourth you get nothing. The teams I have seen are Crayford, King's Lynn, Coventry, Hackney, Wimbledon, Newcastle, Eastbourne, Poole and Oxford.

I like to see the speed and skill of the riders. They know when to overtake, how close to get to other bikes and how far to bend and lean on the corners. I would like to ride in Speedway, but it is very expensive. It costs about £350 for a second hand bike plus new tyres every two rides for maximum grip round corners.

This is very important. The leathers are also very expensive. Most people need sponsors in order to compete. So at the moment I have to be content with watching. But even this is exciting and full of suspense as you never know who is going to win.

Speedway . 1.(Draft)

as the engens started up the riders came aut af the pitch. as the came up to the tapes wating for the tapes to go up the raff *the enjens.* ~~had and the small af the faullrns ar~~ lovely The tupes go up they ~~latt~~ go of the cluch and aff the go sliding around the fast baned gravel flas away in the night skey, ~~and the~~ as they came to the final band the rides back are ~~clos~~ close to tother and after the tapes they go to win the *first* ~~fast~~ but then back to the pitch to gine they bicks a rest and the next ~~lad~~ come out to start it all afver ~~gane.~~

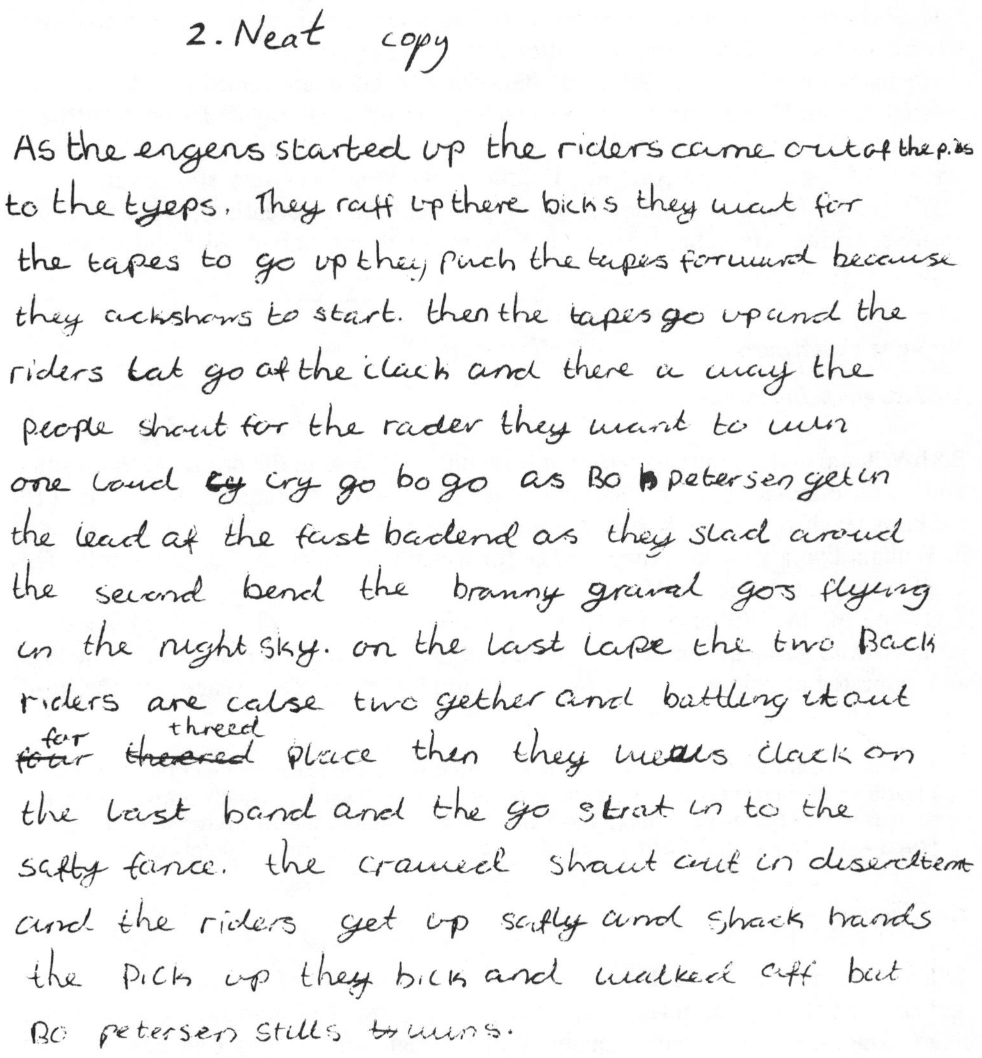

2. Neat   copy

As the engens started up the riders came out of the p.is
to the tyeps. They raff up there bichs they wait for
the tapes to go up they pinch the tapes forward because
they ackshans to start. then the tapes go up and the
riders lat go at the clack and there a way the
people shout for the rader they want to win
one loud cy cry go bo go as Bo b petersen get in
the lead at the fast badend as they slad aroud
the secand bend the branny graval gos flying
in the night sky. on the last lape the two Back
riders are calse two gether and battling it out
for   threed
four ~~theered~~ place then they wetts clack on
the last band and the go strat in to the
safty fance. the crawed shaut cut in diserdtem
and the riders get up safty and shack hands
the picks up they bicks and walked aff but
Bo petersen stills to wins.

Figure 2.21 Mark: draft and neat copy of free writing

WILLIAM

I first met William when I took him for a remedial lesson because his teacher was absent. He was initially very bashful about his reading and spelling, had a strong country accent which caused him to be teased by other boys, and was rather homesick. Once talking about his animals at home on the farm, however, he could laugh, warm to his subject, and show a genuine, honest character of great charm. He later chose to come to me for lessons permanently.

William was 13 when he was statemented for special educational provision for dyslexia. He had a reading age of 7 and an enduringly severe spelling problem. He scored an IQ of 124 on the WISC(R) intelligence test.

His behaviour was always excellent. He had a well-balanced, genial personality at school, and good pupil–teacher relationships.

He had been identified early, but had not had adequate remedial help. He was crossed-lateral. He became a most warmly appreciated head boy under rather difficult circumstances, and started an extra year which he did not complete. After leaving, he started work but then entered an FE college, where he was very successful.

His special talents and interests were sport (equestrian eventing), woodwork and creative writing. He achieved well in O-levels (with an amanuensis) and CSEs (see results on p. 107).

Negative experiences

Inadequate help/neglect

Both William and his parents reported total unhelpfulness in the primary school situation, with supposed specialist help that was in fact given to other children or used for the class teacher to mark books. Complaints about this and school friction resulted in William living with his grandmother for a while in order to change schools. This is all documented (see p. 155).

On top of this William's headmaster actually encouraged him to avoid work and get away with gardening/practical pursuits all the time. William had a teacher he liked and respected at primary school before spending the next four years with the headmaster. This caused problems:

> He was a pushover. The only thing wrong was that we had to learn the times tables, which I learnt and forgot every day. He used to let me do what I wanted, usually practical things such as woodwork or gardening, 'cos I enjoyed doing things outside. After a while I got bored with doing it, and much preferred to stay home on the farm and do my animals . . .

Humiliation

William did not suffer much from this, probably because of his early identification and removal at early secondary stage to a special school environment. In the questionnaire exploration of embarrassment, William mentioned a girl (see next section), shopkeepers and also a teacher:

> Then the second year Science teacher said to me, 'Are you stupid, can't you read?', when I stood in the wrong queue with really high-up notices about the school you came from on. I was talking to a kid I knew, and didn't realize. Shopkeepers sometimes do it to you, 'cos you don't bother to read notices.

This is a common habit of dyslexics, who even when they can read quite fluently have an aversion to written notices.

Teasing/persecution

William only had one incident to mention when talking about embarrassing moments in response to Q15, *Have you had any embarrassing experiences through being dyslexic?* This involved an unfortunate start to his secondary education, when a girl upset him:

When I first went to comprehensive, you know, I had to put a title of a subject on a book, and a girl took the mickey. ('Don't you *know* how to spell *that*?') I never spelt it [Maths] wrong since. She called me thick and stupid. Silly little bitch.

Associative reactions

Truancy/school refusal

William made serious attempts to avoid school, but unsuccessfully at primary level:

This is when I really started trying to miss school. About a year before this, I started acting ill and trying to miss the bus, but my mum always knew when I was faking, and always made me go, even when I *was* ill, 'cos she never knew if I was faking or not! Missing the bus never worked, because my dad threatened to make me walk, and it was a long way!

The thwarting of his attempts at school refusal brought on outbursts of temper. This is from his response to Q24 about anger over school:

I remember getting annoyed about school, and always trying to get away from it. I do remember getting annoyed and despondent about junior school, I used to threaten to run away, I'd run out behind the barn and stay there until someone found me. I used to take it out on my dad when he told me off. It's the frustration, isn't it?

Even William missed lessons, though not whole days.

Isolation/alienation

William was not at all an isolationist, but he did feel he had become polarized against and distanced from his father. This was partly because he felt his brother who was left at home did everything right and was closer to Mr W., who himself felt that William could be very temperamental and obstinate to deal with (comment on Open Day 1983). Obviously, boarding school exacerbates any sibling rivalries latent in any situation because of the erratic time-schedule involved in relationships.

Lack of communication

There is no mention of William being lacking in communication at school, though his mother said on Open Day 1983 that he never told them anything at home about how he was getting on at school. The whole family were pleasantly surprised by reports of his academic progress and exceptional behaviour.

Lack of confidence

William described himself as: 'Someone who worries about what people think about you. Slightly shy, until I know people.'

I found on taking him to work experience at a garage that he was extremely worried about coping with new people. He took a deep breath and said: 'Oh no! A whole load of new people to get to know and get on with. I hate that, I really hate that situation. Can I cope? Oh, well, here goes!' This nervousness and lack of assurance surprised me as he had then been head boy for a full year, used to reading in church, and making presentations to public audiences. The garage was in fact delighted with him, as his work experience report showed.

His mother felt exam success had done a lot for him:

> Being intelligent, William was thrilled with exam results which put him on equal terms with members of his immediate family plus cousins and friends, doing a lot better than some and I know he felt this was important. William was very hurt when not asked what 'O' levels, etc. he was taking when there were family gatherings. He hates anyone to think he is different because of his dyslexia.

Self-doubt/denigration

William was worried about college, for the same reasons as Trevor. Would he fit in? Would he be able to cope alongside 'normal' students?

He was uncertain about his own abilities when asked:

Q19: *How would you describe your intelligence?*

Wouldn't like to say, it's a matter of opinion, isn't it? I suppose I must be average, 'cos I've got O-levels, well; but most people get CSEs so I must be above average, 'cos I've got 1's not 4's.

He had always felt anxious about intellectual status:

Q25: *Have you ever felt worried about school exams?*

Yeah.

Prompt: *When?*

At this place, I've always wanted to do best. I've always been worried about being put in with the thick ones, the ones who aren't normal.

Q26: *Have you ever felt very angry about school?*

Yeah.

Prompt: *Explain?*

When I've not been doing very well, or when teachers are getting at you.

Q27: *What is the worst thing about being dyslexic?*

You're never sure if you're going to make a fool of yourself or not.

His file shows that when he was 10 he was very afraid that he might be placed in the special ESN unit when he commenced at the secondary school. Yet this is a boy in the superior category of the WISC(R) intelligence test both on Verbal and Performance levels (IQ 124). This is even with depressed sub-test scores, as usual for dyslexics in Coding and Digit-span. He scored as very superior in verbal reasoning and comprehension.

Competitiveness disorders

William was extremely dogged in determination and ambitious in his desire to compete and win. I include him here because he is the only one I felt had got the levels of competition balanced. I do not feel his competitive attitude was a disorder, but it was extreme. I had a slight fear he might overwork in later years, perhaps become a workaholic, but I was sure he would be successful.

William felt the most important factor in coping was this:

> You want to always have a goal, don't you, you don't want to get disheartened, you never want to be put down; except I found, if they did put you down, it made you determined, you always wanted to be one better. You always want to prove people wrong.

Asked whether it was important to have brothers and sisters who were helpful and understanding, he said, 'This helps, but is not essential, 'cos you can then try to better them.'

On special talents, he replied, 'Yes, this is important, because you need to be able to show people up, and prove that you are good at something.'

About knowledge of dyslexia his opinion was:

> This is good, because you know other people are similar, and you're not the only one; you know most dyslexic people get on better in the long run, at work, and in later life, despite what people tell you in school.

Asked about his progress, he was very positive: 'I have recently got on well at school, because I proved people wrong and got my O-levels, but I wanted higher pass grades.'

I would then have described William as a young man in a hurry, and one bound to go far. I was right.

His mother said, 'He is very determined to succeed in all he does and probably more determined to prove himself, not wanting anyone to know about his dyslexia.' When asked if he foresaw any future difficulties he said, 'In business, yes, but I *will* overcome them I should say ... I'll have to be very successful and get a secretary.'

He felt his teachers would view him: 'As an intelligent person who wants to get on, succeed and get on as far as possible in life.'

This has been borne out by the fact that, having discovered and developed his great talent for equestrian three-day event competition, he is now in the top 25 young riders in Britain, with possible Olympic prospects. He has reached the level of expertise to merit being sponsored formally by a company, and trains with a famous showjumper and eventer.

It is no accident that many dyslexics run their own businesses and are very successful. The proportion of special school parents involved in that is dramatic. See also the comments of eminent dyslexics in many fields in Hampshire (1990) about their determination to succeed.

Sensitivity to criticism

William's sensitivity manifested itself at home on the farm. Boarding school absences may well have made him feel he had to assert himself in order to retain his position in the family. After William left school Mr W. commented:

He's really calmed down a lot over the last six months. Used to really fly off the handle when you had to pick him up about something. He'd really storm off and shout and get on his high horse about it.

William reserved this outlet of emotion and fieriness for home – at school he was placid, sensible, calm and easygoing, as would befit the head boy. He would be deeply concerned about matters affecting the boys and take action, but he never manifested real tension or any outbursts. He was a perfect gentleman.

Behaviour problems

There is no specific record of William behaving badly at school, and he himself said he used to take the frustration out on his father at home. However, the potential was obviously there and dangerously close to manifesting itself.

When William was 11 years 2 months old, the report by his educational psychologist said this:

> His social adjustment has improved a great deal. Originally his frustration resulted in some behavioural difficulties ... The gap between his intellectual potential and his ability to express this either in reading or writing will undoubtedly militate against him far more seriously when he is expected to deal with the curriculum demands of a secondary school. He is certainly not a child who would function happily in the ordinary remedial department consisting of slow learners and there is a distinct possibility that under the greater frustration in this situation, his behaviour might again become more destructive or he may alternatively find the stress of a secondary school too great for him.

The report by his head teacher on referral states about his relationships with adults: 'Can become aggressive when frustrated, but this is infrequent.' On special characteristics, however, it was noted that 'Apart from already mentioned, is very reliable, co-operative and often shows initiative. Organizes a small group of "gardeners" and can be trusted to be left unsupervised.' It also said that 'Fortunately William's above average intelligence and maturity has helped him to come to terms with his problem for the present.' The school expresses the hope that 'a school can be found that can challenge his intelligence and yet offer a sympathetic understanding of his reading problem.'

His psychological report for special educational provision mentions his reliability and qualities of leadership, pointing out he was only hard to handle 'in situations relating to his known difficulties'.

It was stressed that he needed an environment 'capable of fostering and developing his intellectual development without depending on reading and writing skills to the extent usual in an ordinary classroom setting'. An urgent warning note is again sounded:

> Should he not be challenged intellectually in this way and achieve satisfaction in developing his areas of competence as well as receiving appropriate remedial help, then his frustration and consequent anger are likely to give rise either to quite serious behaviour problems or to a tendency to opt out of the learning situation altogether.

At home, the difficulties were more pronounced:

William was easier to live with when kept occupied with plenty of interesting tasks to do. We often had to remind him about things he was planning to do . . .

William's dyslexia affected the rest of the family when he became explosive and difficult to reason with, often over trivial problems. This tended to have a knock-on effect. He needed a lot of moral help and time.

I remember the exact response of William's parents to praise of his behaviour at the 1983 Open Day already mentioned: 'Well, you know, they *all* say that and you'd never believe it! – still, better that way round for his sake, getting on. It's a bit hard on us though!'

From his dignified status as head boy William did admit to some disruption. Also he did threaten to blow up one of his teachers when at primary school. In answering about his ability to forget school problems he said:

It's hard to forget about it if someone's chasing you; you have to think your way out of it, if they set you extra work 'cos you can't keep up with the class. That's bad, it's a hindrance and does not help you . . . as long as teachers get off you mentally, you're alright. But stupid thick teachers chasing you over trivial things is bad . . . it makes you more despondent, and you come not to care about school. Homework nagging, a childish approach to you, they haven't grown up, treat you like a stupid little school kid, showing you up in front of the class. These are all the things that make you anti-social, and you never bother doing anything again in that teacher's lesson. They can get the knife in and twist so you get yours out too. You can be better at it, too, and that gets you into more trouble. The teacher always comes out on top, though, 'cos they can call in the headmaster.

Appendix

Public examination results

Summer	1984	CSE	Integrated Science	1
			Technical Drawing	2
			Woodwork	1
		GCE	English Literature	C
			History	C
			Woodwork	C
			Geometric and Technical Drawing	U
Autumn	1984	GCE	Geometric and Technical Drawing	D

Career/occupation

William studied Accounts and Bookkeeping at FE college, and obtained a BTEC diploma in Business Studies. A qualified riding teacher, he now runs his own equestrian eventing yard, at which he has been very successful. He is looking for sponsors to develop even further at national level.

Work samples

Four of William's poems are reproduced. They contain some very original descriptions and a boyish appreciation of nature.

Just Die!

I was just led there.
My wheels had been ripped off,
My paint was coming off,
My doors are bent and buckled.
There's leaves and muck all over me,
The rust nibbles at me.
Because of this you only have to touch me,
And I fall apart.
Oh what doom!

The Berry Snow

You can see the trees,
As if they have just seen a ghost.
You can see the car,
Coverd with snow like a piece of old furniture.
That has been in an attie.
The blue-tits fluttering as if they are on a hot plate.
The snow falling like jetpropelled rain.
The squirrels are dancing in the snow.
In the distance you can see a dog,
Sliding in the snow after a crystal stick.

The Shadow Tree

The trees are glimmering in the sun light
Which shines onto the water.
You can hear the water trickling down
And rushing into the rapids.
The banks look dead and still
Except for the odd animal moving in the leaves.
When the wind blows you can see leaves
Falling in to the fiery water.
From the top of the trees you can hear pigeons
Fluttering as the trees move.

The Tile Waves

The tile waves,
The tiles wet with rain
Shine in the wetness,
Shaped as waves,
The sparrows run up and down the waves,
Stopping and picking out the odd,
Loosened insect, by the rain.
Bang! (They're all gone!)

OLIVER

I taught Oliver as part of a CSE Language group, and his attitude to staff was always intelligent and co-operative, if rather laid-back. Small in stature, he had learnt to fight by using his brain in scheming activities and developing a devastating precision in hurting other boys with words singling out their weak spots. He was so good at this that we only found out he had the reputation of being something of a tyrant with younger pupils after he had left!

Oliver came to special school at the age of 14, with his reading age at parity. He scored 112 (Visual scale) and 131 (Verbal) on the BAS intelligence test. This means he was in the top 15 per cent in general intellectual ability, and the top 2 per cent of the population in verbal skill. He was only a residual dyslexic by this stage. His behaviour was excellent towards staff, but could upset other boys. The staff impression of his personality was that of a quiet pupil who operated two codes of behaviour. He was diagnosed as dyslexic when he was aged 4 and at pre-school in Little Rock, Arkansas, USA. He had private tutorial help in maths and reading. His family returned to England when Oliver was 7. He was a prefect at the special school, and went on to FE college to improve his grades at GCE.

Negative experiences

Inadequate help/neglect

Although Oliver had effective help from an early age, he developed a loathing for remedial reading material:

> *Dick and Dora* . . . I mean, that's one of the worst kind of books you could ever make a kid to read, if you're about six or four – I mean, so boring, it can't really encourage you; you just think, 'Oh God!' I mean, you're quite proud that you can read that, but I think they could do something probably a bit more imaginative.

Humiliation

Oliver attended a small private preparatory school, which he felt helped and made him work. He felt under pressure to avoid humiliation, however:

> If you're dyslexic, if you're in a big school it's going to be much harder, you can be just put in a corner and they kind of forget about you. I was in a small primary school so I got made to work hard, so I guess that's why I'm not quite as badly dyslexic as some other people are, because I had no choice but to work. I reckon when you first start and you're made to work hard and they're not that sympathetic with you – well, that worked for me, I'm not sure it would work for other people; but after a while if you're severely dyslexic you need *some* sympathy, and you need people to recognize it so that people just can't call you thick.

He developed a kind of competitive doggedness eventually: 'At my primary school I probably worked my hardest, 'cos if I didn't I'd get called thick and dumb for the first time, and that was an incentive, because things were more competitive then.'

Teasing/persecution

> The worst problem I've had at school was at primary school when I first went there 'cos
> I got the mickey taken out of me a lot. I didn't mind that, but it was *all* the time; but
> after a while I learnt to ignore it and give it back and it was alright after that. In America
> that never happened . . .

Oliver's parents independently gave a very similar picture of the problem in England:

> The village population was largely middle class and rivalry was inevitable. Oliver was quite
> unable to cope competitively, either with his work or, unfortunately, with sports as his
> physical co-ordination remained poor. Teasing was frequent and his self-confidence was
> very undermined. He inevitably asked himself whether he was 'thick' or even 'normal'.

Oliver had this to say also, in answer to the question *What's the worst thing about
being dyslexic, for you?*:

> Dunno. Probably not being able to spell properly. You get angry about that sometimes,
> you can't spell a word. You sit there for hours thinking, 'How do I spell that?' Or you've
> done a piece of work and it comes back with all corrections; you know, why do you
> bother? Sometimes it gets you down, it makes you feel angry. Why are you dyslexic? I
> think the worst thing is spelling or having to read out in front of people. Just like, getting
> embarrassed about it.

He felt particularly bad about reading aloud as a junior:

> Yeah, maybe . . . people could hear . . . some of the books you got made to read, like
> *Dick and Dora*. They were boring to read anyway and people could see . . . people com-
> pare books . . . Longer words equals harder. People go, 'Oh, I read that book ages ago
> when I was in infants,' . . . and they try to embarrass you.

Associative reactions

Truancy/school refusal

Even Oliver, who had markedly less negative experiences, and is also less severely
dyslexic, had attempted school refusal. He was asked the question *Have you ever
played truant or refused to go to school?*:

> I used to pretend I was sick, make myself puke, and say I don't wanna go today. I used
> to get in the car, like when I first went to a school in America, they had like a guard
> in the back of the car and I'd sit in the car and wouldn't get out. They had to get someone
> in the boot and someone in the door and I kept crawling back and forth 'cos I didn't want
> to go.

Lack of confidence

Oliver was additionally vulnerable to lack of confidence because he was between two
very academically successful sisters in family status and age. In his parents' perspective
within his Statement of Special Educational Needs (SEN) it emerges about his elder
sister that:

> In the one year they were at primary school together he received little kindness or support
> from her and the normal sibling jealousies took a harsh form with derision and cutting

comments. His younger sister was reasonably bright and extrovert and represented a 'challenge from behind'. Oliver's pain and frustration at his many 'put-downs' were apparent in spite of our efforts to protect him without smothering him.

Oliver's mother noticed very bad effects in English primary school at age 7. It was a small village school, and very socially and academically competitive. She commented, 'I think he suffered a lot of mockery and bullying at that time which permanently damaged his self-confidence.'

Going to a special school did not help Oliver either in this area.

Special school at first boosted him, but eventually the lack of expectations caused him to 'sit back' on his disabilities rather than fight to overcome them. When he left there he felt as if he was a permanent 'thicko', as he put it.

It was observed that this feeling was very persistent:

[It] pervades his whole thinking about himself. Great lack of self-confidence, and aggression in the sense of attack on life generally. Very happy and content if he is left alone to be amiably idle with no expectations of performance of any sort made upon him. Copes fine with things he knows he can do. Dislikes challenges – either intellectual or even physical.

A clear sense of unfairness is observed by his mother:

Oliver seems not to understand at all that nothing comes naturally easily to *anyone*. It is as if he feels the only person in the world to whom difficulties occur, everyone else can succeed without trying.

The effect of dyslexic problems on Oliver's outlook seems to have been fairly devastating: 'Bit as if he is handicapped and will always be a lame duck I suspect. Low self-esteem.'

It is thought also that his father's successfulness makes him feel he could never match up. He has recently taken the initiative of applying to a kibbutz in Israel, however. His parents are all in favour: 'We recognize, as he does, that in order to enhance his self-confidence or self-esteem he needs to be away from home.'

The annual progress review in his statement comments:

In a small-group boarding school setting Oliver had made progress with his reading and increased in confidence though he still experiences learning difficulties in relation to spelling. He responds well to a consistent, secure environment.

Self-doubt/denigration

Despite small-group teaching, happiness in America, and the regular remedial help at an early age, Oliver still doubted his intelligence:

I think my parents knew I was dyslexic, but I didn't. I just thought I was thick. When I first came here ... was when I realized I was dyslexic – I just thought I was slow. My parents said I'd got learning difficulties and I thought, yeah, they were trying to smooth it for me, but when I got here I realized it was probably true.

Competitiveness disorders

Oliver's mother strongly reports a disinclination to compete or to sustain his effort once involved in competition. He seems to lack 'staying-power'. She mentioned his highly competitive primary school where he first suffered. Then he seemed to do well on entering new establishments for a while. She commented:

> Bursts of enthusiasm and progress in schools when placed in a new situation, e.g. starting secondary school, starting here . . . starting sixth-form college (quite a good year) and finally at college of secondary education, very good first term. When the going gets a bit tough, however, and work is demanded on time, etc. he retreats into failure and apathy. Basically because he is quite able and stable, the new situations represented an opportunity to prove that he *is* okay and normal [to himself].

The idea already mentioned under 'Lack of confidence' above is also relevant here – that Oliver feels everyone else finds success easy except himself.

The problems of feeling in competition with clever sisters and a highly successful father also add pressure and frustration. This occurred inevitably without any parental design. His mother said that they had 'always tried to encourage his interests and enthusiasms. This has been exasperatingly difficult because they flag so quickly when he feels he isn't brilliant at whatever it is straight away.'

I know how hard this is through similar experiences with my own dyslexic daughter, whose difficulties were complicated by a younger sister who instantly seized on the same interest and tried to make herself even better at it. Unquashable siblings can be very jealous of any extra attention, and get emotionally upset in their own right, especially when very young.

In describing his school work Oliver himself said he sometimes felt in a giving-up mood in maths: 'But I guess I give up too easily . . . Quite a lot of things I give up when I can't read, that's why I can't be bothered. If it doesn't work out quickly.' His mother stated, 'I don't think he has coped yet. In some ways I think our early recognition and [particularly my] concern with it has in some ways been counter-productive.'

Sensitivity to criticism

Oliver's mother was really worried about his reaction to her urging him to work harder for his exams and arranging holiday tuition. He interpreted her help as lack of faith in his abilities, reacted negatively, construed this as criticism, and a miserable holiday followed for the whole family. She wrote then:

> I think his present, depressed and negative state arises, at least in part, from mismanagement by me. For obvious reasons he lacks self-confidence, which I have always endeavoured to overcome by affirming and reaffirming my totally sincere belief in his abilities . . .
>
> I suspect the consequence of these policies [holiday tuition] has been to overpressurize him with heightened expectations and to blow up his fear of failure out of all proportion. As a result, I feel he is despairing about his work, particularly Maths, and worse, becoming negative generally about himself. This latter he displaces on to circumstances around him. Exhortations to try harder (from me again!) have probably intensified the vicious circle.

One can sympathize with the dilemma of the caring parent whose agonized efforts to help are rejected as unjust criticism at best, and at worst as a debilitating attack on the child's competence.

Behaviour problems

The most noticeable feature of Oliver's behaviour, which I only learnt about after he left, was a tendency to pick on and victimize another boy. Many staff thought very highly of Oliver, but several boys, juniors amongst them, gave quite different views of him once he had safely left. 'Evil' was one description of his reign as a prefect. This was not just hearsay; consistent and convincing accounts were given to me by boys from disparate social groups and cliques, just on mentioning that I was having difficulty tracing Oliver for follow-up work to my original study. Some jealousy may have been present because Oliver got on so well with the staff, but some detail seemed authentic and came from trustworthy boys. Also for a physically small prefect to exert control he may have been forced to be hard on juniors. I mentioned all this, but the boys remained adamant that he enjoyed punishing them unduly and was the most feared of the prefects.

Trevor mentioned it when asked what was his worst time at school and gave an intensely painful account of Oliver's techniques (see page 38).

Trevor fought back and got some critical reports about hostility to newcomers through it, as Oliver got on so well with staff and was also quite able and verbally adept. I feel Oliver defeated Trevor, who had religious scruples and was not skilled at devious attacks. It must also be said that Oliver had suffered badly himself; and as staff we have noticed that when they first come boys who have had a particularly bad time may have a general field-day, because at last they find people academically worse or more withdrawn and vulnerable than themselves.

They tend to stop when it is rammed home to them how they are simply taking out on the underdog what has been done to them previously; but it takes time, and you have to catch them at it. Oliver never got caught. Boys smaller in stature, as Oliver and Clark both were, also tend to develop woundingly sarcastic tongues in order to defend themselves. Bear in mind also how Oliver's elder sister had treated him with derision and cutting comments.

I feel it is a shame this aspect never came to light, as Oliver had such a pleasant side to his character as well; and the less desirable side might have been smoothed out. Oliver was aware of it, to some extent, himself. When asked about his personality he said, 'Shy at times, quite cheerful I guess. A bit of a stirrer . . . Well, with an argument, I can make it worse or cause one. Or just wind people up. Everyone does that here anyway.'

OLIVER **The Smugler**

The light flashed three times, from the headland. The clatter, & ocasional sqeeck of the sails, & blocks and tackle, seemed unsaly loud, It seemed to bounce of the hills of the bay, like a regostrad ing musket ball. My nerves felt as if some one was twisting them into a ball, I had a horrible sickfeeling in my stomuck, The ancore slipped into the water, A small splash, & a flash of white.

Sudelnley & silently the boat was sur onned by silent men, packages, of lace brandy & silk where passed down to them. Destined, for an celtiril, or fine country gentlemens house, may be one that would hang, or trunspot us if ~~we failed~~ they caught us. Nithir seemz fair or right to me.

I slipped over the side of the lugger, I caught my breath as the cold water, spreeel up my body, some of the men smiled, & gave a nod, ther teeth, white in the darkness,

My feet crunched on the pebles, the horses, two strings of them, snorted & stumpeel ther feet, As if they to wanteel to be away before first light, Ther masters, would find them back in ther stables, hot & sweety, put a parcles of lace, & a bottle of brandy.

Figure 2.22 Oliver: sample of free writing from CSE coursework

Appendix

Public examination results

Summer 1985	CSE	English Language	2
		Geography	2
		Science	2
	GCE	English Language	E
		English Literature	B
		History	C
		Maths	U
FE college	GCE	Maths	successful
		English Language	successful

Career/occupation

Oliver had just finished at an FE college, and intended to visit a kibbutz next. He will possibly look for a business or commercial opening in the long term.

Work samples

Figure 2.22 gives a sample of his free writing for CSE coursework. It should be noted that there was a 13 per cent spelling error rate in the first 100 words.

Chapter 3

Summary of Results

The tables have been compiled to give the reader as much information about each individual as possible. The evidence may be independently evaluated, and this can allow people to check, compare and follow up factors which interest them and on which I may not have focused.

Table 3.1 contains information on a range of educational facts, behavioural tendencies and special abilities which have been gathered from records, reports and participant observation.

Table 3.2 gives an analysis of the different ways data were collected, and indicates which sources were most profuse or productive in each (e.g. Gareth's questionnaire transcript ran to 25 pages, whereas John's was only 4).

Table 3.3 concentrates on testing, giving a detailed breakdown of relevant IQ factors, psychological and developmental variations and the referral procedure for each student. Thus individual patterns of dyslexic factors can be tracked across the table, whilst general trends can be observed by tracking down the columns.

Table 3.4 collates the findings on negative experiences and the emotional reactions caused by them, showing the prevalence of each type of incident and the extent of damaging psychological consequences.

From the evidence shown, it would be logical to state that all dyslexics can expect to suffer from inadequate help and neglect, undergo humiliation and be teased or persecuted within the present school system. As a direct result of this, they lack confidence, doubt their intellectual ability and develop behaviour problems. This prognosis is based on the experiences and results held in common to all eight cases. Other painful experiences such as being the victim of violence or unfairness affected the majority of students.

The majority expressed their dissatisfaction by truancy or school refusal, found themselves unable to communicate, felt isolated and became unduly competitive or anti-competitive. In a minority of cases (yet over one third of the sample), the stress and trauma built up by the whole experience of being a dyslexic in school led to the extreme reaction of clinical psychosomatic illness. This whole syndrome and its repercussions for a person's life and career prospects are dramatic and dangerous, as

Table 3.1. *Background of pupils (17 factors considered)*

	Age at start of study	Age of entry to special school	Degree of dyslexia	Reading age on entry	Early identification	Early help	Age first helped	School provision	Regularity	Years at special school
John	15	11¾	very severe reading & spelling	7.2	✓ immediate problems	✓ Private	7	records misleading	very irregular	5¼
Trevor	15	12	severe spelling	7.4	✓	✓	7½	remedial group & 1:1	1:1 for 1 hr daily (2 yrs)	4
Gareth	15¾	14	average for school	8.7	✓ dyslexia unrecognized	✓ not suitable	8	disabled & ESN school	1:1 twice weekly	6 general 2 dyslexic
Clark	15	14	severe reading	7.8	✓	remedial	8	senior 1:1 30 min./day	1st yr, 1:1 2nd yr, group of 13	3
George	15½	14	very severe reading & spelling	7.9	×	×	9 (told at 15 dyslexic)	2 yrs remedial class & 1:1	1:1 twice weekly	3
Mark	15	14	average for school	9	×	×	9	private & senior school	1:1 twice weekly	3
William	15	13	severe spelling	7	✓	×	8	records misleading	very irregular	3⅓
Oliver	15	14	residual	at parity	✓	✓	4 (USA)	private help	1:1 varied	4

	Behaviour impression	Personality impression	Compensatory talents	School responsibilities	Extra year	Sixth-form teacher relationships	FE college attended
John	variable	extrovert	all sports, pottery	head boy	✓	erratic (extremes)	–
Trevor	excellent	complex, sensitive	art, creative writing	deputy head boy	–	excellent	✓
Gareth	strong-willed	quiet, bluff, genial	mechanics, practical	under-prefect	✓	some minor difficulties	✓
Clark	variable; staff complaints	rascally extrovert	art, woodwork, creative work	fire-prefect	✓	erratic, extremes	–
George	14+: fine past: trouble	introvert; tough image	sport, karate, weight-lifting	prefect	✓	good, but often withdrawn, shy	–
Mark	erratic	extrovert in moods	sport, football	prefect	✓	erratic (extremes)	✓ one term; left
William	excellent	balanced	riding, poetry, woodwork	head boy	✓ only 1 term	excellent	✓
Oliver	excellent (staff) upsetting (boys)	ambivalent boys/staff	wit, sarcasm	prefect	–	good	✓

Table 3.2. *Source, type and amount of data elicited per pupil (18 sources)*

	Free interview (no. of pages)	Questionnaire (no. of pages)	Parental interview	Primary school Reports	Primary school Assessment	Senior school Reports / School type	Senior school Assessment	Statementing documents	Educational psychologist assessments	County review procedure
John	✓ Typed (3)	✓ Typed (4)	✓ mother: telephone	✓	✓	special	– stayed down (transfer special)	✓	✓	✓
Trevor	✓ Taped (3+)	✓ Taped (7)	✓ mother: typed	✓	✓	✓ comprehensive	✓	✓	✓	✓
Gareth	✓ Taped (7)	✓ Taped (25)	✓ mother: taped	–	✗	✓ disabled	✓	✓	✓	✓
Clark	✓ Taped (14)	✓ Taped (16)	✓ mother: typed	✓	✓	✓ comprehensive	✓	✓	✓	✓
George	✓ Typed (2)	✓ Typed (12)	✓ mother: telephone	–	–	✓ comprehensive	✓	✓	✓	✓
Mark	✓ Typed (5)	✓ Typed (7)	✓ mother: typed	–	–	✗ school lost them (comprehensive)	–	✗ private	✓	✗
William	✓ Typed (1)	✓ Typed (5)	✓ mother: typed	✓	✓	✓ comprehensive	✓	✓	✓	✓
Oliver	✓ Taped (2)	✓ Taped (17)	✓ mother: typed	✓ from parents (USA)	✓ via parents	✓ comprehensive	✓	✓	✓	✓

	Special school subject reports	Remedial assessments	Club reports	Pastoral reports	Participant observation	Work experience documents	Exams taken	Career details
John	✓	✓	✓	✓ bad then good	sport, pottery	✓ – non-participant	5 CSEs, 3 GCEs	bricklayer/heavy blockwork
Trevor	✓	✓	✓	✓ opinion varied	art, drama club	– non-participant	5 CSE, 5 GCEs	(FE college) A-level Art, Maths, Photography; BA degree
Gareth	✓	✓	✓	✓ good	computer clubs/duty	✓ 2	4 CSE	FE Forestry (City & Guilds) after agricultural engineering
Clark	✓	✓	✓	✓ opinion varied	riding, fishing clubs	✓	2 CSEs, 2 GCEs	varied; then skilled wood-turning
George	✓	✓	✓	✓ opinion varied	weight-training, karate clubs	✓ 2	2 CSEs, 1 GCE	family business: driving/delivery
Mark	✓	✓	✓	✓ opinion varied	football, duties	✓	4 CSEs	FE Building Studies: left after one term. Varied; then car valeting
William	✓	✓	✓	✓ excellent	riding club, duties	✓	2 CSEs, 5 GCEs	riding instructor (Equestrian eventing); FE BTEC Business Studies
Oliver	✓	✓	– none joined	✓ good	duties	– non-participant	3 CSEs, 4 GCEs	FE extended O-levels (4) with O/A Geography. Possible Business Studies

well as unnecessary. The final chapter on recommendations gives simple suggestions as to how this suffering could be prevented and the condition of dyslexia could be better managed by the authorities.

AN EXPLANATION OF THE DYSLEXIC BURDEN

Any one of these quite extreme yet understandable personal reactions to the way a child is treated by the system could have very damaging long-term impact on a person's achievement of success in society. Obvious deficits could arise through lack of basic skills acquired in school, unstable job prospects and promotion possibilities, or difficulties forming satisfactory relationships. Problems, originally attributable to dyslexia, can be magnified in life after school because attitudes to oneself and others are often consolidated in the teenage years.

Bear in mind that three boys (John, Gareth and Clark) suffered all five of the negative school experiences this study identifies. The minimum experienced was three adverse categories of stressful incidents. All the eight students displayed multiple adverse associative reactions, the minimum being a cluster of six. John, Clark and Mark all displayed eight symptoms of emotional/behavioural damage, and poor George showed the total reaction across the scale with nine out of the nine possible manifestations of emotional trauma.

It must *not* be supposed, however, that damage is irreversible, or that difficult or disruptive personality traits and behaviour are a permanent feature of the dyslexic's emotional make-up. Remember that much of these personal revelations and documented disasters were a surprise to me as a researcher, and unknown to me as a teacher, tutor and member of care staff. I was well known to the boys and dealt with them on a daily basis, often in one-to-one remedial teaching situations and during the more relaxed and informal conditions of extra-curricular activities. Yet the ordeals which they had been through and the damage they had sustained had rarely if ever been mentioned; the scholastic scars and torments of their pasts were hidden, buried and frequently disguised with bravado or eccentricity. Thus the type of emotional injury which dyslexics sustain is an insidious thing, and leads people to misjudge and misunderstand this type of student in his minority position. If a teacher sees only one child of this type in a class of thirty, he is unlikely to recognize the behaviour patterns unless trained to do so. Only three of the reactions reported involve pupils acting out or taking control/initiative over their problems – truancy, disruptive behaviour problems and competitiveness disorders. The other six responses tend to be private, introverted signs of misery which could even be interpreted by someone unaware of literacy problems as moodiness and irritability – lack of confidence, lack of communication, self-doubt, a sense of isolation and an extreme sensitivity to criticism. Psychosomatic pain has no tangible proof either, and as it is often linked with school phobia it can also mean a child is thought of as odd, deliberately skiving or just being plain awkward. The boys recorded as prone to bouts of psychosomatic pain were only diagnosed as such because the symptoms were severe enough to warrant hospitalization investigation. In a classroom the deep damage is masked, strenuously defended, and may be protected by as many clever diversionary tactics as a highly intelligent and desperate mind can devise. A strong rapport between pupil and teacher rates very

Table 3.3. *Results of assessments*

	IQ test	Type	Verbal	Performance	Points gap	Strengths (as shown on sub-test scores)	Weaknesses (as shown on sub-test scores)	Crossed laterality
John	✓	WISC(R)	134	117	17	V: similarities, vocab, comprehension; P: 4 of 5 average	V: auditory memory; visual memory	✓ REye, LH, some ambi
Trevor	✓	WISC(R)	117	137	20	V: abstract thinking; P: 4 of 5 above average	auditory ST memory; visual seq. memory	✓ R/L Ear, RH (ambi), RF
Gareth	✓	WISC(R)	97	112	15	V: comprehension 14; P: spatial & LT visual memory	V: auditory ST memory; P: visual perception	? RH; not on statement
Clark	✓	WISC(R)	96	139	43	not quoted	auditory seq. memory; visual seq. memory	✓ REye, LH, RF
George	✓	WISC(R)	Full scale only 102+		Not on statement	not quoted	auditory memory; visual memory	? not on statement
Mark	✓	BAS	Erratic scores; 'sub-tests higher on reasoning'; 96+			comprehension & concepts; visual mode	writing speed; visual ST memory	✓ LEye, REar RH*, LF (ambi)
William	✓	WISC(R)	112	129	17	V: reasoning & comprehension; P: 4 of 5 superior	V: general knowledge; P: visual memory	✓ REye, LH, LF
Oliver	✓	BAS	131	112 (visual)	19	V: abstract reasoning; visual: spatial	auditory ST memory; visual seq. memory	? not on statement

Table 3.3. *(cont)*

	Child guidance attended	Reason given	Time spent	Early language delay	Speech therapy	Originally referred by	No. of educational psychologist reports	Private educational psychologist reports	Statement labels 'maladjustment'
John	✓	no progress & truancy	2 yrs, 1 afternoon a week	–	–	optician	1	–	✓ socially to peer group
Trevor	–	–	–	–	–	parents	4	2 Dyslexia Institute	✓ mildly; behaviour & psychosomatic pain
Gareth	–	–	–	✓	✓ 6 years	mother	2	✓ Dyslexia Institute	–
Clark	✓	truancy & disruption	not given	–	–	child health	1	–	✓ truancy & disruptive behaviour
George	–	–	–	–	–	school	1	–	–
Mark	–	–	–	–	–	parents	2 incl. neurological	1 + Aston	–
William	–	–	–	not given	✓	child health	2	–	–
Oliver	–	–	–	–	–	pre-school (USA)	3	1	–

Key
BAS: British Ability Scale
WISC(R): Wechsler Intelligence Scale for Children (Revised)
  Average score, full scale = 90 to 109
  Average sub-test score = 8 to 12
V: Verbal
P: Performance (non-verbal skills)
seq. = sequential
LT = long-term
ST = short-term
ambi = ambidexterity
L = left
LF = left-footed
LH = left-handed
R = right
RF = right-footed
RH = right-handed

Note:
*Mark was forced to use his right hand, and his assessment suggests this caused his problems as he was extremely LH.

Table 3.4. *Results: Findings*

Negative experiences

	John	Trevor	Gareth	Clark	George	Mark	William	Oliver	Total (out of 8)
Violence from teachers	✓	–	✓	✓	✓	✓	–	–	5
Unfair treatment/ discrimination	✓	✓	✓	✓	–	–	✓	–	5
Inadequate help/neglect	✓	✓	✓	✓	✓	✓	✓	✓	8
Humiliation	✓	✓	✓	✓	✓	✓	✓	✓	8
Teasing/persecution	✓	✓	✓	✓	✓	✓	✓	✓	8

Associative reactions

	John	Trevor	Gareth	Clark	George	Mark	William	Oliver	Total (out of 8)
Truancy/school refusal	✓	–	✓	✓	✓	✓	✓	✓	7
Psychosomatic pain	–	✓	–	✓	✓	–	–	–	3
Isolation/alienation	✓	✓	–	✓	✓	✓	–	–	5
Lack of communication	✓	✓	–	–	✓	✓	✓	–	5
Lack of confidence	✓	✓	✓	✓	✓	✓	✓	✓	8
Self-doubt/ denigration	✓	✓	✓	✓	✓	✓	✓	✓	8
Competitiveness disorders	✓	–	✓	✓	✓	✓	–	✓	6
Sensitivity to criticism	✓	✓	✓	✓	✓	✓	✓	✓	8
Behaviour problems	✓	✓	✓	✓	✓	✓	✓	✓	8

highly in the accounts of dyslexics about what constitutes good schooling. This was revealed in responses to questions three and five on the pupil questionnaire (The questionnaire is reproduced in the Appendix towards the end of this book.) This essential rapport enables the dyslexic student of any age to suspend hostilities, call a cease-fire with the enemy education, relax and seriously set about building up the strong foundation literacy skills so badly needed.

THE POSITIVE SIDE OF THE DYSLEXIC PERSONALITY

The case-study research which I am explaining in this book was never intended to give dyslexics a public reputation for being difficult to deal with. It was an attempt to explore their experiences from the inside, in order to gain clearer knowledge about the priorities in how to teach them, and to give them a chance to air their own views on education, putting forward some proposals for improvements. It was hoped in this way to lessen the chances of a dyslexic child's complex condition being unrecognized, under-resourced or misconstrued as maladjustment by teachers who might be struggling with a debilitating work-load, and county authorities subjected to economic cut-backs and political pressures. Maladjustment labelling had been officially applied to three of the boys in my study sample of pupils, when in fact it could be strongly argued that it was the school system itself which was maladjusted to the urgent needs of many of its captive clientele.

This section is an echo of my original intention of demonstrating what personality or situational factors helped my resilient and often admirably brave pupils to survive emotionally. It illustrates what I would paraphrase from John's account as the 'bounce' factor, the ability to endure hardship and yet remain humane.

The hopeful, helpful qualities of personality which dyslexics appear to innately possess can redress the balance within the personality portrait I have presented, if they are given enough opportunities to display and develop them.

I have learnt about the constructive elements of personality tendencies in dyslexics in the course of interviewing many dyslexics and parents of dyslexics over the years. These occurred both formally and informally, in schools, at conferences, in social situations or for the Arts Dyslexia Trust. I must also acknowledge the contribution made by my two dyslexic daughters to my general understanding whilst they were growing up, and the insight given by my son-in-law Steve, who had no recognition or assistance whatsoever concerning his severe dyslexia from his comprehensive school.

Success obviously heals many wounds, strengthens the self-image, and repairs a battered ego. Career success is a particularly powerful remedy, and vocational strengths were often mentioned as under-valued motivators by the students in this study when they were asked about any changes they would like to make to the school curriculum. Answers to questions 28 to 35 on the pupil interview schedule were often related to this issue (Edwards, 1990).

Stemming from our work with outstanding professional and student artists/ designers for the Arts Dyslexia Trust, Susan Parkinson and I will be publishing material from a wide range of interviews we have carried out which highlight the way the same intellectual architecture which can devastate a child's morale in school proves to be an advantage in specialist visual/spatial occupations.

Support from family and friends can give balance and stability to a person whose confidence has been undermined by continual classroom failure. This can be a crucial factor, allowing ambitions to be achieved instead of lost. Dyslexic friendships, where similar interests and difficulties are held in common, were often cited as the most essential and productive relationships by both adolescents and adults in personal interviews.

ATTRIBUTES OF CHARACTER RECORDED

Sensitivity, intensity and loyalty are mentioned in reports and by mothers and friends as rewarding personality traits possessed in the extreme by the dyslexic, although this is often qualified as being selectively applied to a limited few people for whom a deep trust or respect has been formed. These observations fit in with other comments like those of George's, Clark's and Mark's mothers who each felt that their son was very suspicious of people until they were well known. Clark's father also felt that this applied to work situations after his son left school.

Stubborness was another part of the personality package regularly noted. It seems to develop as a determination bred from surviving scholastic disasters and social embarrassments, and the attitude permeates the style and content of all the interviews in this book, in varied forms. A profound dislike of being 'pushed around' emerges; and this surely contributes to the rebel image which tends to get the self-defensive individual into trouble with authority or the establishment in any of its representative personas. These can include teachers, parents, employers, shop-keepers and even the police.

Interestingly enough, this deeply entrenched individualism is spontaneously mentioned by students and their parents as a factor which propels them towards self-employment success. It recurred in Arts Dyslexia Trust interviews, driving artistic originality to reach its goals in the design world. It also features in accounts given by scientific/technological innovators about their work, such as Per Udden who invented the electronic wheelchair (Edwards, 1993).

Survival humour. Many specialist teachers familiar with dyslexics, or people who have dyslexics in the family, will be aware that these characters can be extraordinarily good company when they are free from the pressure which causes bouts of depression. In my experience, it seems likely that the well-documented unusual dyslexic brain-structure of scattered cells which often produces visual/spatial strengths and original concepts frequently gives rise to a quirky, off-beat, rather dry sense of humour which is startlingly effective. Dyslexics often seem to possess the ability to turn ideas topsy-turvy, with the unexpected comment, the surprising story or sharp observation, the sudden insight or unconventional perspective which is often at the heart of alternative comedy. The masterly sarcastic put-down, either spontaneously born of anger or carefully planned in its delivery, also features largely in the mental repertoire of the dyslexic. It does not contribute to their popularity with teachers, or a peaceful life-style, as anyone who has been involved in their pastoral welfare will know.

Stimulating intellect. One of the compensations of teaching dyslexics is being amongst people who continually present you with unusual ideas and perceptions on a diverse range of subjects. These pupils can have lively, divergent and rather revolu-tionary minds which scatter challenging thoughts and unusual questions. Their com-prehension skills may be acute, and their problem-solving abilities can reveal a fast-thinking practical intellect.

Sympathy for others. The trials which dyslexics have been through tend to enhance their ability to empathize with others who are suffering. Several times family or friends of students taking part in this study reported unexpected kindnesses or soft spots for those in trouble from individuals whose image projected quite the reverse. Consider 'toughie' sportsman John making tea and toast for home-sick juniors, Mark's mum saying how he hated to see anyone upset by his playful comments, and Gareth the Giant's tender concern and practical help for the physically disabled. Trevor's mother also commented on his deep understanding of others who had problems, and his sincere desire to help them. They *all* wanted to improve the lot of others in the school who would be coming after them. It would be easy to go on giving examples.

Sixth sense. Dyslexics have reported heightened perceptual ability of a kind beyond the normal measures quantified in intelligence tests. They can display an advanced ability to sense people's moods or feelings, and tend to pick up emotional vibrations very effectively at an intuitive, non-verbal level. Other people can sometimes be unsettled by this, but I find it more akin to the advanced sensitivity and observational skills which small children and animals possess. It is an awareness which is often lost to adults. In neurological dissection dyslexics are found to have generally *larger* brains, with *more* and *unusual* connections between neurons than in ordinary brains. Many dyslexics report unusual dream-patterns or phenomena, being able to take control of and plan their dreams in advance, or knowing that something is going to happen well in advance of an event.

Many teachers find dyslexics disturbing to teach – but if you are prepared to listen to their point of view in an open-minded and accepting way instead of giving the impression that teachers are always right and know all the answers, you can learn a lot from them. They have a habit of turning situations around for you as their teacher, and you can begin to feel as if you are looking through the wrong end of a telescope, or down a strange microscope while different lenses are being adjusted, or perhaps a more fitting image is that of seeing through a kaleidoscope for the first time. They have an uncanny knack of reversing the roles so that you feel the instrument of analysis is suddenly turned on you who are supposed to be its master, instead of you using it purely to study them.

Spontaneity. The typical dyslexic has a reputation for bursts of dynamic action, and parents of younger children often complain about this, worried that it is bordering on hyperactivity. In my experience, unless they are depressed or really tired, mature dyslexics tend to be fairly restless individuals who like to juggle several activities at once and pack a lot of experiences into a short time span. Whilst they often find it difficult to organize all their enthusiasms, or even their personal lives, appointments and belongings (which can be highly exasperating for those who have to live with them), they are rarely boring people!

NEGATIVE EXPERIENCES

Many teachers and parents will be deeply shocked, as I was, by the severity, extent and multiplicity of unpleasant experiences which pupils in my study had undergone. One obviously did not expect pupils with literacy problems to describe their past school lives in glowing terms, but the skeletons which emerged from the school cupboards of childhood memory were indeed grim and frequently similar across the group.

Figure 3.1 has been formulated to show at a glance how pressure can build up on all sides for a dyslexic child, both educationally and socially.

Violence from teachers

Five out of the eight boys studied had been on the receiving end of violence from teachers, John and Mark sustaining actual bodily harm in terms of severe bumps and heavy bruising from attacks with sticklike weapons (a broom-handle and walking-stick). Mark was left with a dramatic teacher-phobia which lasted into adult life.

John's attack at age 6–7 was by a female teacher. Two other attacks came from women; another of John's teachers at his private prep school specialized in rulering knuckles to the point of numbness. Clark's music teacher at secondary school during the first and second year frequently smacked him around the face.

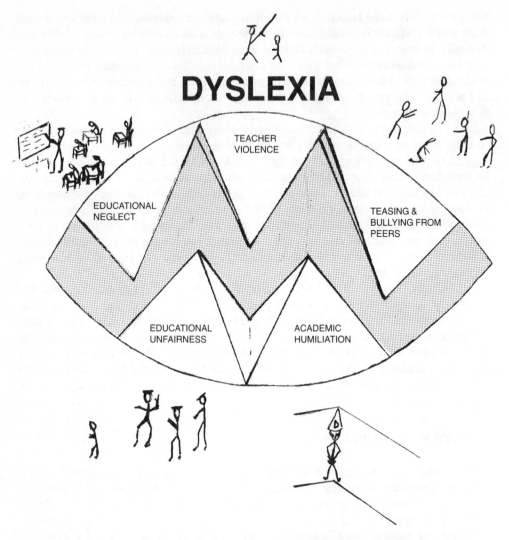

Figure 3.1 *Negative experiences: the dyslexic can be swallowed up into an emotional void by academic stress, literacy strain and accumulated pressure*

All the accounts are documented in detail in the students' own words in the case study portraits. Twelve separate incidents were mentioned spontaneously, although no specific question was asked on this subject. Some of the rough treatment was habitual, and much of this abuse was repeated, with the children not telling parents. This was possibly because they wanted to avoid more trouble, were trying to escape from the grim school situation whilst at home, did not want to upset their mothers, or felt they should cope with it in their own way.

George was only 9 years old when his elderly remedial teacher pushed him into a corner so hard that he banged his head. Clark was attacked from age 10 upwards by four different teachers in three separate schools. The first thump in the face came when he could not play the recorder as he could not read the music, so mimed along. It seems to have been his face which teachers aimed at, possibly because of his cheeky grin and later dogged defiance of being bullied.

Gareth was punished with thong and cane at secondary school and had a teacher actually break a metre-long plastic ruler over his back, which woke him up!

As the majority of my case studies had suffered in this way, how was it that the other three escaped? Trevor, William and Oliver all presented themselves at special school as fairly quiet individuals, and the first two boys were certainly sensitive. None of them were ever in trouble with staff for bad classroom behaviour, direct defiance or refusal to work. They all ended up in academic groups studying for public exams, and were good at oral work, appearing keen to please and anxious to achieve results. They were all socially skilled in conversing with professional adults, and came from upper- or middle-class family backgrounds in the country or suburbs. They all attended FE colleges and gained qualifications. They had all been identified early, though William received inadequate help despite that. There were no outstanding factors in common which they possessed in terms of IQ which the others lacked, and only Oliver had achieved an average reading age. Trevor and William had special talents, but so did the other group.

The battered group of pupils are classified in terms of personality impression in Table 3.1 as three extroverts, one bluff and genial character, and one introvert with a tough image. In their final-year staff relationships, three boys were rated as erratic, with two tending to extremes. One other was described as having minor difficulties, and the last as rather withdrawn. Four descriptions of their behaviour impressions could be summed up as variable, and the last as strong-willed. Only two had been identified early as dyslexic, and only one had received early specialist help. Two had attended child guidance clinics for truancy and had been labelled maladjusted. One of the other group had also been labelled mildly maladjusted, however. All five had come from working/own business backgrounds. Three lived near large cities and two came from the north. In terms of conversational habits, I would say they were all quite selective about speaking to staff/adults and tended to stick to their peers more. All five were definitely more interested in and enthusiastic about the interests, sports and hobbies they excelled in than in their school work. They were all capable of putting across a hostile attitude to adults, but expressed it in different ways. Four of them tended to do it by sarcasm/cheek whereas George could project it silently. From observation I would describe all of them as often cautious or guarded in their relationships with adults.

I would like to give two quotations which I feel explain the different treatment these two groups received in school. The poignant words of Steven Bonfield in Osmond and Morrison (1992) seem to me to sum up the experience of the quieter type of dyslexic, represented more by the first group of pupils. The three students in my study were definitely academic perfectionists who wanted to do well and prove themselves. For this type of student tension and anxiety build up and are bottled up, which can manifest itself in a sense of isolation, shyness and social withdrawal, or even unsociable verbal attacks in the case of Oliver. Mostly, however, these pupils just suffer in silence and misery in the classroom. To quote Steven:

> I was always a very well-behaved child, I was very quiet and twee and no one took any notice, no one noticed me, so I was happily glossed over and ignored, which made everyone's lives except mine somewhat easier . . . Home was sanctuary . . . but by the end

of junior school even when I was at home, the time between then and when you started thinking 'God, it's going to be tomorrow soon' sort of creeps up until eventually you are thinking it almost all the time. And then you've got *nothing*, because even the things you enjoy are spoilt.

Chasty (1993) definitively charts the way the more extrovert dyslexic personality can stir up the authoritarian teacher:

> You can get a verbally very able student who does not handle word shapes and word patterns very effectively, though he talks and communicates very well in class. He doesn't read, write or spell; he becomes very frustrated, very anxious and perhaps even aggressive in class when these activities are required, and he is the student who tends to get himself into trouble in school because he is very questioning, with a very alert mind. He can be presumed to be cheeky, he will argue with his teachers, he will take them on in an argument and he's usually sharp enough to win – and he's the one who seems to stand out as the troublemaker in the class.

This is the child who will stand and fight those who he feels have made him suffer, and who will not back down. The desire to have the last word, not to be humiliated in front of their peers, and to maintain their image is so strong in these pupils because it is all they have left of their self-respect. This is how many of the dead-locked potentially violent situations I have encountered or had described to me seem to arise. It must be said that emotional head-on collisions with pupils do tend to be more of a male-to-male phenomenon in my study, in the proportion of 1: 3, and that is despite the higher incidence of women in the profession. An official of the National Union of Teachers who talked to our staff stated that allegations of brutality or abuse were six times more likely to be made against male staff than female.

If teachers were initially trained at induction stage how to recognize dyslexia and deal with the stresses and tensions it can cause in children, perhaps none of the violence and intimidation reported in this study would have occurred.

Unfair treatment/discrimination

Over half of the group of students I studied had without doubt suffered unfair treatment at the hands of the educational system, and from teachers in particular. John had a hypocritical 'pose' of help from his primary headmaster, paying lip-service only to the idea of personal remedial help for him on a regular basis. John's anger was quite obvious. This situation was confirmed by his mother's remarks on a separate occasion.

Trevor was discriminated against in drama, being inexplicably left off the rota for main casting and assembly performances, rather than given help to succeed in them. As drama was an enduring love of his, and something he excelled in, his resentment was strong. In his middle school he was denigrated in Maths despite superior test results and felt 'totally shattered'. The justification he was given later was that the teacher he had respected thought he could not cope with the reading. Trevor and his parents finally suspected that the trouble they were having getting the authority to provide remedial help had been reflected in the treatment received by him in class. The school records contain some very disparaging and unnecessary opinions about the troublesomeness of Trevor's father, actually blaming his attitude for Trevor's difficulties, despite professional assessments giving objective evidence of profound and specific literacy defecits. These records then went on to his special school, and could have done irreparable damage to future parent–teacher relationships. Trevor's parents are in fact extremely charming professional people who had to fight extremely doggedly for any help for their son. For them to be insulted for their determination and to have to face hostile interview situations on top of the deep worries they had about Trevor's desperate unhappiness and learning difficulties is absolutely outrageous. I had dealings with Trevor's parents on many occasions over the years and found them totally reasonable.

This sort of scapegoat resentful attitude from the educational establishment probably has a lot to do with the allegations that dyslexia is a middle-class invention; I am sure that any parents who were less socially or academically confident and less dynamic than Trevor's would have been scared off from receiving the help they are legally entitled to. Hence it has sometimes been the case that vocal, confident middle-class parents have eventually succeeded in obtaining boarding special school placements for their child; whereas traditional working-class or even deprived children have frequently been noted to reach the statementing and transferral stage only when schools themselves find them too difficult to cope with in terms of disruptive behaviour. Speaking from fifteen years of experience, it seems that it is easier for the middle-class or deprived child to get specialist help, owing in the first case to parental competence with bureaucracy and in the latter to the existing financial involvement of care agencies. In the course of general social contacts I have often personally identified many dyslexics from working-class backgrounds who were completely overlooked and written off at school because nothing was expected of them. They were frequently placed with disruptive or slow pupils in the 'dustbin' class and routinely became difficult to manage because of boredom, frustration, misunderstandings and communication breakdowns. Those whom I have met triumphed over this disadvantage, and sometimes spectacularly, only *after* leaving school through sheer ambition, hard work and practical intelligence. This fits in with my theory that for many dyslexics life in the occupational or business world is easy in comparison with school, where they suffered so many social knocks and emotional set-backs at a vulnerable age. This view is supported by case studies across the social strata reported by Hampshire (1990) and Osmond (1993). I put forward the notion, however, that it applies even more to the social group I have mentioned within the state system.

Gareth's placement within a special school for the handicapped for five years is a glaring episode of unfair treatment. The sudden disappearance of all his exercise books from the comprehensive school prior to his legal hearing over special provision cannot surely be considered as anything short of corruption.

Clark's attitude of cynicism, so strongly commented on in assessments and reports, is likely to have developed initially from his early first-hand experience of the unethical cover-up over teacher violence towards him regarding the recorder incident. He was certainly very bitter about the incident of grammar school selection exam pass slips found destroyed in the classroom bin, with more socially acceptable names having been substituted. It is disheartening to think that such Dickensian social discrimination can survive under modern conditions even at a local level. It is unnerving to wonder what Clark's remarkable non-verbal WISC(R) performance IQ of 139 might have achieved if he had received specialist help for gifted dyslexics from the start of his education. That is not to imply that a career in woodwork is not worthwhile, but it should be mourned that a superior intellect could find no academic channel of opportunity.

William suffered a severe misuse of his hard-won remedial provision which amounted to withholding his special help and spending it on others in the class at the teacher's convenience. It is difficult to imagine how anyone could justify such flagrant disregard of official allocation and specific priority, or to pinpoint who was directly responsible for it. Was it the class teacher clawing back some personal non-contact time out of a sense of grievance over something else? Did the school place more urgent priority on the needs of the girl William referred to as 'dopey' rather than on the dyslexic child? Or was it considered to be a time perk because of having to deal with the management of a dyslexic, with the 'special help' being seen as an aid for the teacher rather than for William personally? The final responsibility must rest with the headteacher, who should have ensured effective delivery of the individual remedial programme designed for William. William's family were unanimous in laying the blame at the door of the head, as William was actually in his class for four consecutive years in the junior school. William's mother spent a vast amount of time in appointments trying to reason with various headteachers throughout her son's school career and make them notice, understand and *do* something about his literacy difficulties. The family even went to the lengths of moving William to stay with relatives in a different school catchment area to get better remedial help. The effect of this unfair treatment on William's morale was appalling, and he says in his interview that the time wasted in junior school represented the most unhappy period in his life, when he used to let out the frustration of it all on his father in temper tantrums and attempted truancy.

Inadequate help/neglect

This was the first of the negative experiences to be a total one, applying to all pupils across the board. This was a surprise, given the knowledge that three-quarters of the group had been identified as having special needs by the age of 8, and of these five were already recognized as dyslexic. Over half of them had also received remedial help, though in only three cases was it specialist. One would have anticipated that the help was not entirely successful or intensive enough because most of the boys had severe dyslexia and finally ended up in a special school, but I had expected it to be satisfactory within the financial limitations of the local authority. I was not prepared for the catalogue of disasters which the boys and their parents poured out.

John's criticisms of the special provision he received were withering. He felt that he did learn something at his prep school, but suffered from intense unhappiness; its memory alone induced 'dread', and the only special provision he mentioned was violent punishment, daily detention for slow boardwork copying, and being asked to leave so that he did not spoil the school's exam pass rate record at 11-plus. He then slated the state junior school with descriptions of uncaring class teachers, a hypocritical head, inaccurate records of help given, and a total lack of control over the children's behaviour. He also had a very low opinion of the teacher at a famous specialist unit he attended, but did imply that he noticed an improvement in his skills by the end of his course of lessons there. His mother's account of the trials and tribulations of attempts to get help for her son were even more dramatic and depressing. She had several remedial teachers wash their hands of John, one of whom then decided to leave teaching altogether. She travelled long distances, took him to the child guidance clinic where he was given an intensive course in sand-play (presumably for therapeutic reasons), and was even told by a doctor that dyslexia was simply the middle-class name for a backward child. However, she bravely continued to fight to get to the root of the problem. She related how she had to get three medical opinions from different medical councils before she could get John properly placed. She had to prove that John could not be taught by normal methods, and that took her years. The whole process was particularly fraught with difficulties for her as she is also severely dyslexic, and yet she tackled finding out from the libraries about dyslexia as well as trying to cut through the bureaucratic red tape of assorted government departments, taking on a spectacular battle with teams of hostile professionals. Throughout, she displayed an amazingly resilient sense of humour, and also provided one of the most moving accounts which I have ever heard of how deeply the dyslexic trauma cuts into the soul. She remembered as a child in Sunday school praying about it all, the horror of reading and writing: 'Oh God, you made me different to them. Why, oh why? Why can't I do it? Please, one day before I die, please let me understand *why*!' Having watched the 1985 *Horizon* television programme by the eminent neurologist Norman Geschwind about dyslexia, she felt that at last she really understood how it came about.

It is worth noting that all these desperate parents except one set had other children, some with demanding problems of their own. The stereotype of the over-anxious mother which emerges from many different children's records seems particularly prejudiced to a person experienced in bringing up dyslexic children of their own, or in a boarding situation. The parent of a dyslexic faces the continual strain of having to watch helplessly while your child suffers, often while the authorities blame you for the problem, which would be unthinkably brutal with any other form of handicap. Add to this the stress of having to spend huge amounts of time and energy trying to convince teachers and assorted experts that something is wrong and that the child will not just magically develop delayed skills 'in his own time' or 'when he is ready'. Colour the picture further by imagining the pressure of perhaps a husband who is not convinced, or who has similar difficulties which he feels guilty that he might have passed on, or the nightmare of reliving disastrous experiences of one's own schooldays. On top of this families find themselves involved in expensive private lessons, independent psychological reports, extra travelling costs, and educational equipment or books to purchase. Jealousy from siblings over the extra attention the dyslexic child gets is a common report. The endless drag of parents' evenings where teachers list your child's academic shortcomings, and tell you off for their behaviour; the jibes of other smug parents rejoicing over their child's advanced reading book to be taken home whilst your child runs out in floods of tears as the only one in the class not allowed a reading book as she cannot even read the cards; long hours spent struggling with an exhausted emotional child over words and symbols, tables and sums, facts and tests; the panic over public exams and limited career options, the school insisting she cannot do Art for GCSE despite it being her career choice, the day the failure slips come through the door despite the school reports giving B grades, praising coursework, insight and oral intelligence; days spent dissuading her from a career as a waitress; going bankrupt over private school costs to mend some of the damage – these are the memories that parenting a dyslexic child consist of. And in the background, nagging all the time, is the pain of knowing your child can sparkle with brilliance, imagination and sensitivity, and that the spectre of school – a grey, factory-minded ghost of education – haunts her, banishing away the positive aspects of the child you nurtured, bright and happy until snared by school. The experience might induce a nervous breakdown in the most level-headed of parents.

Another pattern which emerges is that in all of the cases studied it was the mother who took the dominant role in the initial move to get help, and even in responding to my questionnaire. This occurred despite the fact that five of the mothers worked full-time, one worked part-time, and six had very supportive and competent husbands. This struck me as quite surprising in 1993, where men might be expected to take a more equal part in child-care matters, especially when dealing with problems. Perhaps it is a sign of the times with women expected to fulfil more roles in life, or even a sign of increasing female confidence in dealing with reluctant authority. I suspect, however, from the tone of their interview responses that it is more likely to be strong protective maternal instinct which ensured that it was predominantly the mothers who acted. Two of them were divorced, one being happily remarried with a new baby, and there was only one who was married yet received no support over the problem from her husband. This was largely because he had the same problems as a child and could not cope with it in his son; he was actually hostile to the boy, and resentful of the mother's sympathy towards her son.

Trevor assessed his remedial provision at age 8 as unsatisfactory owing to the abrasive uncaring personality of the tutor provided, whom he came to hate. He felt he made no progress, and also resented being withdrawn from his favourite lesson and teacher. The situation did not improve at his middle school, where he had a group session with an English teacher he regarded as useless and hysterical. He also reacted against 'the remedial attitude' at boarding school, after initially finding such teachers caring and providing someone to talk to. As he got older he found them 'patronizing and two-faced'. His opinion is supported by his mother's statement that he made most progress in school work during his first and last years at special school. His own account stresses the crucial importance of a positive teacher–pupil relationship.

Gareth had developed a remedial phobia, and simply refused to attend them at boarding school. He found the work 'pathetic' and babyish. He felt these lessons were even more damaging within a comprehensive school system because they would draw attention to someone's difficulties, lead to teasing, and then directly to truancy. He considered himself lucky never to have been given remedials whilst at comprehensive. His account proves how differently the recipients of our hard-won provision can view it from our own perspective on help, and why it is so important to open a frank dialogue with them about the sort of help they want. Gareth and all the others in this study were quite clear about what they found most useful; for Gareth it was small-group English work based around coursework, classwork and CSE exams.

At primary school Clark was left in the pitiful position of endlessly copying work from the board which he could not read and which was never explained as he got no help. He approved of individual help, but severely criticized the use of babyish methods. He stressed the importance of counselling about dyslexia and effective professional-class English tuition from a teacher who could be related to. He also mentioned the danger of teasing in a comprehensive school.

George felt that to be labelled 'remedial' in the state system meant you were treated like 'scum'. He gives an account of utter boredom, humiliating work and no progress made.

Mark highlighted how confusing a lack of consistency between class and remedial teaching methods was for him in the state system, whilst Oliver complained of the intense boredom of non-imaginative reading schemes.

Humiliation

This proved to be another very common experience, being recorded by seven out of the eight students.

In his account John described the gap between the literacy skills of his classmates and himself at prep school with deep mortification and hostility. Being asked to leave because of this was a traumatic end to a miserable experience.

Trevor found that his time spent at middle school from age 9 to 12 was the most humiliating. He was repeatedly insulted and demoralized, especially by a History teacher over his academic prospects. Gareth also found that it was the teacher's attitudes and put-downs which were the most hurtful, and made him feel like giving up. This worsened at comprehensive school, where a woman teacher actually tore up a piece of homework which had taken him a very long time to produce, just because it was late. He felt goaded and tormented by the staff.

Clark felt badly debased by staff, being called thick repeatedly by them at primary school. The head is reported to have told Clark that he would be 'lucky to be a dustman', a socially prejudiced remark as well as an intended put-down.

George vividly recalled the embarrassment of being deprived of his shoes and socks at primary school so that he could not run away, and standing in the corner at lunch-times, face to the wall. At secondary school the severity of his difficulty hit him hard, especially as the school was unaware of it. He lived in continuous fear of his dyslexic disability being used to degrade him in public. His account of how people stared at him when they suddenly realized he could not read was poignant. The worst thing for George was being put on the spot by a girlfriend who asked him to read something, and trying to wriggle out of the situation. He felt that the biggest advantage a special school could offer was that teachers did not laugh at you or show by their expression that they were horrified by the inability to read. He also felt very relaxed, at last, to have friends who understood and had similar literacy problems. He was quite happy to read or write in front of them, although in the past he had been deliberately trapped and shown up by 'bored' teachers who taunted him for the amusement of the class. He felt that this kind of cruelty could turn pupils bad, and gave a direct example of how it had affected him personally. He was equally sensitive about literacy difficulties making him feel shamed in front of relatives.

Mark's experiences of humiliation from teachers who refused to believe he had a problem or tried to discuss his difficulties in front of the whole class led him to behave vengefully or disruptively to avoid reading. As already reported, he found situations so distressing that he became school phobic, needing sedation and hypnotherapy.

William received remarks from shopkeepers and some teachers which were designed to make him self-conscious; they related to notice-reading and queuing, e.g. 'Are you stupid, can't you read?' His mother commented that socially he never wanted anyone to know about his dyslexia, and he told me the name of his special school embarrassed him so much with people he met because it sounded like a borstal that he invented an alternative title for it. His mother also said he got very hurt when the family gathered and did not ask him what public exams he was taking: 'He hates anyone to think he is different because of his dyslexia.'

Oliver felt threatened by the possibility of being shown up in public whilst at a small private school, and worked very hard to prevent himself getting 'called thick and dumb'. The word 'thick' or 'thicko' is frequently repeated in his accounts, and seems to haunt him. His mother felt this idea pervaded his whole thinking about himself and caused him to avoid long-term challenges.

These humiliations were clearly remembered in painful detail by the subjects and also given great significance by their mothers in terms of later repercussions on personality. Those registering the most damage from these incidents were George, Clark, Mark and Gareth, all of whom came late to a specialist school at the age of 14. Oliver entered at the same age, but was by then a resolved dyslexic with a reading age commensurate with his chronological level, though not in keeping with his advanced IQ.

Teasing/persecution

All of the boys suffered from this, and evidence emerged throughout their interviews although no specific question was asked.

John was particularly, teased at prep school, and implied that the continuous pressure of such a situation could drive a child to the edge of sanity. George, facing the same situation at comprehensive school, resolved it by taking direct and violent retaliative action. Mark's mother described him as 'tormented' by children calling him thick and by teachers accusing him of being useless and lazy. He also resorted to physical retribution to stop jibes from other pupils at comprehensive school.

Trevor and William both cited girls as causing most grief at middle-school age, directly mocking and taunting them whilst hiding behind feminine immunity to violent reactions. Mark, however, actually snapped and hit a girl who called him thick at primary school and was 'well shamed up' for it.

Trevor was repeatedly involved in defensive playground fights retaliating to group persecution and chanting. He also felt victimized by Oliver at boarding school, but this was perhaps more of a reaction to Oliver's own bullied past and a personality clash rather than being caused by literacy struggles. Records suggest that Oliver felt threatened academically by the newcomer who showed signs of outshining him. Trevor was also perhaps more vulnerable as a victim because of the extreme group bullying in the past, whereas Oliver had overcome his reading difficulties and only endured sarcasm at home from his sister. It seems a fairly classic example of projecting the situation you fear most on to somebody else to release bottled-up resentment at being treated that way previously. Like John, Oliver mentions the strain of being the subject of mickey-taking *all* the *time*, at primary level. His mother describes it as 'mockery and bullying ... which permanently damaged his self-confidence'.

Gareth effectively adopted the class clown strategy to avoid ridicule at his comprehensive. However, exam failure drew intense attention to him and made him the butt of continuous jokes, finally causing avoidance of school altogether.

Clark found that diagnosis and official visitors made him an obvious target for mockery, as before that he had successfully disguised his reading problem to classmates by distractive disruptive behaviour at comprehensive school. Then his planned placement at 'dunce school' got him goaded by his peers unmercifully.

The overall picture given by the boys is a depressing one, and most of them only found relief from the shadow of fear and oppression by taking refuge in residential school. Surely this argues eloquently for a greater emphasis on public awareness of the talents of dyslexics, and a more enlightened attitude within schools about what the condition means.

Associative reactions

I will deal with these in order of their most common incidence amongst the group. I do not intend to quote from accounts the boys gave on these nine reactions to the problems they had encountered, as their own personal case comments make very vivid and powerful reading. I felt, however, justified in recapitulating on their treatment from the educational establishment in order to show what the pressures upon them were which made them develop these irregular patterns and habits.

Figure 3.2 is a pictorial representation intended to show the effects upon a dyslexic's behaviour and personality which the frustration of school failure can produce.

Lack of confidence

Lack of confidence affected the whole sample, despite five of them having very superior IQ scores which they knew about, and the other three having perfectly respectable levels. Bear in mind that they had all experienced social success and responsibility status within the special school, and five of them had also had triumphs within extra-curricular or cultural activities such as art, drama or sport. All the boys had very understanding, concerned mothers, and fathers lent their full support in six cases out of the eight. There were notably helpful siblings in five cases, though two sets of siblings divided into helpful sister and concerned but disciplinarian brothers or 'preferred' brother. Two boys reported damaging sisterly competition, confirmed by the mother, one sister being most hostile. Only one case was an only child. Therefore, one would have expected confidence levels to have improved dramatically hand in hand with social/literacy success. This was not the case. Four mothers reported distinct, worrying lack of confidence with paperwork after their sons had left school, despite having passed public exams in English. Their sons relied totally on them for information-gathering, form-filling and bookwork. All four mothers were reluctant to fulfil this role, wanting the young men to use their hard-won skills, knowing they could read/write adequately if desperate, and all were worried their son's skills would deteriorate through lack of practice.

Seven students registered extreme lack of confidence in new situations involving

ISOLATION

TRUANCY

PSYCHOSOMATIC
PAIN

LACK OF
COMMUNICATION

BEHAVIOUR
PROBLEMS

SELF-DOUBT

COMPETITIVENESS
DISORDERS

SENSITIVITY
TO CRITICISM

LACK OF
CONFIDENCE

Figure 3.2 *Dangerous associative reactions: the dyslexic burden*

unfamiliar people. Oliver was the only exception here, finding new placements stimulating at first, though he slid backwards once the novelty had worn off, apparently lacking staying power. Seven out of the eight felt being with other dyslexics greatly improved morale; again Oliver was reported as the exception in sitting back on his disability and feeling demoralized by the special school image and the severe difficulties of his classmates. I feel Oliver's milder dyslexia would have been better served by an integrated unit within a public school. He would then have compared himself with other bright, achieving mild dyslexics instead of finding himself top of the class in literacy ability with no competition and less reason to work hard like the others. Whereas the relaxed, sociable environment of special boarding suited severe cases who could unwind at last, and so achieve, Oliver needed a disciplined, demanding system which would contagiously propel him forward. He needed jolting into gear from a lethargy born of rather cynical disillusionment bordering on pessimism. Whilst his case and responses sometimes looks the mildest, it masks some disturbing damage.

Two out of the three boys who were involved in the work experience programme were reported as lacking confidence, one to an extreme degree. This was obviously worrying, as employers were well used to normal adolescent nerves, and the boys displayed unusual nervousness and reticence. Their past academic difficulties were being carried with them into the world of work, although the workplaces here were carefully selected for their kind and understanding approach. This foreshadowed difficulties others experienced later, as mentioned by Clark, Mark and George's parents with employer attitudes.

Six sets of observations in the records from educational psychologists and teachers directly linked lack of confidence and frustration to incidences of behaviour problems in the classroom and playground.

Six mothers felt their sons were more caring and sensitive to other people, especially those with problems, because of their own past distress. Two mothers felt some self-blame over their extreme concern for their son's welfare in the past, and were aware it could have dangerous effects on the developing personality in terms of spoiling/over-indulgence/smothering in one case and overwhelming pressure over results in the other. One mother also felt paternal conflict over the learning problem contributed to her son's damaged morale and personality effects.

Self-doubt/denigration

It has already been stated that, as a sample, the group of eight boys had an intelligence level well above average, despite the erratic scatter of peaks and dips within their sub-test profiles. They had been informed of this. Yet all eight boys were diffident and disbelieving about their ability levels, placing more weight on their personal experiences of school failure than on the factual test-score ratings they had been given. All of the boys spontaneously mentioned believing themselves 'thick' for years. 'Slow' and 'stupid' featured strongly too. Two boys said they would be on the dole if it had not been for the special school; and another two only believed in dyslexia once they met others at special school. Before that they thought it was just a kinder name, or people trying to cheer them up. One felt only his parents' belief in his intelligence had saved him, and another was haunted by the horror of being put in with those who were 'not normal' (meaning mentally retarded). Another had blamed himself utterly for his inability to read, feeling he was lazy and bad because he could not do it. Two of the five who started at FE college admitted experiencing real panic at the thought of returning to mainstream education in terms of whether they could keep up with average people or fit in, and two were seriously worried about college or City & Guilds exams. One left after only a term because he felt the attitude and treatment he received was just as bad as at comprehensive school; he felt he was learning nothing of practical value, and personality clashes with lecturers resulted.

None of them when asked to estimate their own intelligence level initially viewed themselves as above average. The majority showed great uncertainty, and took refuge in jokes, complaining about the question.

Without exception, all the students studied undervalued their intelligence for significant periods of their school careers, and tended still to be insecure about it.

Sensitivity to criticism

There were reports of acute sensitivity to criticism about all of the group consistently. Comments and examples came spontaneously from six parents (four mothers and two fathers) and repeated remarks from different teachers in school reports. Five of the boys tended to confine these emotional outbursts to home situations. Two of the parents were particularly worried about their son's attitude to employers in the world of adult work.

It seems clear that many dyslexics develop a dislike of authority in general, and that this can be displayed either at school or at home in attitudes to correction by parents or teachers. It was found to be singularly difficult for parents in the boarding school situation, who were often separated from their offspring for up to three weeks at a time, to resolve the correction conflict. In the special school this touchiness syndrome was often seen as pupils taking classroom comment personally, staffroom comment about boys with 'a real chip on their shoulder', 'storming out' behaviour, feelings of a particular teacher (various) trying to persecute them, and a lot more tears than one would normally expect from boys of secondary school age. I have heard one teacher tell another not to correct a new boy's work because he would burst into tears instantly. I clearly recall my first day teaching in a special school when six different 12- to 13-year-old boys burst into tears on me at some point during an individual lesson; it occurred usually in connection with not being able to read a word, stuttering, missing a line out, repeated 'sorry' comments, or even just on me opening a book. I was well used to teaching this age-group, and being particularly gentle as they were new. Nobody could classify that as a normal reaction amongst boys, many of whom hailed from large cities. In general, we noticed that special school dyslexics were prone to feel rejected and disliked if they had to be corrected socially. The one-to-one reasoning chat, very calm and low-key, appealing on a professional, adult level worked best. Small groups with a teacher–pupil ratio of 6 : 1 (or maximum 8 : 1) meant that this approach could be easily adopted. Also as a pastoral tutor and head of English I found that a lot of my time and energy was expended on negotiating between aggrieved staff who had been abused or defied and tutees who thought they were being picked on. Matters could usually be analysed in discussion, resolved by a cool letter of explanation from the pupil, and clarifying to the teacher exactly what triggered the pupil flare-up from the student's point of view. Often it was a grievance which had magnified over time, or a simple misunderstanding. This strong tendency of vulnerability to criticism within the dyslexic personality necessitates careful and delicate handling of correction and general management techniques.

Behaviour problems

This is the last of the associative reactions which all the group fell prone to, and perhaps the most dramatic and damaging. Hostile, disruptive actions towards teachers, aggression and cheekiness were already being exhibited at primary school in five cases. This ranges from sabotaging the ladies' loo as revenge on teachers to hitting other pupils and playing dangerous practical jokes.

In summary, seven out of the group got involved in fights, four mentioned petty theft (two of them being at primary school at the time and undetected), and there were two habitual pranksters. Deliberate destruction of property was related by five boys, though one destroyed a loved possession of his own out of sheer frustration. Classroom disruption was confessed to by all eight subjects, with varying motives, but often linked to dislike of the teacher's methods, boredom with the subject matter, inability to do the task in hand, or direct mutual confrontation and conflict with the class teacher. Impertinence in class, diverting attention away from literacy difficulties by clowning, and trouble in the playground were common comments from schools, though several related the incidents directly to situations where the boy was teased or difficult to handle because the task was exceptionally difficult for him. Several schools, psychologists and a doctor mention the severe frustration levels endured by exceptionally bright dyslexics in large classes, and make direct causal links.

With some of the records, such as Gareth's and George's, the school pleaded mitigating circumstances despite the complaints, being at pains to explain why the bad or irritating behaviour occurred; with others, such as Clark's, the teachers were obviously at the end of their tether, feeling hostile, and were determined not to endure this particular pupil's disruption any more.

Senior school behaviour problems included fights where the dyslexic sustained hospitalizing injuries, vandalism to staff property, shouting abuse at staff, and undue aggression in sports. Three boys had maladjustment mentioned on their statements, two of whom felt they would have ended up fully delinquent if they had not come to special school, as did a private pupil. Another was already in trouble with the police and almost turned down for entry to the special school because of his file records of behaviour. Another was mentioned as in danger of his social adjustment disintegrating under stress if he went to a state secondary school.

Explosive or destructive behaviour at home was mentioned by six families, usually coinciding with the most stressful phases of school trauma for that child. A tendency to deliberately bully a particular sibling or classmates was independently mentioned by two subjects who had perhaps been more vulnerable to physical punishment in the past owing to relatively small stature.

The extent, range and commonness of behaviour problems was a surprising finding. It was a constant feature of the boys' past reactions, even in students we had found totally amenable and responsible at special school, where one might have expected problems with lots of teenage boys away from home, friends, girlfriends and social life. Four of the boys had never been in any trouble at special school, two calmed down very quickly, and one was only ever in trouble for smoking. Only Clark still had staff complaints about behaviour made against him, and perhaps that is not surprising given that he had the highest of all the Performance IQ scores and the lowest Verbal, with a gap of 43 points; this means he could act disruptively with consummate skill, whereas he would find it more difficult to use sarcasm or oral weapons. He himself described himself as stuck in his old 'skiving' behaviour patterns. Oliver was alone in being reported unimproved via special education by his family, either in behaviour or in confidence, although he passed two GCEs and three CSEs. The susceptibility to behaviour problems shown by my sample is worrying because so many of them feel they could have gone completely off the rails and destroyed their futures. Their opinion is justified by independent records, and highlights another potential pitfall for wastage of talent, family suffering and unnecessary community expense as well as personal ruin.

Truancy/school refusal

Truancy occurred in combination with school refusal, and was common to seven cases. Trevor was the only stoic who never tried it, possibly because of his strong background training in moral/religious principles and ethics. Truancy and school refusal started as early as infant school for two boys, happened repeatedly whilst at primary school for five, and was habitual at secondary level for five of them. John never truanted at secondary level because he was already at boarding school. Oliver only did it at primary school, where he was teased the worst and could not hide at the back of the class as he later did at comprehensive. William was a frequent refuser, but was out-manoeuvred by a very determined father. Six out of eight boys indulged in truancy heavily, and two blamed that street habit for temptation to petty theft. For pupils of all ages to be out of school not only is a waste of resources, but also puts them at the mercy of boredom, deviant company, street culture and crime. The infant/primary school incidence was a surprise, as one thinks of habitual truants in connection with big, impersonal comprehensive establishments and teenagers.

Competitiveness disorders

Six out of the eight boys studied suffered from some irregularities of attitude. A tendency to give up prematurely and withdraw from the 'failure situation' was noted even at primary school for one student, and persisted throughout his school life even in sports. Two students habitually used clowning to avoid competitive situations. This non-participant attitude was taken to the extreme of avoiding challenges at all costs by three students, according to their mothers. Another also felt dyslexia meant he could never even begin to compete successfully in the employment market. Two boys were, however, desperate to prove themselves successful and worked very hard to ensure they achieved their targets. Where this can become an obsession is difficult to judge, but both of them fulfilled their ambitions in further education, business and degree success. I felt with one of them that the emphasis was too intense to be healthy, but so far I have happily been proved wrong.

Lack of communication

Five boys either kept violent attacks or bad treatment and intense anguish caused by teachers completely to themselves, hid problems from parents, or reported that they found it very difficult to open up and talk to anyone about deep feelings or trouble. There is a tendency for dyslexic boys to isolate themselves within their own problems, withdraw and try to cope with them alone. This seems a very dangerous propensity, as so much misunderstanding within personal relationships can arise from lack of communication and negotiation, and the absence of problem-solving discussions. It has also been suggested that in stressful situations it is often those who bottle up and bury emotions for a long time who explode or crumple mentally. It is also a common complaint from women in divorce actions that communication had broken down. It can alienate family and friends, who may feel excluded in times of trouble. Escape into alcohol or violence can become the only possible release from pressure for those who have no alternative way of coping.

Isolation/alienation

Five of the group experienced this sensation in an extreme form at the most unhappy stages of their school lives. The picture is a miserable one of boys aged from 7 to 13 cutting themselves off within their own distress, hiding, crying, wanting to die, or just feeling completely alone with their disability and unable to fit in – a rejected outsider. No specific question was asked, but the evidence emerged from the boys' recollections, parental accounts or records. Of the three subjects who made no mention of this factor, the addicted smoker made it his main aim in life to get on with the 'lads' socially and mend motorbikes, one took refuge in care of his animals and equestrian pursuits, and the other hid amongst the back row boys at comprehensive. It is interesting to note that four of the five felt like misfits at primary school, and one at middle school. It is obviously an unhelpful and unhealthy state of mind to be in for any child, but, in combination with the other difficulties and reactions already noted, it could be a devastating one.

Psychosomatic pain

This unusual syndrome was reported by three students, and confirmed by records. It proves the extent of the strain these boys were under that over one third of my sample should have been afflicted by a proven clinical psychiatric delusion commonly associated with unbearable stress. This is surely one of the most powerful results in the study which I undertook and must contradict the critics who brush dyslexic stress aside by claiming that all teenagers suffer similar emotional upheaval. Ages this phenomenon struck at were 10, 12, and only one in his teens at 15.

CONCLUSION

Out of my sample of eight, all except one had been pushed to extremes of misery during primary school, and he had temporarily emigrated. All of them had been teased, humiliated and insulted, by staff, children or both, with four examples of extreme violence from teachers, three of which occurred under age 9.

Of those who had not been physically attacked by teachers who could not cope, there was evidence of truancy, total demoralization, psychosomatic pain and isolation, and the risk of permanent physical damage being done while inducing artificial sickness. The boys registered a great deal of intensity, pain or embarrassment in recalling the worst incidents, which showed in voice, gesture, eyes, increased colour, feeling hot, drawing odd doodles, or coffee consumption.

Part II

Technical Data

Chapter 4

Previous Research on Emotional Reactions

This area is important to understand because the emotional stability of the dyslexic pupil is a pre-requisite which underlies all teaching and research, and has never been conclusively documented. There is no consensus of evidence which leads us to a thorough knowledge of how specific dyslexic pupils react to particular teaching methods, remediation styles and school regimes. How can we hope to teach them successfully or explore their cognitive profiles if we have not taken time first to study their typical experiences, and reactions to them? What sort of emotional make-up underlies, or is produced by, the condition of dyslexia? We are all involved in charting the aetiology and manifestation of this condition, often in minute detail; so what effect is observable on the personality?

Existing research falls into five categories as described below.

PERSONAL ACCOUNTS AND BIOGRAPHIES

Hampshire (1981), for example, is an articulate adult account of a dyslexic childhood which describes a gradual build-up of damaging humiliation, classroom misery, and frustration in trying to learn to spell and cope with memory problems. She experienced intense anxiety and recalls, 'just knowing that I was not mentally retarded or lazy, or backward, or emotionally disturbed ... would have made all the difference' (p. 55).

Attempts to cope with severe feelings of inadequacy are listed, like desperate over-helpfulness, giving extravagant gifts, pilfering and attempting to barter friendship for homework-copying. It is stated that these insecurities are permanent:

> This need to give, for fear of otherwise not being tolerated, has remained with me all my life ... I assumed that no one could like someone as 'stupid' as me ... Nothing has changed: the doubts of childhood remain.

Surprising clarity and intensity are present in the recall of academic disasters from childhood, and hurtful paternal and sibling reactions.

It is noted that even when an adult individual is highly successful in a career, a crisis situation involving dyslexia can develop unexpectedly and destroy confidence levels (see her account of trying to read a teleprompter on page 117 of her text).

OBSERVED AND CAREFULLY RECORDED REACTIONS

Miles and Miles (1983) give a comprehensive overview of the emotional climate surrounding the dyslexic population and their families. They register extreme reactions from children, varying from withdrawal to dogged determination or anti-social behaviour (p. 17). Attention is drawn to the cumulative deprivation of information involved in literacy failure, and lack of stimulation which multiplies hidden general and educational problems and can exasperate sufferers (p. 18). The authors corroborate the view that continuing problems with spelling and literacy failure can compound and accumulate in everyday situations, and their accounts lend support to the view that Hampshire's reaction is typical.

Tomatis (1978) presents some composite case-study descriptions, based on many years of observing dyslexic students and their families. He emphasizes 'how crushing the anxiety caused by all the various possible perception distortions can be' (p. 157). This author is perhaps unique in postulating that emotional reactions can be of primary importance, and he is convinced that dyslexia has a deep origin in early trauma. He takes an audiometric approach with underlying psychotherapeutic principles. As a psycho-physiologist, he believes mixed laterality can represent a specific listening block.

Tomatis gives a child's eye-view of the dyslexic's classroom situation and its repercussions on home life, concentrating on the sense of bewilderment and confusion experienced: 'One thing he could never understand was why the things that were so hard for him seemed perfectly easy for everyone else.' (p. 159). Tomatis charts the pathology of failure, and shows its repercussions as insecure confidence, low morale, and feelings of isolation which result in non-participation, aggression and behaviour problems. He proves this by examining the cases of Gerard, a 12-year-old under threat of expulsion, Andrew, who suffers from acute depression, and Alexandra, who has extreme behaviour problems.

Miles and Gilroy (1986) give case studies of successful dyslexics at college, and show how scars from treatment in primary and secondary school still affect individuals. They indicate that tutor–student relationships can founder due to a back-log of extreme sensitivity (pp. 28 and 29). The cases of S. J. Martin and S. Batty, eventually both highly successful science graduates, show how bright dyslexics can be written off at lower levels of the system, and deeply humiliated. The two show intense bitterness in their comments about denigration at school and, later on, about teachers who told them they were wasting their time thinking about further education.

LONG-TERM FOLLOW-UP STUDIES

Seven negative studies were considered, but an equivalent number of positive ones could not be found. However, five positive studies were examined, and discrepant findings were studied.

Negative studies

Carter (1964), Silver and Hagin (1964) and Preston and Yarrington (1967) all found negative results and low-achievement careers. Rawson (1968) found depressed attainments compared with paternal occupation and IQ expectations even among the successful. Rackham (1972) also found a downward shift in careers. These are documented cases, but apparently no research was being done into reasons, nor recommendations given, at that stage. Similarly, Saunders and Barker (1972) revealed long-term damage to individuals relating to sensitivity, concealments, matrimonial friction and resistance to help which they attributed partially as side-effects of the subjects' dyslexic condition. Yule and Rutter (1976) also found subjects experienced a whole range of adult embarrassments concerning jobs, friendships, social interaction, clubs, committees and even sports.

Positive studies

These relate to the ability of the dyslexic to adjust to his disability and succeed in life. Gottfredson, Finucci and Childs (1983, 1984) found that, amongst adults of professional status who had had a two- to three-year spelling/reading deficit, persuasiveness, initiative and problem-solving were the more important skills, together with confidence in the ability to succeed. Robinson and Smith (1962) interestingly found subjects employed in jobs satisfying to their parents, rather than personally fulfilling. Evidence also exists for good general emotional/behavioural adjustments at follow-up: Abbott and Frank (1975), Edgington (1975) and Hinton and Knights (1971).

Discrepancy of findings

It would be useful to establish whether critical cognitive variables, such as locus of control, self-concept and self-efficacy, interact to determine overall adult adjustment. More research is needed to find out what factors have most impact and to discover which individuals are most vulnerable.

QUANTITATIVE STUDIES

Williams and Miles (1985) hypothesized on aspects of the dyslexic personality and its coping strategies in relation to Rorschach responses. It seemed that the educational and social pressures on a dyslexic child frequently made him lack confidence and so limit the adventurous quality of his responses. Knasel (1982) found that on similarity responses to 'triads' (for example, 'myself, my mother, my favourite teacher') dyslexics displayed fewer constructs. This supports the theory of a personality-based cause for this self-limiting effect.

There are a variety of possible explanations for the differences revealed. Dyslexic children are often reported by parents and teachers to lack maturity, though Halpern (1953) and Francis-Williams (1968) both agree that even during the earliest years at school the number of responses increases for normal children.

Another interpretation is that dyslexics are less in the habit of matching things accurately. The work of Stirling (1978) on inaccuracies of spoken language and confusions of similar words in dyslexics supports this view. She suggested that in word-definition work, however, verbal rambling showed not just lack of confidence about what is known, but insecurity about what is not known, a tendency to go 'over the top' and to extremes. Williams and Miles interpret these findings as a difficulty in giving the socially appropriate response to a situation. The link between extremity of behaviour tendencies, either self-limiting or over-elaborative, organizational problems and severity of dyslexia needs further investigation. This whole theory fits in with Knasel's identification of the dyslexic's 'minimax' strategy to guard against exposure to failure and ridicule.

It is interesting to note that, in fields where dyslexics have been known to excel (such as the scientific, design, mechanical or practical), complexity can be dealt with comparatively easily. It is, however, a more detached, non-verbal, spatial kind of complexity which is more clear-cut than the demands of satisfying a person expecting a fluent response to an academic question.

STUDIES FOCUSING ON SELF-ESTEEM AND SELF-KNOWLEDGE

Rosenthal (1973) provides some clear evidence about low self-esteem in dyslexic children. He lists the pressures and adult frustrations which dyslexics inevitably encounter. Certain reactions to this situation have been noted.

Macdonald Critchley (1970) found compensatory manoeuvres such as efforts to excel in non-literate skills like sport, or becoming the class-room clown because of loss of self-esteem.

Edmond Critchley in Macdonald Critchley (1968) examined aggression, studying 477 delinquent seniors in London, and found reading incompetence in 60 per cent of cases. 'Some of the boys almost certainly had primary developmental dyslexia. There appeared to be a high correlation between acted-out anti-social aggressions and problems in reading' (Rosenthal, 1973, p. 28).

Edmond Critchley describes the stages in development of self-esteem as being (1) how the individual is valued by others, (2) his history of success/failure, and (3) his responses to devaluation. It is clearly shown how this normal development can be damaged at home and school for the dyslexic.

Rosenthal found that behaviour was further influenced by the parents' degree of understanding that dyslexia is a specific abnormality. He also found that friendship-patterns revealed insecurity or low self-image as dyslexics and their families chose younger children or those with obvious difficulties, though of other types.

The work of Stott (1978), though not writing specifically about dyslexics, shows how teaching styles and children's individual learning strategies can clash in the classroom and cause permanent damage to ordinary pupils in terms of their perceived image, potential and behaviour-patterns. This is relevant because of the adverse classroom response many dyslexics document.

Sylvia Farnham-Diggory (1978) records the effect an adverse learning situation for children with learning difficulties can have on both pupils and teachers. She gives examples of pupils treated with mental cruelty by teachers who could not cope with continuous chronic failure, and accounts of clinical psychological problems induced by school failure.

The work of Freya Owen is also given fully in Farnham-Diggory. Owen researched parental reactions to a child with literacy problems. She found that parents perceived the learning-disabled children as having a range of problematic tendencies concerning global perseverance, verbal and motor skills, self-control and organization. Relative to siblings, they were also thought lacking in general coping ability and anxiety control. Parents were negative about school experience even when a special programme existed. It was only for educationally handicapped children that mothers tended to withhold affection if the child was irresponsible or disorganized. Fathers, however, withdrew affection if that child was apathetic or worried, lacked concentration or showed lack of control. This did not apply to siblings. Academic pressure from fathers was related to their views of the learning-disabled child's perseverence and ability to carry responsibility.

Farnham-Diggory's chapter on case studies conveys the holistic nature of a dyslexic child's hardships in considering family attitudes, school systems, personality, and forms of assessment and treatment. In the case of Jack, she details the confusion and multiplicity of approaches which can exist even after full diagnosis and recognition. Peter, Sammy and Luke are all charted cases which illustrate the range of damage sustained by literacy-failing children in school.

CONCLUSION

The majority of these authorities, from their different disciplines and perspectives, converge in projecting dyslexic students as seriously affected at both home and school by academic failure. Within their works there are 12 confirmations of severe lack of confidence, eight authors recording behaviour problems, and three documenting profound self-doubt and humiliation. Two studies report a finding of extreme sensitivity, and there are individual confirmations of communication problems, unfair treatment and competitiveness disorders.

My study identifies a full set of eight students matched for current school environment, social success, status and age. This is unlike the case-study work listed, which is largely individual. It thoroughly cross-checks information across 18 sources, including personal interviews as well as parental and professional comment. It systematically corroborates existing findings on lack of confidence, behaviour problems, self-doubt, humiliation and unfair treatment. It confirms less frequent results noted on sensitivity to criticism, communication problems and competitiveness disorders.

Through free interview and questionnaire techniques it identifies three additional negative experiences dyslexics undergo: violence from teachers, inadequate help/ neglect, and teasing/persecution from the peer group. Three associative reactions to these experiences never examined before are given: truancy/school refusal, psychosomatic pain and feelings of isolation/alienation.

The five long-term positive studies listed above (see p. 147) are the only exceptions to the mass of negative evidence. Amongst these it is interesting to note that Gottfredson *et al.* examined only adults of professional status, so one might argue that they had already disbarred those who failed dramatically. The Robinson and Smith study is really a comment on susceptibility to parental expectations rather than an endorsement of success. This leaves three positive studies on emotional adjustment weighed against thirteen which record serious damage through the dyslexic experience. Surely this finally gives a conclusive consensus of opinion when taken in conjunction with my own findings.

Chapter 5

Research Methods Used

SAMPLE

All of the eight boys I chose either had volunteered to stay on at school for an extra year or were prefects in responsible positions, two achieving the status of head boy. I felt this proved they had overcome their aversion to schools to a large extent.

I deliberately picked out fairly tough 'survivors' as I felt it might be damaging to a very withdrawn or nervous child to dwell upon his experiences. Knowing the individuals so well because of the complete holistic view facilitated by boarding placement gave a unique opportunity for a relaxed discussion/conversation about personal matters and views. These boys were at the end of their school careers, but still attending, so that school life was fresh in their minds and strongly felt. This seemed the ideal situation in which to look back and review their school careers.

I had taught most of them for at least three years on an individual basis, on a class basis for two years, and as a personal tutor involved in many varied social situations with them.

APPROACH

I chose the case-study approach as most suitable to my purpose. I conducted an initial 'free interview' where I simply asked, 'Tell me about the schools you went to, what you thought of them, and how you felt.' I hoped this would give their own spontaneous recollections and opinions an opportunity to surface untainted by constraints of questions, and that the most memorable relevant situations would emerge naturally. I thought the boys might find it hard to just talk in this monologue way, but in fact they proved to be extremely lucid and talkative, as I ought to have expected from their generally strong characters. I was surprised by their willingness to reveal quite personal experiences, and I deemed this a success.

CASE STUDY

I selected case-study methods as a means of examining the dyslexic emotional experience for many reasons. As a procedure it offered flexibility to explore the subjects' views and feelings, and invited communication and the expression of personal reactions from the unique individual under study. Thus I hoped the reader would become involved with the people described, and would experience their situation. I felt a statistical analysis of many dyslexic people would show trends clearly, yet at the same time encourage a detached attitude towards them, like studying and counting the properties of aberrant bacteria under a microscope. I wanted to look at each person as a whole and try to discover what particular elements in his career helped him to cope with his difficulties better. Ideally, I intended each boy to tell his own story, and support or clarify this by documentary fact and the opinions of his parents and teachers. The experiences of the dyslexic become more comprehensible to the observer when examined through several different perspectives.

Emotional scars and reactions to dyslexia have been largely ignored in the struggle to remedy the academic problems; yet confidence, attitude, motivation and the self-concept deeply affect the learning process. To isolate factors which help these children survive better could well alter and improve our treatment and handling of them.

Case study, then, is essentially 'a systematic investigation of a specific instance' (Nisbet and Watt, 1978, p. 5) concerned with the interaction of factors and events. It attempts to give a detailed three-dimensional picture of an individual unit. Nisbet and Watt believe the aim of a case study to be portrayal: 'The style to aim at is that of an anthropological study, which portrays what it is like "to be there" . . . but avoids explicit or implicit judgement on it' (p. 19).

There are obvious problems inherent in this approach. If the researcher is asking personal details of a sensitive nature, the mutual relationship and atmosphere of trust must be very strong for the subject to be willing to explore his opinions and feelings. This is why participant observation is useful, because it is a more natural way of learning about other people. After all, it is only with the best of one's friends that most people drop their everyday 'mask' and talk about areas where they are vulnerable. I have been observing my cases informally for years, just as they have been studying me. I was convinced the depth of answer I required would emerge only after a two-way long-term relationship of this kind. For example, consider John's stress reaction described in his case study when talking about unhappiness at prep school. I am quite sure the interview would have ended there, and painfully for the pupil concerned, if we had not known each other so well and been able to laugh about this and talk about how people cope. It could well be dangerous and damaging for a stranger to pry into a sensitive area.

MODE OF RECORDING FREE INTERVIEW

I allowed each boy to choose the mode of recording. I had at first decided to use a tape-recorder, but several boys groaned heavily and said, 'Oh, no,' 'I freeze with one of them,' 'Do we have to have that on?' or 'I'll feel a pratt with that on.' I revised my method; half of the boys chose a tape situation, and the other half opted for me typing whilst they talked. They could then clearly see and read what was produced, and felt I was participating too instead of just watching them. The boys who were speaking had time to think, expand their comments or rephrase them whilst typing was in progress; surprisingly the noise did not bother them. A few preferred hand-written notes read back to them.

STRUCTURED INTERVIEW

I applied the same approach to the structured interview, which was obviously more formal, being guided by what I wanted to know, but proved equally enlightening. Some boys were more at ease with the free situation, others spoke in more detail over the questionnaire. This was quite interesting in itself, their style of answering varying very much from individual to individual.

PARENTAL INTERVIEW

Parents were given a choice of writing their answers to a short questionnaire, or discussing the questions by phone or in personal interview. It was more difficult to get an answer from them because of their lack of availability and their other com-mitments. Also, I realize I was asking them to do something quite difficult – to stand back and objectively analyse their son's personality, and the effects upon him of his whole education. I had free access to boys' records for analysis, comparison and cross-checking facts (see the section entitled Triangulation procedures and examples on pp. 154–5).

It is important to maintain a scientific, methodical approach, writing up key points and quotes from interviews instantly whilst the words of the subjects are fresh in the mind. Tape-recordings facilitate this, but they may inhibit the interviewee and spoil the atmosphere. In my situation I felt parents would become very embarrassed at being tape-recorded, whilst they volunteered quite fascinating aspects of their children's careers and behaviour in the context of informal conversations and progress discus-sions. They were very forthcoming about the problems they and their children had encountered when they knew you were listening with genuine interest and were involved positively in the educational process. To write notes after a warm exchange and then check them over with the parents at a later date has a different relationship ethos than to coldly tape-record and analyse, which could have made people feel suspicious and intruded upon. This did not apply so much to boys who knew their teacher well, but I felt parents who had often been battered and humiliated by officialdom required special consideration.

PARTICIPANT OBSERVATION

Additional insight was given to me by participant observation. This included striking reactions to situations out-of-school, boys' behaviour, comments and confidences occurring naturally during extra-curricular situations in a social environment, and interesting casual comments from other boys. These needed to be carefully checked and explored, but often gave clues which were fascinating to follow up. Staff-room comment had to be treated in the same way. Consider Mark's comment about John as a team captain tending to give up immediately he began to lose in competitive sports (Mark's specialist area) and how angry it made him. This led me along a path of enquiry which proved useful. It became evident from checking through sports reports and asking various sports masters that this was a pronounced feature of John's attitude. Indeed, sports reports became a useful check on an individual's character tendencies in a non-academic field. Sports comments in the staff-room also provided clues about levels of sensitivity to criticism which could be confirmed by reports. An example of this occurs with Trevor and PE:

> Trevor always performs well, but he finds it difficult to cope with defeat on a personal level. If he is caught in the wrong, he will not accept a reprimand. He must learn to accept advice and criticism.

Both competitiveness disorders and sensitivity to criticism became major features in the negative associative reactions identified within the study. This was sometimes taken to extremes, as can be seen by individual accounts (for example, Mark threw away his hard-won football medal because his team came second in the league, and the worry of Clark's father about his son's ability to get on with his potential bosses was also significant).

I had to use the same procedure in reverse to corroborate boys' comments about Oliver as an over-zealous prefect capable of cruelty. Here I checked facts from Trevor's transcript with other teachers, care staff and junior pupils. Reports also testified to the friction and conflict between the two boys (tutorial comment on Trevor, spring 1983).

The work-experience situation for William and the speech exam conditions for George contributed evidence towards hypotheses about lack of confidence. In a pastoral context, casual comment from George about feelings of panic and inability to read under stress conditions was confirmed by disparate test results with external professionals in reviews of progress.

TRIANGULATION PROCEDURES AND EXAMPLES

A problem with case study can be a dependence on the verbalization skills, insight and self-knowledge of the subjects, and their ability to remember and analyse their own feelings and experiences. Is this the complete truth? The researcher is subjectively interpreting subjectively expressed memories, which we all know are liable to distortion, especially over time. This can be remedied or at least assisted by documentary evidence, cross-checking with parents and different teachers, and by asking the same kind of question in a different form over time (for example, with questionnaires). This must eliminate some mood-colouration effects on the data. Triangulation techniques must be an important feature of a case study if it is to be authentic, systematic and scientific enough to base a theoretical analysis upon. Cohen and Manion (1980) state: 'Triangulation may be defined as the use of two or more methods of data collection in the study of some aspect of human behaviour' (p. 208). The term originates in the efforts at physical measurement by navigators, for example pinpointing a single spot by using several locational markers.

Confidence in the validity and reliability of results is substantiated if different methods yield similar conclusions. For example, if my questionnaire showed the same sentiments at a later date to the open preliminary interview with the boy, findings were consistent. If this correlated with his parents' recall and the accounts in his detailed records, I felt reasonably secure. If other teachers agreed with my conclusion about this child, it made my case stronger. The right of the subject to read or hear the account of his views must also have added consistency.

Triangulation processes yielded interesting contrasts for me. In a long conversation about John, his mother was telling me what a bad time he had in school, and how the police were always returning him to school at the tender age of 6 because he truanted and was found by the canal. This happened regularly; yet the school records did not mention it, only how in the afternoon his remedial work was undertaken by his class teacher *daily*. I was also discussing reading age progress with this boy and showing him his chart over his whole school career. I pointed out how many hours special teaching he had had at this primary school, yet had not progressed as well as at Unit E. His amazed response was, 'They never gave me no special teaching! I was never there in the afternoons.'

Thus it appears the primary school was glossing over its problems with John, though quite independently he and his mother recalled things in a different light. This was also supported by the rates of fluctuation in his reading progress, which always shot up when given individual lessons. Establishing the true provision made for John was like detective work. Yet, previously, I had set a lot of confidence in the very full, professional-sounding school accounts – as much as in the parental memory.

Another similar case arose when records showed William had a peripatetic remedial teacher personally provided for him by the county psychologist. No reading age increase had occurred. The remedial teacher had been asked to take a group of others. Some of the class were set work, and the dyslexic was supposed to get special help from the class teacher, who used the time to mark books, according to the boy. Independently mentioning the shortcomings of past schools, William's mother cited this incident as the main reason for removing her son from school and sending him to live with his grandmother in another area.

REPORTS FROM TEACHERS

I used less formal testing procedures than I thought I would, as the other approaches yielded such a mass of material. I did use the Pupil-Rating Scale (Myklebust) Personal–Social Behaviour section, given to various teachers to complete, to gain a supplementary second opinion on how individuals presented in class. This was useful to check overall impressions of a student's personality, to cross-check whether their own impressions of staff attitudes towards them were correct, and compare their behaviour in one teacher's class with another. Generally, these forms confirmed student perceptions. The notable case was Clark, who gained widely divergent ratings from different teachers and within different subject areas. His school reports support this.

Finally, however, I found individual teachers' behavioural reports, collated across time on an inter-school basis, much more productive. They were obviously deeply felt, written at the time of some notable event, and often carefully observed. I have quoted many of these comments in Chapter 2, discussing behavioural tendencies and explanations. One advantage was that a teacher had been free to give full expression to an analysis of a pupil's difficulties, unconfined by categories. The teacher was uninvolved in this study, unaware of later developments in a child's school career, and uncoloured by knowledge of the hypotheses under scrutiny.

STATEMENTING DOCUMENTS

Statementing procedural documents from schools were frequently perceptive, highlighting problems which even sympathetic schools encountered in dealing with dyslexic pupils (see George's secondary school comments on behavioural problems on p. 87).

Educational psychologists gave extra insight or controversial alternative views that were useful to consider (see Clark's county adviser's remark on his attitude to his special school on p. 71).

CONCLUSION

Overall, a clear but complex picture seemed to emerge from an integration of the various sources combined with the transcripts. My chief problem was the organization, collation and presentation of this material once I had obtained all the data.

their reactions – simply that they have a hidden multiplicity of problems to cope with; these build up and interconnect, and that makes them more vulnerable and volatile in their emotional reactions.

Like all Clark's teachers I was totally unaware that he had been the subject of teacher violence and humiliation as a small child. I had heard such stories from other pupils not involved in this study, but had assumed they were just unlucky. Over ten years of teaching and discussion with all my pupils, the frequency of this seemed rather high. Not until this study, however, did the significant fact strike home that over half of the sample of pupils had been physically hurt by staff at school. This surely cannot be construed as normal educational experience.

Another point which marks Clark's experience out as particularly damaging is the fact that his lack of O-level C grades (he has a B in Art) will permanently prevent him from being able to take up a college place for art, even if he should wish to do so in maturer years. An ordinary person of Clark's IQ could study at night-school and pick up the minimum four GCSEs now. Because of his dyslexia, however, Clark would find any academic subject exceedingly difficult without expensive individual tuition, which in itself would not guarantee success now the amanuensis facility has been removed and 100 per cent coursework syllabuses have been killed by John Major's prejudiced attack. Could Clark go to college for an intensive year? No college catering for severe dyslexics to retake or collect basic qualifications exists. Nor do there exist any open-learning courses at a lower level than Open University. This is a recipe for frustration. Fortunately, Clark has found his own satisfyingly creative and lucrative outlet in handcrafted woodwork. Will he feel bitter about his lost opportunities in later life? Has the education system done anything for him at all, commensurate with his innate ability? This study inevitably throws up more questions than it answers, and I hope they will be pursued, researched and answered.

GEORGE

George chiefly suffered from lack of confidence owing to dyslexic illiteracy and behaviour problems. All the professionals involved with his case connected the two together as cause and effect. His difficulties with literacy were severe and debilitating, and he struggled for seven and a half years in mainstream education, suffering acute frustration and embarrassment as a daily ritual unless he truanted. Surely he should have been given specialist help earlier? One wonders what this shrewd and physically talented, well-motivated pupil could have achieved if given an early opportunity to progress, since he changed so much with just two and a half years of help. One can also see clearly the kinds of dangers lying in wait for dyslexics who cannot find a socially acceptable area in which to gain some recognition and an identity.

MARK

Being an outgoing type of personality, Mark's behavioural outlets for tension and frustration were truancy and disruptive action, though he had also displayed spells of withdrawn behaviour. He was a notable school phobic, having required professional help for this. His lack of confidence assisted his feeling of failure in academic pursuits and led to occupational dissatisfaction, as he never felt able to attempt his real dream of becoming a PE instructor. Yet this boy was the most well-motivated I ever met, and very intelligent and resourceful in formal discussions. There was a strong current of disillusionment and bitterness flowing through Mark's account beneath the jovial surface, and school failed him both practically and emotionally.

WILLIAM

Whilst William had no adequate remedial teaching, the early identification of his difficulty must have helped him to achieve his undoubted stability. In contrast to the high levels of violence, humiliation or unfair treatment experienced in the classroom by six out of seven of the other cases, the way in which William was treated must have led to his comparative security, drive and confidence. Reports from his schools are understanding. If they did not provide him with any help, at least they did not belittle or degrade him. Had others received equally sympathetic handling and not endured adverse encounters with adult professionals they too would have been less tense or lacking in confidence, and overall more successful. Obviously, William's warm, solid, commonsense farming background helped him adjust, as did his fascination with animal care, success in show-jumping, his interests and considerable intelligence. His very supportive mother emphasizes his dramatic improvement at special school, with reading ability, happiness, teachers' dedicated care and exam success as crucial factors. Entering special education at age 13, he also avoided the explosive third year in state education mentioned by George and Clark.

OLIVER

Oliver is interesting because he is only mildly dyslexic, yet his mother feels that his personality has been strongly affected by this. It must have had a lasting effect on him to be 'written off' academically as he describes so well in the last page of his free interview when speaking about his comprehensive school. Oliver felt his progress was hampered by being sent to a special school and under-stretched competitively. He raises the issue of whether merely residual dyslexic individuals are better served and motivated by being educated in integrated units.

STRESSES ON THE MILD DYSLEXIC

To be a mild dyslexic can be disorientating because the goals are almost within reach, and may even be easy on a good day. Yet frequently the child can feel confused as to why he cannot integrate skills enough to consistently achieve the excellence of which his intellect is capable. I saw this daily when I was head of two separate integrated units supporting a majority of mild dyslexics with superior IQs in public schools of high attainment (Carmel College, Oxfordshire, and Stowe School, Buckinghamshire). I have had many cases of undiagnosed mild dyslexics who were deeply frustrated by the disparity between the excellence they occasionally reached and inexplicable sporadic failure areas. One boy thought he was going mad – 'losing it' was the expression he used. This seems to reflect the unusual heights and dives on the IQ profile which can be very confusing for the owner if he is unaware of its occurrence or meaning. It explains why dyslexics can suffer from extreme and shifting self-images which are unrealistically over-inflated in some areas or moods, and non-existent in others. Once fully instructed about their own learning profile of strengths and weaknesses, however, and given specialist advice on specific skills, students went on to achieve confidence, GCSEs, and A-level and degree success.

GENERAL COMMENTS

What factors prove that the reactions of these students were due to their dyslexic condition and experience rather than being a normal part of adolescent reaction? The evidence is in Table 3.4. Consider the section 'Violence from teachers'. Would anyone seriously contend that 62.5 per cent of ordinary children are physically attacked by teachers? That is the generalized conversion of the findings. Would anyone suggest that 100 per cent of children in schools suffer inadequate help or neglect? That is what the Section 'Inadequate help/neglect' suggests. It should be borne in mind that schools covered a wide range from private prep school to inner city comprehensive. It is obvious that these children have a different and malevolent pattern of educational experience. They have these problems as well as the normal ones involved in growing up or in home circumstances. This produces an emotional overload which leads to permanent scarring. Considering these experiences, of which all pupils registered more than half, it is only surprising that the personality damage was not far more serious.

Picture the 'normal' adolescent, then examine the 'Associative reactions' part of Table 3.4. Is it sensible to suggest that 100 per cent of them lack confidence, doubt their intellect, are hypersensitive to criticism, and have behaviour problems? My own experience of comprehensive and public school teenagers suggests the reverse. Where is the 'typical' arrogance, the superiority of youth, the 'don't care' attitude, the apathy? None of these things were said about this dyslexic sample, though I suggest these kinds of comment fly around many staff-rooms about teenage pupils.

The parents of these children are very experienced in what is a normal reaction as they deal with non-dyslexic siblings, extended family or teenagers occupationally. Amongst them are a teacher, a social worker, a football club trainer, a youth club worker, and employers. One also has an extensive family for comparison. Only one pupil is an only child, and he has many cousins of his age. They were convinced their dyslexic showed particular reactions, and were very definite, clear and chronological in their statements.

The teachers whose comments form substantial amounts of evidence within the categories and patterns of reaction are used to age norm comparisons and come from varied schools. Yet the statements echo and reinforce each other. Often the level of teacher anxiety over these strong emotional reactions is instrumental in propelling the child towards special educational statementing.

So does it follow that all dyslexics have this syndrome of connected and predictable reactions? The key to this question is in the ability of the adolescents to change under more favourable educational conditions. Not one of the five pupils labelled as disruptive or at risk of delinquency displayed this tendency seriously when given adequate literacy help. In fact, they were all given posts of great responsibility and fulfilled them admirably. So failure and scarring is not an innate and integral feature of the dyslexic. profile. It is induced by adverse treatment conditions, and in this study had to be delved for. I reiterate that these pupils had had a large and dramatic input of specialized help, even if for half of them it had come at the very last minute. These boys, unlike the majority of adolescent students who leave school at 16, appreciated, needed and volunteered for an extra year of education. One might expect far more extreme reactions amongst comprehensive or private school dyslexics who had never been identified, or who had been identified and not helped.

The dyslexic experience and the attitude of teachers and other pupils to it definitely affected the outlook of these students, but with varying amounts of impact and damage sustained. The combinations and severity of reactions displayed varied with degree of dyslexia, length of time exposed to mishandling by schools, and balancing compensatory talents. It is interesting to note that Oliver, perhaps the most generally unfulfilled of all the sample, had no recognized and acceptable special talent.

An effective description of the dyslexic, his talents and how easily he can be overlooked was given to the Orton Society by Vail (1990) in her account of Foley's Rocks. She likens dyslexics in the academic context of school to apparently unexciting brown rocks, which glow with colour and brilliance underneath ultraviolet light. 'Our job is to find them and shed that light' (p. 7). She identifies ten special traits dyslexics possess which can enrich learning and later life but may cause friction with staff. They are the rapid grasp of concepts, awareness of patterns, energy, curiosity, concentration, exceptional memory, empathy, vulnerability, heightened perception and divergent thinking. I would add talent in art and design, multi-dimensional thinking, originality and problem-solving. She urges teachers to cater for these individualistic gifts, and not waste intellectual potential because it does not fit into preconceived stereotyped majority moulds.

This present study shows the damage which can be done if dyslexics are not catered for effectively. The results are a powerful indictment of the way pupils with dyslexic special needs are treated by the modern English educational system.

Chapter 7

Recommendations

After reading the students' individual accounts of the worst parts of their school careers and the few contrasting highlights, and studying Table 3.4, there is likely to be a consensus of opinion asking what can be done practically and quickly to change the educational ethos surrounding dyslexic pupils in general so that the misunderstandings and traumas these pupils suffered do not have to be relived by others.

Much can be done to stop teacher violence, child humiliation and persecution by peers. The responsibility must rest with individual teachers, the educational system and the government.

A. THE INFORMED TEACHER

Teacher hostility seems to hinge on the lack of recognition of the condition of dyslexia and lack of knowledge about how to handle/treat these complex and sometimes contradictory or reluctant pupils.

1. It is essential that full information about dyslexia should be given to student teachers in training colleges across all specialist subjects and age ranges. They should be given some idea of how the dyslexic problems of memory, sequencing, directional orientation, divergent viewpoints and the organization of thought present themselves in different subject areas. Training courses on special needs often deal fully with physical handicaps, yet the incidence of dyslexia is higher as well as being present in every classroom. Half the severely dyslexic pupils within this study, finally sent to special school, spent up to nine years in mainstream classes. However, on recently applying for special needs posts in further education and teacher training, I was told that no dyslexia input was required, and only physical handicaps were dealt with.
2. There should also be an urgent, intensive and local programme of in-service training centring on the awareness of dyslexia, its recognition, its processing and the specialist teaching methods useful in alleviating its effects.

3. A diagnostic approach to all remedial education should be adopted, based on the analysis of specific problems, and the build-up of individual learning profiles or coherent group programmes to work on known patterns of weakness and use obvious strengths. This provides a much more scientific basis to special needs provision than the sometimes watered-down and simplified primary-school type of learning diet, or rather patronizing 'now-colour-in-this-worksheet' (because we know you cannot read it) sort of work frequently offered to bright but semi-literate groups of varied special needs pupils in the senior mainstream situation. Essay-writing and reading analysis check-lists (see material in boxes) can be a useful pointer to teachers as to what features to look for, as they show how the dyslexic pattern of difficulties builds up in terms of literacy errors and pinpoint exactly what is going wrong, rather than a teacher having a general impression of a poor or con-fused piece of work or low reading skill. These lists should therefore help non-specialist teachers to extract individual error patterns to work on one by one rather than slating the whole piece of work, the child's attitude or ability in a destructive, punitive way by a face-to-face confrontation or with the threatening blood-red pen.

4. Structured, cumulative, multi-sensory teaching methods should be used which have inherent logical step-by-step progression of content, and include varied repetition, visual representation of facts, and memory training as well as giving outlets for the creative imagination. Oral communication skills to build up confidence and the development of independent study skills are also essential com-ponents for any programme designed to cater for dyslexic pupils. Keyboarding skills and the use of electronic spell-checking aids complete the picture.

5. A basic training in counselling skills, practical methods of managing and training difficult children displaying behaviour problems, and recognizing the tell-tale signs of low self-esteem would also be very great assets to many teachers preparing for life in classrooms today.

B. TEACHING METHODS

1. Teenage dyslexics deeply resent any attempt to give them juvenile work, or to take a primary school attitude towards them. They want above all to be treated as intelligent semi-adults and not 'talked down' to.

2. They feel a need for individual attention, to have their say and be listened to. This could be considered as a two-way yet counselling relationship.

3. Dyslexic boys strongly stress the importance of warm, trusting teacher–pupil relationships as paramount in their learning. Individual boys gave particular importance to *the outstanding teache*r – a special person they could relate to – during the course of their school careers. (Trevor, William and Mark all gave glow-ing accounts of an encouraging teacher who had helped them.)

4. Basic literacy work can be more acceptable to older boys when centred around their personal interests and hobbies, on which they are frequently experts. The 100 per cent coursework GCSE exams (now defunct) facilitated this in English Language, where an individual flavour could enrich a folder and creative, factual discussion and explanatory work could reflect personal topics.

5. Free time and holidays should be preserved whenever possible, without interrup-tion (advice from Tomatis and Hampshire; also interviewees in this study).

C. THE SCHOOL ENVIRONMENT

1. School ethos, the degree of respect toward its pupils, and a friendly regime are felt to be crucial by the boys in this study.
2. The students felt a strong desire for stability of environment and method – a fast rate of changes within the system disturbed them (Mark especially).
3. Continuity of teaching styles between the remedial process and class teaching was important. (Mark stressed this.)
4. 'A school should change with its people – they should have a say, a real council' (Mark). This highlights the need for pupil participation, especially for older pupils.
5. An interesting school environment is essential for distressed pupils with feelings of failure. 'A really good school will be both friendly and well cared for, bright with ever-changing displays of [pupils'] work. Pictures will be well chosen and well framed and every school is a warmer and more congenial place for the presence of flowers' (Clegg and Megson, 1973, p. 89m). In support of this view they quote the beliefs of Edward Thring, a famous public school head, who professed that his greatest achievements were made by attention to details of this kind because of the effect they have on the morale of pupils, and on the general atmosphere of the school (see Parkin, 1898). The general atmosphere of the school, the tone and level of concern among the staff for the problems of their pupils, and their attitude and approach to these pupils have great impact.
6. An holistic approach to the pupils' talents and welfare should be more prevalent within the school context. Several boys in this study bitterly mentioned gold stars, tests and being last in the class. Competition should be only to encourage the pupil and show individual improvement, not as public condemnation or congratulation (see Bettelheim, 1971 and Oakeshott, 1973 on damaging competition; and Clegg, 1973 on the emotional 'descending spiral' effect).
7. Every opportunity to praise success across a wide area should be taken advantage of. Achievement in non-academic fields of endeavour can improve confidence and self-esteem. Consider the Duke of Edinburgh Award scheme, English Speaking Board exams, karate belts, sports colours, drama, and community service awards. Certification exists for many extra-curricular club activities to show excellence.
8. Creative work in English, art, music, drama and practical subjects can be therapeutic and help communication (see Oakeshott, 1973 and Winnicott, 1964 on rationale and methods).
9. Careers guidance is especially necessary for dyslexics. My interviewees stressed the need for schools to develop their real strengths towards employment whilst balancing this with hard work upon their problem areas (George especially).

D. THE EDUCATIONAL SYSTEM

1. Early identification can prevent unnecessary hardship and worry for children and parents. Teachers could do this (see Stott, 1978, p. 3).
2. Screening at age 7 alongside the normal medical checks of hearing and eyesight should be introduced across the board. Dyslexia would then be identified and accepted as a specific disability rather than some kind of attitude or mental problem. At senior school, LEAs test IQ with Cognitive Ability Tests. Yet how

often are discrepancies in individual achievement acted upon? How easy it would be to slip in diagnostic tests with these general ones. Pre-school checks of speech development predictive patterns, such as verbal sentence structuring, the ability to distinguish rhyming words, and the rapidity of word repetition ability, could be very useful. The work of Bradley (1989) and Fawcett (1993) is interesting in analysing the connection between dyslexia and these frequently noticed verbal difficulties.

3. For those families 'at risk' for dyslexia because of hereditary factors, additional thorough pre-school checks of co-ordination and motor skills should occur.

4. Those found to have a strong deficit in age norm skills should receive a specialist nursery school 'head-start' on a limited but regular basis.

5. Upon identification, specialist treatment of an intensive nature should follow immediately. (Some families in this study had to wait six years.)

6. Dissemination of knowledge about dyslexia to the individual and the family concerned can be critical (see Rosenthal, 1973, p. 37). This should be made the responsibility of a specific agency. It could prevent the strong self-denigration evident in individuals throughout this study. Boys were unaware of their IQ levels and ability profiles.

7. More assistance and awareness in FE colleges and universities would be helpful for dyslexic individuals (see Miles and Gilroy, 1986). When I enquired on behalf of applicants from my unit, it was often clear that universities and the former polytechnics were making no provision at all.

8. More awareness of the pastoral needs of dyslexic individuals is desperately needed at all levels of the educational system. The dearth of reference material on this subject accentuates this point.

E. THE BOARDING SITUATION

1. Older boys seek status and responsibility. This should be catered for, and include *all leavers*.

2. Boys need a refuge and some privacy, with free permission to be in their own dormitory as seniors, rather than always being in a crowded common-room situation (Gareth).

3. A cohesive attempt should be made to broaden boys socially, and bridge the gap between school and work. Work experience can do this (Gareth).

4. An after-care and support service that dyslexics could turn to for advice in any crisis after leaving school is very important. This can be formal or informal. Boys should be made familiar with facilities of the Citizens Advice Bureau.

5. It could be most helpful to have living quarters away from school for a real change of atmosphere (Trevor).

6. If boarding schools are the only economical and practical policy solution for these students' problems, co-educational provision should be considered (Trevor).

7. Sport, music, hobbies and activities to alleviate boredom are important.

8. Contact in sporting competition with other schools is desirable to prevent a feeling of claustrophobia and insularity (Mark).

9. A family atmosphere should be aimed at and any sheltered situation should be widened with sympathetic visitors, for example old teachers, old boys and staff families. A major social event can be planned at least for every term whether it be an exhibition, Christmas pantomime or Spring play.

10. There needs to be strong parental involvement and discussion in order to lessen the gap between home and school which can develop.

11. Dyslexic girls, a minority within a minority, are often left out of specialist boarding provision. A day unit or separate houses would help these individuals for whom far fewer non-academic job opportunities exist.

F. NATIONAL/POLITICAL ISSUES

1. *Ongoing publicity about the condition of dyslexia and how to get help, at a national level, is still required.*

Intensive effort is expended every year by the Dyslexia Institute and British Dyslexia Association, both national charities, to familiarize the public with dyslexia. They have co-operated in launching National Dyslexia Awareness Week, gaining substantial press coverage. Celebrity involvement such as that of Susan Hampshire has allowed many actors and famous figures to talk openly about their problems, and so inspire other sufferers, showing how problems can be survived and overcome. The Arts Dyslexia Trust has also been active, arranging exhibitions to publicize the talents which are often part of the dyslexic cognitive pattern. Expert professional support such as that of Sir Roger de Grey, President of the Royal Academy of Art, has lent strong backing to these campaigns.

What, however, has the government done? How many children still slip through the educational net and leave school illiterate? The figures given in estimates and surveys vary, often because of different views on how severe a literacy problem needs to be before it is classified as illiteracy. There is no doubt, however, that a serious problem exists.

The Adult Literacy and Basic Skills Unit (1988) estimated that there are 400,000 adults and young people in this country 'who cannot read at all' (p. 3). In 1987 it was estimated by a Manpower Services Commission survey that at least 20 per cent of long-term unemployed had substantial problems in literacy and/or numeracy. Osmond and Morrison (1992) quote 45 per cent as the estimated proportion of prison inmates who could be dyslexic. Experimental evidence suggests that this is actually the amount who cannot read, write or spell. In all these figures, the pure dyslexics will obviously be a smaller sub-group amongst those affected by other factors such as ethnic/language background, social deprivation or primary emotional/behavioural problems. Yet the fact that we do not know how many of the literacy casualties amongst these statistics are attributable to dyslexia, or whether its incidence is over-represented within these socially vulnerable groups, is a piece of national ignorance which is worrying in itself.

The pupils described in this book came to a realization of what their difficulty was by very varied means. John was put on the trail of dyslexia by his optician, who suggested this might be the problem when he was having his eyes tested and named lots of letters back to front; his mother acted on this. Trevor, Mark and Gareth were also identified by their mothers. William and Clark were referred by the child health department. Oliver was diagnosed at the pre-school stage in America. George was the *only* subject to have been diagnosed by his school. This reveals an appalling lack of educational awareness.

The government has done little to fulfil its obligation to promote the welfare of this educational minority group. There are still local education authorities who do not recognize dyslexia, there are state special schools where staff are totally untrained and unprepared to deal with it, and professional specialism is too often left to charity provision or is only available in the private sector.

All too often children in state special schools are inaccurately or vaguely diagnosed, worried parents are intimidated by committees of harassed, over-worked and under-funded professionals, and the nature of the difficulty is not clearly explained either to parents or to the child. Learning difficulties of very different sorts, such as slow learners, dyslexics, behaviourally disturbed and severely deprived children, are treated as a homogeneous 'special' group even when their needs are directly conflicting. The slow learner is often highly literate, but cannot comprehend the facts read technically correctly, write coherent sense, form links or solve problems. Often the dyslexic can do all of these sophisticated processes, but is bewildered by the printed or written manifestation of the material.

State provision for these pupils is often confused and inadequate – witness the reports of the eight cases in this study. It is not enough to classify dyslexia as a handicap under the 1981 Education Act, or to give occasional subjective, long-winded highly discretionary grants to individuals via bureaucratic means. Dyslexia *is* the only handicap which is not obvious, where sufferers may doubt their intelligence or sanity, and which is not provided for adequately under medical services. It is a specifically educational and social disadvantage, and this seems to be why it falls between clear categories of funding. Its prevalence, social dangers and expensive wastage of potential and employability merits a public campaign on the scale of those conducted by govern-ment departments on road safety, Aids, or the dangers of cigarettes. The crucial dif-ference may be that by alerting the public to dyslexia the government would be creating an expensive demand for care rather than alleviating it!

Government campaigns in other areas were obviously aimed at genuinely saving lives via prevention. Whilst dyslexia is obviously not a fatal affliction, there are, however, many arguments which can be used to justify a campaign. There are no statistics available on the incidence of suicide or mental breakdown because of failures linked with dyslexia. Nevertheless, I am personally aware of three cases where profound dyslexia and its accompanying frustrations played an undoubtedly tragic part. Pumfrey and Reason (1991) also refer to the case of a dyslexic student who passed GCSE and 'A'-level exams but committed suicide after failing his first-year exams in college, even in an institution with good welfare services.

Osmond and Morrison (1992) made a very powerful documentary of eight main dyslexic cases drawn across the full age range and social strata of society. Dangerously extreme misery was prominent. Consider the words of Peter Bradford, who found out about dyslexia only when he was retired and his grandson was diagnosed. He had felt hounded all his school life, failing his exams again and again.

> But at 19 I really was suicidal. I felt that there could be no place, no job which I felt I could do. There was nobody who would have the confidence in me to employ me.

Geoffrey Holliday, now withdrawn from his primary school, was described as so traumatized by his experiences of failure and misunderstanding in the school system that he was 'on the point of a nervous breakdown'.

Steven Bonfield was so withdrawn and distressed about his experiences that he had to have a year of counselling on top of specific intensive literacy help. He had been school phobic. Like Trevor in my study, he had become isolated and depressed. His account of how mental pressure builds up on the quiet dyslexic is poignant and convincing (see pp. 127–8).

Other cases make equally disturbing connections. Ian May believes he would not have ended up in prison for burglary if his dyslexia had been discovered. Colin New painfully describes how dyslexia destroyed his chances of promotion, in an otherwise successful career. Mrs Spenser highlights the nightmare disruption to family life which dyslexia can cause, and the strain imposed on parents who are forced to watch their child go downhill educationally and suffer personality damage. Full accounts of these experiences are given in Osmond (1993).

There is also the case of a boy who was placed in a special school in East Sussex because he had had a full nervous breakdown at the age of 11 when he transferred to a huge comprehensive school and was teased and bullied over dyslexia. These sad events happened despite specialist intervention.

The link between the stress and frustration of dyslexia and behaviour problems shown in this study has been used as key research in a 1992 court case by Dr Harry Chasty regarding a 15-year-old boy wrongly placed in a school for maladjusted pupils.

The severity of the misery and depression described by the students in my study is dramatic. Think of Trevor, aged 12, hospitalized and imagining he was dying from some incurable disease. He was on crutches for up to ten days at a time with severe psychosomatic pain which the doctor connected directly with the frustration of dyslexia. At age 10 Clark suffered similar severe pains in the abdomen, for which no cause was found. At secondary stage he used to spend long periods alone in a wood, truanting, 'till I run out of tears and just used to roar and want to die . . . I want to die, please let me die.' He felt he would have started stealing and getting into serious trouble if it had not been for his parents who kept him going. Mark was in such a severely stressed state that he developed a full-blown school phobia necessitating hypnotherapy and tranquillizers. Gareth went to the extreme of having his friend beat him up in order to get time off school. These are just brief examples from interview transcripts.

The official neglect and erratic treatment provision which surrounds this condition are likely to worsen under increasing financial decentralization. Local management of schools is also likely to limit the funding available for the expensive individual or small-group teaching provision dyslexics require, and may even affect their placement.

It is time to end the diplomatic lip-service paid to the notion of dyslexia by governments over the last thirty years. It is time that education ministers put their money where their mouth is, and provided access to adequate practical help for children who are potentially high achievers, and many of whom have outstanding measured IQ scores. This is indeed the politics of failure. The local compartmentalization of funds on issues of central national concern and the immediate profit and loss constraints of the market economy applied to education in general and special needs in particular can only lead to short-sighted policies of financial expediency rather than genuine investment in the future of our children and, therefore, of our society.

2. A big influx of public money into education to reduce general class size within schools would help all remedial groups.

All the government initiatives since the 1960s have cost huge budgets, and been fundamental, sudden, inadequately researched and implemented in a rush to catch votes. Had a fraction of the finance spent on building factory-sized comprehensive schools, introducing GCSE exams or bringing in the National Curriculum been allocated to reducing class sizes or training specialist teachers in any problem areas, we might be looking at far healthier literacy figures and less damaged children.

3. Public money needs to be available to provide more specialist help on a regular basis within schools or to individuals.

All too often comprehensive schools are served by overworked peripatetic remedial teachers who have to travel large distances between schools, and are given little time to liaise with class teachers and co-ordinate individual programmes geared to a child's most urgent needs. Owing to the pressure of demand, they may only get a chance to see a child once a week for half an hour, or end up teaching in a noisy corner, corridor or 'converted' cupboard. An integrated assistance programme often means a pupil is withdrawn from a lesson he likes or will have to catch up work from, and he may be drawn attention to or teased about his absence. It is rare for state schools to have the luxury of 1:1 teaching which drastically cuts down the distractibility factor and has often been the only way dyslexics have made dramatic progress, from their own accounts. Dyslexics need practice in basic literacy skills and memory work little and often, with rules or patterns repeated in different ways every day. They often flounder even in small groups if the learning difficulties of the other children are not compatible with their own, and memory loss over a week spent failing to keep up with written work in large groups can be spectacular. Yet such a service, which just papers over the cracks in the structure of the education system, may be all a poorly funded authority feels it can afford to run. The frustration and high stress levels of dedicated teachers who work in such services and have often funded their own specialist training are frequently evident at remedial conferences, updating lectures and in-service training courses, as well as amongst teachers I tutored on the Dyslexia Institute courses for the British Dyslexia Association Diploma.

Many primary schools are in an even worse state, and do not even have a special needs teacher available, often relying on voluntary parental help to hear struggling children read. General assistants working under a specialist supervisor are also rarely employed in this area, where they might be invaluable assets.

4. More day special schools or integrated units for dyslexics should be established to avoid social problems of boarding.

It seems terribly unfair to inflict family separation, tedious travel and the social problems inherent in residential placement on those who have already been under emotional pressure. If flexible specialist local units were available working in high profile as study skills provision within senior state schools, much family disruption could be avoided. This would necessitate some independent power and funding being at the command of the unit head, and a full co-operative working relationship between the school and the unit. The capacity to influence policy decisions on such matters as curriculum modifications, careers guidance and exam load for individual pupils would be essential. Input on counselling and pastoral care would also be an advantage.

This would require an unusually enlightened and flexible structure within the main school, but would surely be a positive influence on teaching methods, resource development and staff training if handled diplomatically. It would surely pay for itself in terms of increased effectiveness in literacy areas and the early identification of special needs, as well as lessening the disruption caused by distressed pupils within classes. I have run such a high-profile integrated unit at Carmel College, Oxfordshire, and the system could be adapted to use by the state system. It offered everything from full assessment and parental consultation to cross-curricular exam support and homework assistance.

5. *Greater access is needed to adult literacy assistance specifically for dyslexics in addition to the other ranges of problems. Public funding and paid staff should be provided, with more individual help being made available.*
Many adult literacy services fulfil a great need, are staffed by volunteers, and provide an opportunity unavailable otherwise locally. This service could be better funded and expanded to provide a specialist-trained diagnostic facility within local communities, heightening awareness of special needs and doing outreach work. The framework, dedicated staff, facilities and goodwill are already available – all that is required is substantial funding.

6. *An open learning situation for dyslexic adults who wish to gain public examination recognition should be provided for those who are intelligent but were not adequately helped in school.*
David McLoughlin has recently set up the Adult Dyslexia and Skills Development Centre in London in order to help adults achieve their full potential and younger dyslexics to make the transition successfully. He gives full psychological assessments, counselling and career advice. There is a great need for such help, but yet again it should be state funded rather than private provision. Then it would be available to all dyslexics, and not in danger of becoming an extra financial burden or out-of-reach luxury for average families who are already paying into the state system which often fails them.

CONCLUSION

1. Teachers underestimate the damaging emotional effects of classroom failure on dyslexic children.
2. The fact that attitudes still need to be enlightened regarding dyslexia is obvious from the suffering the interviewees in this study went through. At present dyslexia is frequently equated with actual disease or mental retardation.
3. This fundamental ignorance reaches also into the staffroom, where attitudes can be dismissive, disbelieving and even hostile. It is conceivable that some lecturers at teacher training college share these attitudes.
4. If early screening for dyslexia was widespread, the public would become acquainted with the problem, as would other children. This would lead to less bullying by teachers, less teasing by peers, and less worry for the individual.
5. Dyslexia should be as socially acceptable as any other disability commonly suffered by schoolchildren such as shortsightedness, asthma or diabetes. It should carry no stigma, especially from teachers, but be considered seriously for its far-reaching cognitive and emotional complexities, as this study has established.

Appendix

Interview Questions (Pupil)

1. What do you know about dyslexia?
2. What do you think is most important in helping a dyslexic child cope with school? (Choice of cards: select from

    Having helpful parents
    Having brothers and sisters who understand about dyslexia
    Being good at something else
    Knowing you are not stupid
    Having sympathetic teachers
    Knowing about dyslexia
    Getting individual help
    Getting extra help with English
    Being able to forget about your problems.)
3. What do you think makes a good teacher?
4. What do you think makes a bad teacher?
5. What do you think are the best qualities a school can have?
6. What is your earliest memory of school?
7. What is your best memory of school?
8. What is your worst memory of school?
9. What is your best school subject?
10. What is your worst school subject?
11. How do you feel you are getting on at school now?
12. Do you like reading now?
13. Do you feel you can cope with spelling now?
14. Was there any particular age you felt especially bad about school?
15. Have you ever had any embarrassing experiences through being dyslexic?
16. What do your friends think about you being dyslexic?

17. What do you think your family felt about you having problems with school work?

18. How would you describe your personality?

19. How would you describe your intelligence?

20. How would you describe your school work?

21. Have you ever had nightmares about school?

22a. Have you ever played truant?

22b. Have you ever refused to go to school?

23. Have you ever deliberately disrupted a class?

24. Have you ever smashed anything up on purpose, because you were upset about school?

25. Have you ever felt really worried about school exams?

26. Have you ever felt very angry about school?

27. What is the worst thing about being dyslexic?

28. What is the best thing about being dyslexic?

29. How would you describe your school life on the whole, looking back?

30. Do you foresee any difficulties related to dyslexia in your future life?

31. Do you think you have ever tried harder in other things because you did not at first do well in school?

32a. What do you think is the best way of helping dyslexic people to make the most of their talents?

32b. Which of these do you think would be best for a dyslexic child?

    (i) Ordinary comprehensive schooling with remedial help?

    (ii) A special unit attached to a comprehensive school, with some lessons shared, or day release?

    (iii) A specialist boarding school?

33. Why?

34. Describe yourself as a teacher might see you.

35. What do you think is the worst thing a school can do to a dyslexic person?

36. Why did you stay on at school (despite the bad time you had had in the past)?

Written work analysis

This pupil displays the following features in written work which indicate specific learning difficulties or dyslexia:

A. Spelling

1. A varied error rate of   per cent in free writing. ☐

2. Whole words that are indecipherable, not just spelt phonetically. ☐

3. Frequent letter reversals, e.g. b/d, p/q, f/t ☐

4. Spatial rotations of letters, e.g. f/t inversion, c/u. ☐

5. Whole words reversed, e.g. was for saw, on for no. ☐

6. Letters within words out of sequence, e.g. 'sdie' for side. ☐

7. Difficulties with homonyms, words that sound the same but have different meanings and spellings, e.g. their/there. ☐

8. Problems remembering spelling rules, e.g. when to double letters, 'puding' for pudding. ☐

9. Confusion identifying vowel sounds, e.g. 'rashed' for rushed. ☐

B. Structural faults

10. Incorrect sentence structure, including phrases written as sentences, e.g. '... did. A few hours later. They ...' ☐

11. Lack of punctuation. Punctuation used, but incorrectly. ☐

12. Ideas out of sequence in content, jumbled or non-existent planning/forethought shown. ☐

13. Words left out of sentences, incomprehensible sense. ☐

C. Handwriting problems

Look for inconsistencies, e.g.

14. Irregular letter sizes. ☐

15. Confusion between short and tall letters. ☐

16. A mixture of capitals and lower case letters within a word or sentence. ☐

17. Top line ripple in letter flow (irregular height). ☐

18. Base line ripple, with letters floating above the line erratically. ☐

D. Problems reproducing script or text

19. Numbers reversed even when copying script, e.g. ⴕ for 7.   ☐
20. Letters omitted even when copying, e.g. 'teacer' for teacher.   ☐
21. Endings such as 'ed' left off.   ☐
22. When copying, identifying letters wrongly, e.g. 'vuhen' for when.   ☐

E. Concentration

23. Distractible on written tasks.   ☐
24. Reluctant to start.   ☐
25. Needs reassurance to continue.   ☐
26. Slow to complete.   ☐
27. Unhappy with result.   ☐
28. Tendency to deface work with blots or crossings-out/destroy it.   ☐

F. Cognitive level

Strengths are often shown here:

29. Original ideas.   ☐
30. Outstanding artwork.   ☐
31. Knowledge of interesting facts.   ☐
32. Distinct difference between higher oral level and written output.   ☐

Reading analysis

This pupil displays the following features in reading which can indicate specific learning difficulties or dyslexia:

1. A high varied error rate of   per cent. ☐
2. Whole words guessed at and misread. ☐
3. Over-reliance on pictorial clues. ☐
4. Frequent letter reversals and mirror-imaging, e.g. b/d, p/q. ☐
5. Spatial rotations of letters, e.g. f/t vertical inversion, c/u anti-clockwise twist. ☐
6. Whole words read reversed, e.g. 'was' for saw, 'on' for no. ☐
7. Letters within words out of sequence, e.g. 'sdie' for side. ☐
8. Syllables read out of sequence, e.g. 'license' for reasonably. ☐
9. Inability to break words into syllables, or blend them together when split. ☐
10. Inability to pronounce words in accurate sequence, even when able to read the syllables, e.g. 'arrage', 'avage', 'agerave' for average. ☐
11. Slow speed, hesitations, stutterings. ☐
12. Inability to recognize high-frequency repeated sight-memory words like 'they', 'was', 'call', 'because'. ☐
13. Tendency to process words by outline shape only, e.g. 'leave' for live, 'wasted' for washed. ☐
14. Confusion over basic sound/symbol correspondence, e.g. 'uh' sound for a. ☐
15. Lack of grasp/retention/application of spelling rules to assist reading, e.g. 'Mick' for Mike, in Magic e rule. ☐
16. Failure to register punctuation. ☐
17. Perseveration, adding extra sections to words, e.g. 'serculalarly' for securely. ☐
18. Ellipsis, the omission of letters within a word or of words within a sentence, e.g. 'lily' for lively, I [took] my dog for a walk. ☐
19. Reading the same word several different ways even when it is repeated regularly throughout a text, e.g. 'gosh', 'gust', 'guessed' for ghost. ☐
20. Panic and breakdown of skills/confidence when faced with an unfamiliar word/words or reading aloud, instead of using word-attack skills. ☐
21. Tracking problems, missing out a line, losing one's place in the text. ☐
22. Slight phobia/obsession with books, e.g. buying lots of comics he cannot read, wanting to read books at far too hard a level even when in a 1 : 1 situation. ☐
23. Finding the words such a struggle that he cannot recall the story. Not remembering the start of the sentence. Forgetting the names of characters. ☐
24. Throwing in facts/ideas/anecdotes which show acute powers of comprehension, although the tale may be told in a rambling/disjointed/circumlocutory way. ☐
25. Impoverished vocabulary owing to lack of reading experience. ☐

Bibliography

Abbot, R. C. and Frank, B. E. (1975) 'A follow-up of learning-disabled children in a private special school.' *Academic Therapy*, **10**, 291–8.

Adelman, C., Jenkins, D. and Kemmis, S. (1977) 'Rethinking case study: notes from the Second Cambridge Conference.' *Cambridge Journal of Education*, **6**, 139–50.

Adult Literacy and Basic Skills Unit (1988) *After the Act: Developing Basic Skills Work in the 1990s*. London: ALBSU.

Ames, L. B. (1971) *Adolescent Rorschach Responses*. New York: Brunner Mazel.

Badian, N. A. (1986) 'Non-verbal disorders of learning: the reverse of dyslexia.' *Annals of Dyslexia*, **36**.

Baker, D. (ed.) (1984) 'The neurological basis of the talents of dyslexics.' *Perspectives on Dyslexia* (Medical Research Update, Research Division), August. Orton Dyslexia Society, Baltimore, Maryland.

Bancroft, W. J. (1982) 'The Tomatis Method and suggestopedia: a comparative study.' Revised version of a paper presented at the Seventh International Conference of the Society for Accelerative Learning and Teaching, Colorado, 30 April–2 May.

Bastian, R. T. (1959) In Penfield, W. and Roberts, L. (eds), *Speech and Brain Mechanisms*. Princeton, NJ: Princeton University Press.

Berlin, R. (1887) *Eine Besondere Art der Wortblindheit (Dyslexie)*. Wiesbaden: J. F. Bergmann.

Bettelheim, B. (1971) *Love Is Not Enough*. New York: Avon Books.

Bradley, L. (1989) 'Predicting learning disabilities.' In Dumant, J. J. and Nakken, H. (eds), *Learning Disabilities, Vol. 2, Cognitive, Social and Remedial Aspects*. London: Academic Press.

Bruner, J. S. *et al.* (1976) *Play: Its Role in Development and Evolution*. Harmondsworth: Penguin Books.

Bryan, T. (1983) 'Learning disabled children's language problems.' Paper read to the Second World Congress on Dyslexia, Halkidiki, Greece.

Carter, B. (1964) 'A descriptive analysis of the adult adjustment of persons once identified as disabled readers.' Ed. dissertation, Indiana.

Chasty, H. (1988) 'Check-list compiled for the Dyslexia Institute.' *Sunday Times*, 18 September. Updated in 'Successful learning for dyslexic people', DI free leaflet, 1993.

Chasty, H. (1991) 'Specific learning difficulties.' Psychology lecture for Dyslexia Institute, Staines, Middlesex, August.

Chasty, H. (1992) 'WISC III retest scores.' Table previously provided for G. Trickey, The Psychological Corporation, Sidcup, Kent.

Chasty, H. (1993) Interview given to A. Heath for *Dyslexia*, Studio 1 Films, London; advised by the Arts Dyslexia Trust.

Clegg, A. and Megson, B. (1973) *Children in Distress*. 2nd Edition. Penguin Educational Specials. Harmondsworth: Penguin Books.

Cohen, L. and Manion, L. (1980) *Research Methods in Education*. London: Croom Helm.

Coopersmith, S. (1967) *Antecedents of Self-esteem*. San Francisco: Witt, Freeman, pp. 265–8.

Critchley, M. (1968) 'Developmental dyslexia.' *Pediatric Clinics of North America*, **15**, August, 669–76.

Critchley, M. (1970) *The Dyslexic Child*. Springfield, IL: Charles C. Thomas.

Critchley, M. and Critchley, E. A. (1978) *Dyslexia Defined*. London: Heinemann.

De Fries, J. C. (1991) 'Genetics and dyslexia: an overview.' In Snowling, M. and Thomson, M. (eds), *Dyslexia: Integrating Theory and Practice*. London: Whurr.

Diesing, P. (1971) *Patterns of Discovery in the Social Sciences*. Chicago: Aldine.

Edgington, R. E. (1975) 'SLD children: a ten-year follow-up.' *Academic Therapy*, **11**, 53–64.

Edwards, J. H. (1990) 'Emotional reactions to dyslexia: case studies.' Vol. 1, Text. Vol. 2, Appendices includes full transcripts of interviews with pupils and parents. M.Ed. dissertation, University College of North Wales, Bangor. Copies at St Mary's College Library, Bangor and Central University Library, Cardiff.

Edwards, J. H. (1993) 'An eminent dyslexic: Dr Per Udden.' Interview with the founder of the Rodin Remediation Academy at the Royal Society, London, 22 October. Available in leaflet form from the Arts Dyslexia Trust, Brabourne Lees, Near Ashford, Kent.

Elliot, C. D. (1983) *British Ability Scales: Handbook and Technical Manual*. Windsor: NFER-Nelson.

Euler, C. von, Lundberg, I. and Lennerstrand, G. (eds) (1989) *Brain and Reading: Structural and Functional Anomalies in Development Dyslexia with Special Reference to Hemispheric Interactions, Memory Function Linguistic Processes, and Visual Analysis in Reading. Proceedings of the Seventh International Rodin Remediation Conference*. London: Macmillan.

Farnham-Diggory, S. (1978) *Learning Disabilities: The Developing Child*. London: Fontana.

Fawcett, A. and Nicholson, R. (1993) 'Mental speed, skill and dyslexia.' Paper read to the Rodin Academy Conference on Mental Speed and Reading at the Royal Society, London, 22 October.

Francis-Williams, J. (1968) *Rorschach with Children*. Oxford: Pergamon Press.

Galaburda, A. M., Corsiglia, J., Rosen, G. D. and Sherman, G. F. (1987) 'Planum temporale asymmetry.' Reappraisal since Geschwind and Levitsky. *Neuro-psychologia*, **26**(6), 853–68.

Galaburda, A. M., Rosen, G. D. and Sherman, G. F. (1989) 'The neural origin of developmental dyslexia: implications for medicine, neurology and cognition.' In Galaburda, A.M. (ed.), *From Reading to Neurons*. Cambridge, MA: MIT Press.

Geschwind, N. (1982) 'Why Orton was right.' *Annals of Dyslexia*, **32**, 12–30.

Geschwind, N. (1983) 'Biological associations of left-handedness.' *Annals of Dyslexia*, **33**, 29–39.

Glaser, B. G. and Strauss, A. L. (1967) *The Discovery of Grounded Theory*. Chicago: Aldine.

Gottfredson, L. H., Finucci, J. H. and Childs, B. (1983) *The adult occupational success of dyslexic boys: A large-scale, long-term follow-up*. Reprint No. 334, Johns Hopkins University, Baltimore.

Gottfredson, L. H., Finucci, J. H. and Childs, B. (1984) 'Explaining the adult careers of dyslexic boys: variations in critical skills for high-level jobs.' *Journal of Vocational Behaviour*, **24**, 355–73.

Halpern, F. (1953) *A Clinical Approach to Children's Rorschachs*. New York: Grune & Stratton.

Hammill, D. D. (1990) 'On defining learning disabilities: an emerging consensus.' *Journal of Learning Disabilities*, **23**(2), 74–84.

Hampshire, S. (1981) *Susan's Story*. London: Sidgwick & Jackson.

Hampshire, S. (1990) *Every Letter Counts*. London: Bantam Press.

Healy, J. M. and Aram, D. M. (1986) 'Hyperlexia and dyslexia: a family study.' *Annals of Dyslexia*, **36**, 237–52.

Hinton, C. G. and Knights, R. M. (1971) 'Children with learning problems: academic history, academic prediction and adjustment three years after assessment.' *Exceptional Children*, **37**, 513–19.

Kimbrell, H. W. and Karnes, L. R. (1975) *Dyslexia: A Commonsense Guide to the Diagnosis and Treatment of Specific Language Disability*. Monograph 1, Trident Academy, Mount Pleasant, South Carolina.

Knasel, E. G. (1982) 'Towards a Science of Human Action.' Ph.D. thesis, University of Wales.

Lofland, J. (1971) *Analysing Social Settings*. Belmont, CA: Wadsworth.

Lovegrove, W., Martin, F. and Slaghuis, W. (1986) 'A theoretical and experimental case for a visual deficit in specific reading disability.' *Cognitive Neuropsychology*, **3**, 225–67.

Lowenstein, L. F. (1988) 'Dyslexia: fiction or reality?' *Education Today*, **40**(1).

Masland, R. L. (1990) 'Neurological aspects of dyslexia.' In Hales, G., Hales, M., Miles, T. and Summerfield, A. (eds), *Meeting Points in Dyslexia. Proceedings of the First International Conference of the British Dyslexia Association*. Reading: BDA.

Merton, R. K. and Kendall, P. L. (1946) 'The focused interview.' *American Journal of Sociology*, **51**, 541–57.

Meyer, G. (1954) 'Some relationships between Rorschach scores in kindergarten and reading in the primary grades.' *Journal of Projective Techniques*, **17**, 414–25.

Miles, T. R. (1978) *Understanding Dyslexia*. London: Hodder & Stoughton.

Miles, T. R. (1983a) *Bangor Dyslexia Test*. Cambridge: Learning Development Aids.

Miles, T. R. (1983b) *Dyslexia: The Pattern of Difficulties*. St Albans: Granada Publishing.

Miles, T. R. and Gilroy, E. (1986) *Dyslexia at College*. London: Methuen.

Miles, T. R. and Miles, E. (1983) *Help for Dyslexic Children*. London: Methuen.

National Joint Committee on Learning Disabilities (1988) Letter to the member organizations of the NJCLD.

Newton, M. J. and Thomson, M. E. (1982) *Aston Index (Revised)*. Wisbech: Learning Development Aids.

Nicolson, R. I., Fawcett, A. J. and Baddeley, A. D. (1991) *Working Memory and Dyslexia*. Report LRG 3/91, Department of Psychology, University of Sheffield.

Nisbet, J. and Watt, J. (1978–80) *Case Study*. Oxford: TRC.

Oakeshott, E. (1973) *The Child under Stress*. Care and Welfare Library. London: Priory Press.

Orton, S. T. (1925) 'Word-blindness in schoolchildren.' *Archives of Neurological Psychiatry*, **14**(5), 197–9.

Orton, S. T. (1928) 'Specific reading disability: strephosymbolia.' *Journal of American Medical Association*, **90**, 1095–9.

Orton, S. T. (1937) *Reading, Writing and Speech Problems in Children*. New York: Norton.

Osmond, J. (1993) *The Reality of Dyslexia*. London: Cassell.

Osmond, J. and Morrison, P. (researchers) (1992) *Dyslexia*. London: Poseidon Films in conjunction with Channel 4 TV.

Owen, F. W. *et al.* (1971) *Learning Disorders in Children: Sibling Studies*. Monographs of the Society for Research in Child Development, Serial No. 144.

Parkin, Sir George (1898) *Edward Thring: Life and Letters*. London: Macmillan.

Parkinson, S. E. and Edwards, J. H. (1992) 'Innovative visuo-spatial powers in dyslexics: a new perspective?' Paper presented to the New York Academy of Sciences, Twentieth Conference of the Rodin Remediation Academy, 12–15 September.

Preston, R. C. and Yarrington, D. J. (1967) 'Status of fifty retarded readers eight years after reading clinic diagnosis.' *Journal of Reading*, **11**, 122–9.

Pringle-Morgan, W. (1896) 'A case of congenital word-blindness.' *British Medical Journal*, **2**, 1378.

Pumfrey, P. D. and Reason, R. (1991) *Specific Learning Difficulties (Dyslexia): Challenges and Responses*. London: NFER-Routledge.

Rabinovich, R. D. (1959) 'Reading and learning disabilities.' In *American Handbook of Psychiatry*. New York: Basic Books.

Rackham, K. (1972) 'A follow-up of pupils at one word-blind centre.' *ICAA Word-Blind Bulletin*, Pt 4, 71–9.

Rawson, M. B. (1968) *Developmental Language Disability: Adult Accomplishments of Dyslexic Boys*. Baltimore, MD: Johns Hopkins University Press.

Robinson, H. M. and Smith, J. (1962) 'Reading clinic clients ten years after.' *Elementary School Journal*, **63**, 134–40.

Rosenthal, J. (1973) 'Self-esteem in dyslexic children.' *Academic Therapy*, **9**, 27–39.

Rumsey, J. M., Dorwart, R., Vermess, M., Denckla, M. B., Kruesi and Rapoport, J. L. (1986) 'Magnetic resonance imaging of brain anatomy in severe developmental dyslexia.' *Archives of Neurology*, **43**, 1045–6.

Saunders, W. A. and Barker, M. G. (1972) 'Dyslexia as a cause of psychiatric disorders in adults.' *British Medical Journal*, **4**, 759–61.

Silver, A. and Hagin, R. K. (1964) 'Specific reading disability; follow-up studies.' *American Journal of Orthopsychiatry*, **34**, 95–102.

Smith, H. W. (1975) *Strategies of Social Research: The Methodological Imagination*. London: Prentice-Hall.

Snowling, M. (1987) *Dyslexia: A Cognitive Developmental Perspective*. Oxford: Blackwell.

Stein, J. F. (1993) 'Dyslexia and personality.' In Wright, S. F. and Groner, R. (eds), *Facets of Dyslexia and Its Remediation*.

Stirling, E. G. (1978) 'Naming and verbal fluency in dyslexic boys.' M.Ed. thesis, University of Wales.

Stoll, F. (1977) 'A propos de la dyslexie' (A few observations on dyslexia). Paper presented at the Première Conférence sur la Lecture, France, April.

Stott, D. H. (1950) *Delinquency and Human Nature*. Dunfermline, Fife: Carnegie UK Trust.

Stott, D. H. (1974) *Manual to the Bristol Social Adjustment Guides*. London: Hodder & Stoughton.

Stott, D. H. (1978) *Helping Children with Learning Difficulties*. London: Ward Lock Educational.

Stott, D. H. and Marston, N. C. (1970) *Bristol Social Adjustment Guides*. London: Hodder & Stoughton.

Thompson, L. J. (1969) 'Language disabilities in men of eminence.' *Bulletin of the Orton Society*, **19**, 113–20.

Thompson, M. E. (1984) *Developmental Dyslexia*. London: Arnold.

Tomatis, A. A. (1978) *Education and Dyslexia*. Association Internationale d'Audio-Psycho-Phonologie, Switzerland.

Tuckman, B. W. (1972) *Conducting Educational Research*. New York: Harcourt Brace Jovanovich.

Vail, Priscilla L. (1990) 'Gifts, talents, and the dyslexias: wellsprings, springboards and finding Foley's Rocks.' *Annals of Dyslexia*, **40**, 3–17.

Vellutino, F. R. (1979) *Dyslexia: Theory and Research*. Cambridge, MA: MIT Press.

Walker, R. and MacDonald, B. (1976) *Curriculum Innovation at School Level*. E203, Units 27 and 28. Bletchley: Open University Press.

West, T. G. (1991) *In the Mind's Eye*. Buffalo, NY: Prometheus Books.

Williams, A. L. and Miles, T. R. (1985) 'Rorschach responses of dyslexic children.' *Annals of Dyslexia*, **35**, 51–66.

Winnicott, C. (1964) 'Communicating with children.' *Child Care Quarterly Review*, **18**(3). Also in Tod, R. (1973) *Disturbed Children*. Longman's Papers on Residential Work. Harlow, Longman.

Wolcott, H. F. (1973) *The Man in the Principal's Office*. New York: Holt, Rinehart & Winston.

Wragg, E. C. (1978–80) *Conducting and Analysing Interviews*. Oxford: TRC.

Wright, S. F. and Groner, R. (eds) (1993) *Facets of Dyslexia and Its Remediation*. Studies in Visual Information Processing, Vol. 3. Edited proceedings of the Eighteenth Rodin International Remediation Academy Conference on Reading and Reading Disorders. Amsterdam: North-Holland Elsevier Science Publishers.

Yule, W. and Rutter, M. (1976) 'Epidemiology and social implications of specific reading retardation.' In Knights, R. M. and Bakker, D. V. (eds) *The Neuropsychology of Learning Disorders*. Baltimore, MD: University Park Press.

Index